Never a Dull Moment

Roy and his wife Margaret

Never a Dull Moment

The Autobiography of a Travel Writer

ROY J. SHARP

SERENDIPITY

Copyright © Roy Sharp, 2003

First published in 2003 by
Serendipity
Suite 530
37 Store Street
Bloomsbury
London

British Library Cataloguing-in-Publication data
A catalogue record for this book is available from the British Library

ISBN 1-84394-039-6

Printed and bound by Antony Rowe Ltd, Eastbourne

Acknowledgments

With grateful thanks to my wife, Margaret,
without whom life would be very dull and to my cousin,
Charles Sharp for family history.

Contents

Foreword

by

Lord Charles Forte

I T GIVES ME GREAT PLEASURE to commend Roy Sharp's autobiography *Never a Dull Moment*. Roy has had a varied career and for many years was involved in the hotel and catering industry as general secretary of the National Caterers' Federation and as editor of *The Caterer's Record*, *The Caterer's Journal* and *Food & Cookery Review*. This book provides an interesting record of his life.

Charles Forte

Lord Forte of Ripley in the County of Surrey
FRSA, President, Forte plc (formerly Trusthouse Forte)

Foreword

by

Sir Ray Tindle

FROM WHERE I STAND, Roy Sharp is far too young to be writing his autobiography! Newspapermen like Roy go on forever. Sir Ted Pickering, the Executive Vice-Chairman of the *Times* is 90. Alistair Cook who brings us his *Letter from America* each Sunday morning on the BBC is 93. In America, Randolph Hearst ran his group of papers until he was 89. Lord Beaverbrook ran the *Express* when he was well into his eighties and had a circulation of 4.3 million (it's now around one million).

A glance at a few of the pages, however, will tell anyone why the book is so well worth reading, even if there is more to come at a later date.

Roy Sharp is a 'dyed in the wool' journalist and it shows. What an interesting life.

I first met Roy and Margaret in connection with the *Esher and Leatherhead Courier*. They had launched it in 1966 to cover an important part of Surrey.

Launching a paper requires enormous courage. It really is a case of 'Who Dares Wins'. The Sharps had that courage and enormous tenacity that such a task requires. 'To bring out a newspaper is certainly an arduous undertaking' said John Walter who founded the *Times* in 1785.

They also had the basic skill and that courage and that tenacity to lead such a full life in the newspaper and travel industries, and to write it down in such an interesting manner as Roy has done in this fascinating book.

I have never been to Gibraltar or Thailand, Louisiana or the Mississippi, Denmark or the Caribbean but Roy took me to these and many other places in his book and made me feel I knew them as well as those few countries I have visited on holiday and even better than the parts of the world I served in as a soldier in 1944.

I have never seen wild crocodiles or elephants, even though I was in the Army for two years in the Far East, but Roy brought them to life in his book. I've never had a snake in the toilet but Roy and Margaret have!

You will really enjoy this book. You will be envious, you will want to follow in his footsteps forthwith, and you won't be able to put this book down. This is the real life of a real man who knows his job and knows his world – and can write it down so that you can't stop reading it. You'll never have a dull moment.

Sir Ray Tindle CBE, DL
FCIS, FCIJ, FCI Arb (Chairman)
Chairman, Tindle Newspapers Ltd.,
Publishers of over 125 newspapers

Introduction

WHY WOULD ANYONE want to read about my life? I am not a film star, pop singer, actor, politician or celebrity. I came from a working class family: my father was an engine driver and my mother a dressmaker.

But I have been fortunate and had a varied career. I have never made a fortune but I have travelled the world, visiting over eighty countries; served in the Royal Air Force in Gibraltar during the Second World War; travelled three times on the Orient Express; flown in an airship and been on forty-three cruises including the QE2.

During my life, I have been a local government officer, an incorporated secretary, a radio telephone operator, a school teacher, an exhibition organiser, a public relations officer, a journalist, an editor, a publisher, a lecturer, a food writer, a theatre critic, a lay preacher and a travel writer!

I have been happily married for fifty-nine years and, if we are spared, will be celebrating our Diamond Wedding Anniversary in the year 2003.

My wife, Margaret, and I have stayed and dined in some of the world's top hotels and have met various members of the Royal family. We have had tea with Queen Elizabeth the Queen Mother in St James's Palace; have been presented to Her Royal Highness Princess Anne, the Princess Royal, and to the Duke and Duchess of Gloucester and have had tea with the ex-King Constantine II and his Queen of Greece.

Besides meeting various film and stage stars, we have among others interviewed Laurel and Hardy, Liberace, Tommy Steele and Diana Dors and met a number of prominent politicians, including Prime Ministers Clem Attlee, Sir Harold Wilson and Sir Edward Heath.

But most important of all, we are active evangelical Christians and take part in all the activities of the church, from being Sunday School teachers and Bible class leaders to participating in services, giving talks and witnessing to our faith.

Do you still want to follow my career? Then read on ...

CHAPTER ONE

In the Beginning …

Good beginning makes a good ending.

Fourteenth-century Proverb

M<small>Y ENGLISH MASTER TOLD US</small> that a good essay, prose or literature should have a beginning which will immediately arouse the interest of the reader and his desire to read on. If nothing significant has happened by page ten, then the chances are you will read no further.

<small>SEX</small> – how about that for a beginning? The first thing a mother asks after giving birth is whether her child is a boy or a girl. An Irishman whose sister had just given birth asked what was the sex of the baby and whether he was an uncle or an aunt! 'If it's a girl, we'll call her Denise, if a boy De-nephew!'

Before the Second World War, you knew who was a boy and who was a girl. Apart from pink and blue bootees, little boys wore shorts and little girls wore dresses. Not until boys reached their teens did they resort to long trousers. Jeans and denim had not been invented and you rarely saw a woman in trousers.

Before schools went comprehensive, you started your education as a mixed infant, then progressed through junior school until you were segregated into separate schools for boys and girls. Even when classes were mixed, there were separate entrances and separate playgrounds for boys and girls.

My story begins way back in 1849 in the village of Barkway on the Suffolk–Essex border when my grandfather, Arthur George Sharp, was born. As an adult, he was a renowned horse handler with a reputation as a strong character, physically and mentally. He could look after himself and was a bare-fisted pugilist of note.

With the development of the railways, he moved to Cambridge and worked as head cabman with the Great Eastern Railway Company, making deliveries from Cambridge station to various locations in the district with a four-horse wagon. He became well-known for his reliability in delivering heavy freight from the goods station to business premises in the town, especially to the University. Undergraduates would have a whip-round (minimum 'inducement' required £1) to persuade him to drive his wagon through Trinity College gateway at a brisk canter with only inches to spare. Word would get around and crowds would gather in Trinity Street to watch the challenge. The first part of the act was to place one heavily-booted foot on one of the two massive leather traces that joined the wagon to the horses. The lead horse would then receive a sharp tap of command and the team would move forward, snapping taut the trace and thus propelling driver Sharp upwards. With perfect timing, he would turn slightly forward and land squarely in the driver's seat high above.

This was a very difficult and dangerous accomplishment and it eventually ended in tragedy. Grandfather's mate, whose main attribute was his ability to lift heavy loads, certainly not his horsemanship, was never allowed to attempt such a feat. But one day, in the gaffer's absence, he decided to have a go. He made a hopeless mess of it and landed underneath one of the front wheels of the wagon, sustaining injuries from which he subsequently died. As a result, the authorities banned any further attempts.

One of Grandfather's loads consisted of the large cockerel weather vane which was to top the spire of the Roman Catholic Church of Our Lady and the English Martyrs on the corner of Hills Road and Lensfield Road. It was so large that it only just fitted on to his wagon. The church was consecrated in 1890.

In those days, well-to-do undergraduates often had pianos in their rooms and Grandfather was required to lift them up the winding, narrow college staircases. First, he would uncrate the piano, taking care not to damage it. Once the piano was safely installed in the owner's room, there was the problem of getting rid of the crate. Naturally, Arthur offered to take it away for another bob or two, which he then delivered to a local builder who specialised in making coffins out of it. Thus, one person's discard became a welcome added source of income for others!

When Grandfather's first wife was dying, her best friend was at her bedside. Her last words were: 'Look after Arthur for me, Lizzie'. She did that the best way she knew, she married him and thus became my grandmother. The result, a whole new Sharp progeny was created. Lizzie was a wonderful woman, who gave birth to Ben (father of my cousins Charlie and Arthur), my father Sidney John (always known as Jack), Wall, Charlie, who was killed in the Great War, and Esther.

Among Grandfather's vices was his inclination to cheat at cards and dominos. He smoked a vile selection of clay pipes, which he firmly anchored between his jaws by means of what can only be described as 'holders', fashioned with a penknife out of large cotton reels and wound on to the stem of the pipe with strong thread. He smoked shag which he bought from a 'baccy' shop just round the corner in Mill Road. My father gave him fourpence each week in order to buy his ounce of tobacco. He would make all sorts of objects with wood from orange boxes, using hundreds of nails which he extracted from firewood and then painstakingly straightened.

Another occupation was slicing up pages of newspaper into squares, then threading them on string and hanging them up in the outside toilet! He had a bristly moustache that prickled when he kissed you, an act I hated!

One mystery still surrounds Grandad Sharp – how he sustained injuries to his legs which made it impossible for him to walk without the aid of sticks for nearly half his lifetime. It was said that he was hit by a train one night while walking home late from the railway station. Like most railwaymen who lived in Romsey Town, he never went the long way round over the bridge and down St Barnabas Road but took the short cut along the railway line and getting into his backyard through a hole in the fence. It was the end of his working life and the family went through a hard time. Grandma took in washing to make ends meet, standing at the sink in a steam-filled kitchen, a brick-built copper on the boil, arms in the washtub, singing hymns as though she did not have a care in the world. She did the washing and ironing for the local vicar's wife but tried to find time to visit the Salvation Army, whose Citadel was nearby in Devonshire Avenue. I remember her delicious Yorkshire puddings. She would put the batter in the meat tin and place a joint of beef over the top on a trivet, so that the meat juices dripped into the batter – a wonderful delightful dish! The family would have the pudding as a first course with gravy.

My father and his brothers took turns to push grandfather out in a wheelchair and they delighted in bumping him up and down kerbs and uneven surfaces, causing grandfather to utter some rather strong language!

The family lived in Merry Cottage at 26 Argyll Street. How they managed to sleep everybody in just two small bedrooms and a box room I do not know. This was one of the first houses built in Romsey Town (over Mill Road railway bridge as you come from the town centre) especially for railway workers. Besides my grandmother's children, there were also the children of Grandfather's first marriage – Alf, Bill, Arthur, Nell, Fred, Lou and possibly two others who had died in infancy. In later years, the two families drifted apart and a certain amount of hostility existed among them. Only Bill seems to have remained on intimate terms with grandmother's offsprings.

Cousin Charlie related an incident when he and his parents were visiting Merry Cottage. Charlie's father, Ben, would regularly trim Grandfather's hair and give him a proper shave with a well-honed cut-throat razor. He had reached the stage where only Esther was around to give him a trim with scissors. He looked forward to a real shave from Ben.

On one occasion, Ben was a bit careless and sliced off the lower lobe of grandfather's ear. Blood spurted everywhere and the victim did not remain silent! Ben immediately retrieved the sliced-off portion off the floor, spat on it and quickly replaced it on the ear, holding it firmly in place until the blood had ceased to flow. A bandage was wound round Grandfather's head and he continued to keep up a barrage of oaths directed at his son. There were no complications and when the dressing was removed some days later by a district nurse, the lobe was securely in place. Only one thing marred Ben's prompt surgery – he had replaced the lobe back to front and that is how it stayed until he finally died in 1942 at the age of ninety-six years.

All Grandfather's children attended St Phillip's School up to the age of fourteen. Uncle Ben's first job was an apprentice at a printer's in Trumpington Street but he spent a lot of his time with his father, learning how to handle horses and he jumped at the chance to become a horse-tram driver.

After the war, Ben was offered a job on the railway but he was attracted by the newly-formed Ortona Bus Company which he joined as a conductor. After this company was taken over by Eastern Counties and finally, Eastern National, he continued in their employ.

Some of these early double-decker buses were open-topped and fastened to the back of each seat was a canvas cover which the person behind could hold over his head and lap when it was raining. These buses were later replaced with enclosed upper decks. These had rows of seats for four or five persons and a gangway along the right-hand side to enable passengers to get access to them. There was a step-up to the seats which meant there was little headroom. A notice said 'Mind your head when rising from your seat'. Uncle Ben fixed one of these notices for fun in Grandfather's outside toilet!

There is a photograph in several of Cambridge museums, taken on the 18 February 1914, showing the last horse-drawn tram beginning a ceremonial final journey by the Cambridge Tram Company from the East Road depot to the Senate House in King's Parade and back. The driver was seventeen-year-old Uncle Ben Sharp. A year later, Ben landed in France with the Cambridgeshire Regiment.

In Flanders, Ben met half-brother Alf just behind the front line. As a schoolboy, Alf, the eldest of grandfather's first wife, was a compulsive truant and was always in trouble. His parents were eventually given the choice – Borstal or the army? They decided on the army and boy soldier Alfred Sharp began his adventurous military career. He became a fine foot-soldier but as fast as he earned promotion, so he got into regular trouble – drunken brawls and the like – and was reduced to the ranks. He was one of Kitchener's original army. Back as a sergeant, he gave Ben some practical advice.

'When you hear that bloody whistle blow and it's time to go over the top, get as low down as you can, on your belly if need be, and crawl. That way, you may survive to where you're supposed to be going, so you can go and do it again!'

No doubt following his brother's advice was the principal reason he survived those four dreadful years of carnage. Later in the war, they met again but this time, Alf had made his way up the line to find the Cambridge-shires and Ben. He told him that he had seen his younger brother, Charlie, among recruits just arrived as reinforcements from England.

Ben slipped off to find Charlie during a period of heavy bombardment. They had hardly time to greet one another when a German shell burst almost on the spot killing Charlie outright, whilst Ben escaped without a scratch. A couple of years before his death at the age of eighty-seven, Ben visited Charlie's grave at Ypres, together with his sister Esther.

When he came out of the forces, Uncle Ben married Aunt Gladys and they lived for a short time in St Catherine's Street but then moved into a cottage at 1 Union Lane, the oldest still functioning cottage in what was then the village of Chesterton. They had two sons, my cousins Charles and Arthur.

On the outbreak of World War II, Uncle Ben became a company sergeant at the Home Guard post guarding the Milton Road railway crossing. He was also a full-time member of the Fire Service at Marshall's airfield. Cousin Charles served in the Royal Navy in the Far East. He and brother Arthur both started as reporters on the *Cambridge Daily News* and after the war, they both became editors of regional newspapers. Charles served some time in Nigeria advising on newspaper production.

Aunt Gladys died in 1950 and Uncle Ben remarried and retired to East Dereham, Norfolk.

Uncle Wall was a maintenance engineer for a company in Carlyle Road, known popularly as 'The Scientific'. He married Aunt Ivy and they were awarded the tenancy of one of the first council houses to be built in the immediate post-war development on Mowbray Road. Designed and built to quality standards hitherto unknown, the Borough Council used it as a showhouse. They had four children, cousins Audrey, Pauline, Brenda and Gordon.

Aunt Esther, my father's sister, was a wonderful person who devoted her life to looking after her parents. She never complained and never married. She worked at Chivers Jam factory at Histon, Cambridgeshire, where she contracted a troublesome skin infection as a result of handling oranges.

The family it seems were always squabbling, especially at meal times. One would only have to say 'I don't want this' and the other brothers would grab the said morsel. A favourite dish was a suet jam roly-poly pudding, cooked in a muslin cloth.

'I don't want the end piece' was a universal cry from the brothers, because there was less jam in it. They all wanted a piece taken from the middle.

'Right', said their father, 'your mother and I will have the end pieces' and cut the pudding in half. Whether grandmother managed to eat her half is debatable!

My father was born on Christmas Eve 1896. As a boy, he was always watching the trains. Their house, Merry Cottage in Argyll Street overlooked the railway and the approach to Cambridge station. Each day, on his way home from school, he would peer through the iron bars of Mill Road bridge to watch the trains. On one occasion, he poked his head through too far and got stuck. It required the fire brigade to release him!

When father left school, he started work on the railways – the Great Eastern Railway Company – as a fireman in the Cambridge depot. Because there was a shortage of manpower, he missed the first rung of the ladder, that of engine cleaner. When the Great War broke out in 1914, although he was in a reserved occupation, he joined the Royal Army Medical Corps as a medical orderly. He wanted no part in killing fellow human beings but because his brothers had joined up, he was determined to do his bit.

He was sent overseas and was based in Salonika where he had to treat the casualties from the Dardanelles and Gallipoli Campaign. He told us some of his experiences in Serbia and Greece. He liked the Serbs but did not think much of the Greeks. On one occasion, he and a comrade witnessed a large procession of Greeks going to a funeral. Thinking they were lining up for refreshments, they decided to join them. They eventually arrived at a large house and once inside, instead of refreshments, they discovered a man's body laid out on a table, the owner of the house who had just died. Everyone was expected to kiss the body. Father and his mate decided this was not their scene and somehow managed to escape amidst shouts and curses from the mourners.

His unit formed an entertainment group and Father joined the chorus in their production of Gilbert & Sullivan's *The Mikado*. At home after the war, he was often singing snatches from the opera's most popular songs.

On demobilisation, Father returned to the railways as a fireman and eventually progressed to 'past fireman' which meant, when required, he took over a train as a driver. This counted as a 'driving turn' and you had to complete several hundred such turns before you were a fully qualified locomotive engineer, an engine driver.

Railwaymen had to work three-week shifts – from 6.00 a.m. to 2.00 p.m.; then 2.00 p.m. to 10.00 p.m. and on the third week, from 10.00 p.m. to 6.00 a.m. When Father was on the early morning shift, the 'knocker-upper' would come to the house at 5 o'clock and tap on my

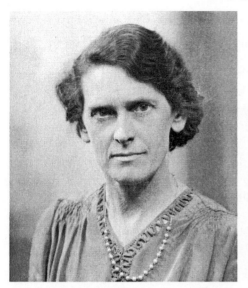

Gladys Valentine Sharp and Sidney John (Jack) Sharp, Roy's parents

parents' upstairs bedroom window with a long pole to wake up Father so that he would not be late for work.

He had a number of fascinating tales concerning his time as a railwayman and these I will relate in the chapter on Railways.

My parents were married in 1922 in St Luke's Church, Cambridge. When they became engaged, they started to look for somewhere to live. They applied to the council for a council house and when everything was agreed and a house allotted to them, Father remarked 'Now we can get married'.

'You're not married?' exclaimed the Council official. 'I'm sorry, but we cannot let you have it. There is a long list of married couples wanting a house, so we cannot give priority to unmarried or engaged couples.' Eventually, they were able to rent rooms in Gwyder Street, Cambridge and so got wed.

My mother's name was Gladys Valentine Rolph and she was born on St Valentine's Day, in 1896, ten months before father was born. I know very little about my mother's family, except that it was large – six boys and three girls. I never met her father and have only vague memories of her mother. Fred was the eldest and worked as a chef in the kitchens of Clare College. On the occasion of a visit to the University of the Crown Prince and Princess of Japan, we visited his kitchen and Uncle Fred let us sample some of the delicacies he was preparing for the Royal party. Fred had a daughter, cousin Vera.

Vincent worked in the Cambridge Instrument Company and he had a son, Ron, who went to Spain with the International Brigade to fight against Franco in the Spanish Civil War (1936–39). I never knew what became of him.

Len was a dental mechanic and his workshop was full of false teeth. He was the youngest of Mother's brothers. Reg was a hairdresser and Harold, who lived in Caldecote, looked after dogs. There was a sixth son who was killed in the war but none of us can remember his name.

Mother was the youngest of the three girls. Her eldest sister, Annie, married a furniture maker, Frank, and they lived in Liverpool. The other sister was Dorothy but she was always called Doll. She married Frank Conder who worked in the University laboratories as a technician. They had one daughter, cousin Dorreen.

Mother's father died before I was born. He was a carter and looked after horses. He was kicked by one of them on the leg and it turned gangrenous. Doctors wanted to amputate it but he refused, resulting in an early death.

Mother used to visit her grandfather who had a large house and garden in the Chesterton district of Cambridge near Castle Hill and he had some peacocks. A roller skating rink was built on part of the land which was later converted into a cinema and ballroom, called The Rendezvous. This subsequently became the Rex Cinema.

Mother could have appeared in the *Guinness Book of Records*, for she was awarded a medal in recognition of her school attendance – seven years never late and never absent throughout the whole of that time!

When she left school, she served a seven-year apprenticeship as a seamstress and dressmaker and worked long hours in a dim light. One of her jobs was to make a dress for one of the guests at the wedding of Princess Mary, the Princess Royal, which took place on 28 February, 1922. She was the daughter of King George V and she married the Sixth Earl of Harewood.

After she married, mother continued working from home as a dressmaker to help out the family income, which in those days was less than £5 per week. She charged ten shillings for a dress, 12s. 6d. for a coat and 5s. for alterations.

On one occasion, she went frantic. She had some very expensive material for a lady's dress spread out on the dining room table, ready for cutting out. Unfortunately, I beat her to it for whilst she went out of the room to fetch the pattern, I wanted to cut out a picture from a newspaper. I spread the paper out on the table on top of the dress material and proceeded to wield the scissors, not only cutting out the picture but also a neat square out of the material underneath. Only by skilful needlework and embroidery was Mother able to invisibly repair the damage.

CHAPTER TWO

Childhood Days

The child that is born on the Sabbath Day
is bonny and blithe and good and gay.

A.E. Bray, 1838, *Traditions of Devonshire*

I was born on the Sabbath – Sunday, 1 April 1923 at 33 Vinery Road, Romsey Town, Cambridge. Bonny and blithe? Yes, maybe. But certainly not 'gay' in the sense it is used in the twenty-first century. I was and always will be a ladies' man!

April the first is known as All Fools' Day. John Heywood, the sixteenth-century playwright, wrote: 'God sends fortune to fools' (1546). I have never had or earned a fortune but in St Matthew's Gospel, chapter six, we are told not to 'store up for yourself treasure on earth ... but to store up for yourselves treasures in heaven'. That is where my fortune lies!

The year 1923 was very special. In the *Weekly Dispatch*, published on the 1 April 1923, it was reported that nobody would buy the memoirs of ex-Kaiser Wilhelm II of Germany. I hope my memoirs do not suffer the same fate!

My father was a renowned practical joker. When I was born, he dashed round to his mother's to tell her the good news. But because it was April Fools' Day, she refused to believe him and it was not until the next day was she convinced and I was officially recognised!

Roy, aged 9 months

I am told I was not a handsome baby! One day, Mother took me in the pram into town to do her shopping. She left me outside Sainsbury's store in Sidney Street whilst she made her purchases. In those days, the grocer would take a whole side of bacon and place it on the slicing machine and cut off rashers for the customer. Butter would be displayed in large barrel-like shapes and lumps would be cut off and patted into half pound and pound portions.

When Mother had made her purchases, she emerged from the shop and, seeing a bus outside, hopped on it and went home. Only then did she remember she had left me in my pram outside Sainsbury's. I was still there when she came back – nobody else wanted me!

On 28 June 1927, my sister Eileen was born. By this time, we had moved from Gwyder Street to 4 Coronation Place, a row of seven terraced houses off St Eligius Street. Just before her birth, I was sent to spend a few days with Aunt Doll, Uncle Frank and cousin Dorreen at 35 Searle Street.

As a pre-war child, you knew nothing about sex until at least the age of puberty. Even then, no one told you anything – not even about the birds and the bees! The first I knew about the intricacies of reproduction was in biology class at the High School when rabbits were dissected in the school laboratory to show us the difference in the sexes. The rest was left to conjecture and one's imagination. Brothers and sisters, of course, made discoveries long before an only child or where the family consisted of one sex only.

However, I discovered the difference when I slept with cousin Dorreen. I was aged four, she was aged eight. As soon as I knew I had a sister, I returned home. 'Are we going to keep her?' I asked my mother. The answer was in the affirmative. There was no question now of my returning to Aunt Doll's, even with the pleasant prospect of sleeping once more with cousin Dorreen!

I was the proud owner of a small tricycle and I would ride all round the four roads which enclosed Coronation Place without having to leave the pavement. These were St Eligius Street, Bateman Street, Brookside by

Roy, aged 3 years

Hobson's Corduit and Pemberton Terrace. I would pretend to be a tramcar and fixed a garden cane to the axle of the cycle and let it trail behind on the ground to provide the 'current' to my make-believe tram, imagining it to be the pole connecting to the overhead cables. I attached a card on the back and another one on the handlebars, announcing my destination, always changing it when I reached my 'terminus' and start the return journey! When I grew too old to ride the tricycle, I would stand on the rear axle and scoot along until one day, I hit a stone and shot over the handlebars, breaking off a piece of my permanent front tooth. I still bear the evidence of this little accident and I have the piece of tooth among my souvenirs.

At one of the big houses on Pemberton Terrace, I became friendly with one of the maids who introduced me to the lady of the house. I had fair curly hair and I wore a smock over my shorts. I had discovered that some people liked girls more than boys, so I decided to pretend I was a girl.

'Hallo little girl,' the lady of the house greeted me. 'What is your name?'

'Joyce Jones' I promptly replied. I was made very welcome and given sweets. I was fascinated with one of those glass paperweights which, when shaken, produce 'snowflakes'. When Christmas came round, the lady of the big house sent a bunch of flowers and a basket of fruit addressed to Mrs Jones. My secret was out! She also sent me a Christmas present. I was hoping it would be the glass paperweight but it turned out to be a whistle with a loud piercing note. My parents were so pleased! After a couple of days, the whistle mysteriously disappeared and I never found it again!

Our house in Coronation Place consisted of a front room, a dining room, small kitchen with a built-in brick copper, a small front and back garden and an outside toilet. We had no bathroom and we all had to use a tin bath in front of the fire in the dining room! We had no electricity and illumination was provided by gas-lamps. There were two bedrooms plus a small box room. Mother and Father slept in the front bedroom, my sister, Eileen had the middle room and I had the box room. Neither Eileen's nor my room had a gas-lamp so we had to use candles. My room overlooked the back garden and the sloping roof over the kitchen. I was able to climb out of my window on to the sloping roof and so get out into the garden.

I had a single bed with brass knobs at each corner. I would make a tent by draping a sheet over the four corners and securing it by unscrewing the bed-knobs, placing the sheet over the posts and screwing back the knobs, that is until mother discovered holes in her sheets! I would read in bed with the aid of a torch, sitting under my 'tent'.

Our neighbours in Coronation Place were all very friendly. Our house was No. 4 and next door at No. 3 was an elderly lady, Mrs Bates who often came in for a cup of tea. On one occasion, Father came into the house from the garden wearing a very old pair of trousers. Mother told him he looked a disgrace but Father replied, 'They're all right, there's plenty of wear in them yet'. He never liked to throw things away.

'Look,' Mother said, 'you've a tear in the seat' and she inserted her fingers and gave it a tug. The tear increased and Mrs Bates joined in and helped to rip his trousers until they were in threads.

'Now you will have to throw them away' commented Mother.

At No. 2 lived a girl a year older than me, named Margaret Cox. She wore her hair in a long pigtail which was very useful for tugging when we had an argument. On the whole, we got on very well and played together.

Mr and Mrs Francis lived at No. 5 with their son Clarence, a year older. His father was a barber with a shop in Lensfield Road who charged three pence for a haircut, four pence for an adult. One day, Clarence told me his father was not going to cut hair any longer.

'Oh, I'm sorry,' I said. 'I always go there and so does my father.'

'Don't worry', was the reply, 'he's only going to cut hair shorter!'

Everybody called Clarence 'Sunny Jim' after the character who appeared on Force Corn Flakes boxes. He was a dandy and wore a monocle. Anyone, we thought, with a name like Clarence must be a bit of a dandy. His mother, however, was always telling people not to call him by his nickname.

At No. 6 lived Mrs Conder, the mother-in-law of mother's sister, Dorothy (Aunt Doll). Mr and Mrs Hinds lived at No. 7 with their son John, about ten years my senior. Mrs Hinds always told people John was a jockey, but he was too tall for that. In fact, he was only a stable lad who used to take the horses for exercise on Royston Heath.

No. 1 Coronation Place was occupied by an elderly couple whose names I cannot remember. This was the line-up in the 1920s and 1930s.

At the end of the passage which ran along the back of our gardens was a gate which was the rear entry to a large house which contained an artist's studio. The occupier was a lady who painted in water colours and on several occasions, she would ask Eileen, me and Margaret Cox to pose for her in different scenarios to represent the four seasons. This would include building sand castles and paddling at the seaside, snow-balling and skating, skipping and trundling hoops, leap-frogging and playing marbles and conkers. She gave us two shillings each for our efforts. This helped to supplement our pocket money which started at two pennies a week and eventually rose to sixpence. From this large sum I would have to save for a visit to the annual Midsummer Fair and to buy fireworks for 5 November. Very occasionally, Grandfather or other relatives would give us a penny!

I was able to earn a little extra from my father. He was secretary of the Cambridge Cage Bird Society and instead of posting letters, show catalogues and notices to members, I would deliver them all round Cambridge on my bicycle, thus saving the Society postage. Father bred Border canaries and had over a hundred birds in an outside aviary in the back garden. During the breeding season, we all had to help and hand-feed some of the chicks. Father won many trophies, cups and other prizes with his birds which he exhibited around the country and at the annual show in the Cambridge Corn Exchange.

On 5 November, I would make a Guy and we lit a bonfire at the end of the garden. I had to buy most of the fireworks myself and I would meticulously make a list of all my purchases and arrange a programme specifying the order in which they had to be lit. My record total of purchases was in November 1938 which came to 165. This reminds me of the young boy who went into the shop with two pennies to buy fireworks and asked the shopkeeper to put in plenty of rockets!

The street behind Coronation Place was called Brookside and we used to catch sticklebacks in the stream which flowed alongside it. The stream was fed from Hobson's Conduit, which was established in the seventeenth century to provide quality water to the town from Nine Wells Springs to the south. Trinity College fountain is fed by pipes from Conduit Head Road which was laid by monks in 1325. Channels along Trumpington Street alongside the kerbs on both sides of the road lead to the fountain on Market Hill. Similar channels ran along St Andrew's Street. We would drop matchsticks into the channels and see who reached the end of the street first.

Opposite Brookside is Coe Fen, a meadow on which cows sometimes grazed, and this leads down to the River. There was also a small brook by the side of the meadow, beyond which were some allotments. To reach these, there were a number of planks across the brook. One day, cousin Dorreen, Eileen and I decided to 'walk the plank' across the brook. Leading the way and each of us holding hands, Dorreen proceeded to cross the 'bridge'. Half way across, she slipped and pulled all of us into the water. Mother was not very pleased. When she was angry with us, she would clout us with a double slap, which we called her backhander. Eileen often got me into trouble then would plead with Mum 'Don't hit him'.

One year, I received a junior carpenter's set for my birthday. After happily knocking nails into the garden fence, Father gave me a piece of three-ply wood and a batten and told me to make a table. I cut off four lengths for legs and nailed one on each corner of the piece of three-ply. I told Eileen we would have our tea on it so she pulled up her small child's chair and placed her elbows on the table. This was too much for my handiwork and the legs spread-eagled and the table collapsed.

'Look what you have done now,' I said indignantly.

'It was not a very good table' was her reply. SISTERS!

One Saturday, Father sent me into town to buy a tin of black enamel paint from Woolworths. I made the purchase all right but dilly-dallied on the way home as usual, talking to tradesmen and shopkeepers. On reaching home, I handed the tin to Father, only to my dismay to discover that I had been holding the tin upside down and that the lid was not fitted securely. The paint had been trickling out all the way home and running down my jacket and trousers, a long, sticky black streak. Mother was furious and threw the tin into the hearth, where it suddenly ignited and set fire to the wooden mantelpiece and the fringe material which everyone had along its border, a survival from Victorian times. Fortunately, Father ripped down the fringe and beat out the flames before the fire really took hold.

Our house at 4 Coronation Place, Cambridge. My bedroom was the small one in the middle and sister Eileen's on the left.

CHAPTER THREE

Schooldays

... the whining school-boy, with his satchel and shining morning
face, creeping like a snail unwillingly to school.

William Shakespeare
'The Seven Ages of Man' from *As You Like It*

BY THE TIME I WAS FOUR years of age, I was ready to start school.
The compulsory starting age was five but my parents wanted me to
start early. They took me to St Barnabas Church of England Infants
School, about a mile from our home, where they had vacancies for
under-age pupils.

I did not want my parents to take me there, I wanted to go by myself,
but Mother insisted on accompanying me on the first morning. From the
next day onwards, I walked there on my own – four journeys a day, as I
had to go home for lunch (it was always called dinner then) and return
to school for the afternoon period. Twenty-first century parents would be
horrified at a four year old walking alone along busy streets.

To get to school meant crossing the very busy Hills Road, the main
road into town from the railway station. My father arranged with the
owner of the hardware shop on the corner of Russell Street and Hills
Road to take me across the road on my way to school. There were no
pedestrian crossings on roads in those days and Leslie Hore-Belisha, who
introduced Belisha beacons, was only thirty-four years of age and not
appointed Minister of Transport until 1934. On the return journey, I
would stand on the opposite side of the road and call out the shopkeeper's
name at the top of my voice until he came out of his shop and brought
me back across the road.

My career as a mixed infant was very eventful and I soon made my
mark. The head teacher's name was Miss Green who would put naughty
pupils across her knee and smack their bottoms. This always caused a lot
of excitement among the rest of the class, especially if the victim was a
girl, because we could see her knickers! Miss Green once threatened me
with the same punishment but she relented and I was let off. I felt cheated!

My granddaughter, Isabella started play school in the year 2000. On the second day, her mother told her to hurry up or she would be late for school.

'I don't have to go again', she said, 'I went yesterday!'

The usual dress for little girls was a frock and knickers made from the same material and boys thought it great fun to lift up the girls' skirts to see if they had knickers to match. Even at infants' stage, sex raises its head!

During my first year at school, we had to be immunised against diphtheria. I did not relish the idea and mother came to the school with me on the day this was to be carried out. I started to resist, saying I did not want it.

'It won't hurt' the nurse said, 'it is only to test if you are immune.' With that she jabbed in the needle in my arm and I howled.

'I thought you said it was only a test', I moaned.

This reminds me of the Tony Hancock sketch repeated on television in the 1980s when he went to donate blood. When told they only wanted a pint, he exclaimed it may only be a pint to them but for him it was an armful!

A second injection was due the following month. This time, I was taken to school by my father and I submitted without a murmur.

Mid-morning breaks were the time when each child was supplied with milk. Each had his own mug or cup, identified with a piece of coloured wool or ribbon. The milk was ladled into the cups from a churn by the teacher. Several years later, the method of supplying milk to schools was in one third of a pint bottle. A cardboard lid was fitted on the top of the bottle with a perforated hole in it. You punched the hole to break the perforations and you inserted a straw. Often this would not work and if you pushed too hard, the whole stopper would go into the bottle and you would be splashed with the milk. We had to bring our milk money to school each week, twopence if I remember rightly, and a child was appointed milk monitor to collect it.

At home, our milk was delivered from Bull's Dairy and we would tell people we drank Bull's milk. The milkman had a horse-drawn float with two wheels, like a Roman chariot and his customers would come out to the cart with their jugs which the milkman filled from a huge churn. When not at school, he would let me ride on the float whilst he made deliveries along the road.

At St Barnabas's, some children took sandwiches to eat with their mid-morning milk. My mother would make up a pack of egg sandwiches for me which were wrapped in tissue paper. All the packages were placed on a table in the classroom when we arrived at school. One morning, one of the girls whom I did not like, wanted to leave the room. The toilets in those days were outside the building. A few minutes' later, she came back and told the teacher there was no toilet paper in the lavatory. So the teacher tore off some of the tissue paper which was wrapped around my sandwiches and gave it to her. I was horrified and when my sandwiches were handed to me at break time, I promptly dumped them into the waste paper basket. But the teacher saw me do so and fished them out and made me eat them. In my imagination, they tasted awful!

I always took my time going to school after lunch. My meal was never ready when I got home.

'Good gracious, is that the time?' my mother would say. She had probably been busy making a dress.

I am a very observant person, even as a small child, and notice things other people miss. I know immediately if a poster on a hoarding has been changed; if a shop has changed hands or altered its window display. This ability must have developed from my school days. On my way to school, I would watch the billposter man sticking up a fresh poster, how the large ones came in segments and how, by using his long paste-brush, he would position them and match up the pieces so they did not reveal the joins or overlap each other. I had my own 'hoarding' on our garden fence and each week, I would ask a shopkeeper for the previous week's theatre poster which he had displayed in his window. This I would cut into two or three pieces then stick them on my board, matching up the cut pieces.

I would speak to the postman, the baker, the milkman and all the other delivery men *en route* to school; watch the gardeners trimming the hedges, the decorators painting and when workmen started digging up the pavement to lay pipes, I would stand watching them for ages, oblivious of the time. I was especially fascinated to see them cementing the pavement after the pipes had been laid and the holes filled in. They would run a metal hand roller with protruding knobs along the wet cement to make small indentations and form a pattern. I got into trouble when I dug a trench along the passage at the back of our gardens to lay my own pipes (garden canes).

Time meant nothing to me. I would set off for school at 8.30 to get there for 9 o'clock, but when it got to 10 o'clock, Miss Green would come looking for me on her bicycle. When she eventually caught up with me at one of my observant stops, she would make me run all the way to school as she cycled beside me. I inevitably got the 'stitch' in my side on the way.

It never ceased to amaze me how stupid teachers were. Each year on Guy Fawkes' Day, St Barnabas put on a display in the school playground and all the children would line up against the wall while the teachers let off the fireworks. Miss Green proceeded to tie two sky rockets to the gatepost. Although I was only nearly seven years old, I knew that was not right.

'You put rockets in a bottle, Miss', I told her.

'Get back', was the reply, 'we know what we are doing'.

She lit the touch paper and the rockets burst into flames, but instead of shooting into the air, sparks and flames shot backwards and set the gate alight. They could not take off because of being tied to the post. In the panic and dousing the flames with water, I doubt if the teacher heard me say 'I told you so'!

Once, when I was caught talking in class, the teacher, Miss King, made me stand up. She pushed down my socks and then left me standing whilst she drank her cup of tea. When she had finished, she came back to me and slapped my legs and then told me to pull up my socks.

'You pushed them down,' I said, 'you pull them up!' She did but not until I got a few more slaps.

At Christmas, the school put on a concert and part of the hall was converted into a stage and hung with curtains. But I knew they did not have it right. Instead of a pair of curtains parting in the middle, they put up a single curtain which was drawn across the front of the stage from side to side. But you cannot tell teachers anything!

I was to play the part of an elf and we were all given wooden hammers to carry with us which we were to tap on the ground and look for diamonds. I had been given a similar wooden hammer at a party and knew that there was a whistle at one end of it. So when on the stage, I blew the end of my hammer and a loud whistle emanated. Other children immediately followed suit.

The teacher picked me out as the culprit and said I could not be in the play. But when I said my mother could make some of the costumes, she relented.

CHAPTER FOUR

A Mixed Junior

Child! do not throw this book about;
Refrain from the unholy pleasure
Of cutting all the pictures out!
Preserve it as your greatest treasure.

Hilaire Belloc, 1870–1953
The Bad Child's Book of Beasts

BOOKS, books, books! My wife complains I have far too many – at least 500! I certainly do not throw them about nor cut out the pictures but use them for reference and pleasure. As a child, I treasured my books. My mother's friend, Miss Winnie Bird, would come for tea once a week and she always brought me a picture story book from Woolworth's costing a few pence. But eventually, I had so many that I would say: 'Got this one'.

I was never short of paper on which to write and draw. Each week, we would go to the local office of the National Deposit Friendly Society. This was a form of social security and we all had accounts in it in which Father deposited a few pence each week. This enabled us to visit the doctor and have treatment when necessary without payment.

'Have you any paper I can have?' I would ask the local secretary and she would always find me some old forms or notepaper.

At the age of seven, I left St Barnabas School and in September, 1930, I was admitted to

Roy – a junior schoolboy
Father's bird aviary is behind

St Paul's Church of England Junior Mixed in Russell Street, just five minutes' walk from my home. The school was built in the late Victorian age and had separate entrances and playgrounds for boys and girls. It was a two-storey building with six classrooms. Two of the downstairs class-rooms were divided by screens which could be removed to form a large assembly hall. The toilets, of course, were outside.

The headmistress was Miss Margaret Chandler. I entered Class One and made rapid progress. I could already print letters and read and was now joining up.

Two terms later, I moved up to Class Two and after a further term, entered Class Three the following September. By the time I was ten years' old, I was in the Top Class Five, the headmistress's class.

Miss Chandler always insisted we sit with our arms folded behind us, not in front, to help us maintain good posture. Girls were not allowed to sit with legs crossed, it was not considered ladylike! Two pupils sat at a desk with a lift-up top and an inkwell and one of the tasks performed in turn was to fill the inkwells. Ink was made up with powder and water and, of course, we wrote with pen and nib; ballpoints had not been invented.

I came near the top in all my examinations and I was put in charge of the school's Post Office Penny Bank. Pupils were encouraged to save a penny a week and I had to keep a record of their deposits. I was also school librarian.

Each week, the vicar of St Paul's Church, the Rev. J. A. C. Ainley, came to give us religious instruction. We learnt the Lord's Prayer, the Ten Commandments, the Apostles' Creed and the Catechism.

The Catechism began by asking: 'What is your name?' Answer: 'N or M'. I never could understand what those letters stood for. The next question was: 'Who gave you that name?' to which the reply was: 'My godfathers and godmother in my Baptism, wherein I was made a member of Christ, the child of God and an inheritor of the Kingdom of Heaven.' It went on to say: 'They promised and vowed three things in my name. First, that I should renounce the devil and all his works, the pomps and vanities of this wicked world and all the sinful lusts of the flesh. Secondly, that I should believe all the articles of the Christian faith and, thirdly, that I should keep God's commandments and walk in the same all the days of my life.'

I cannot recall who were my godfathers and godmother were or that they reminded me of the vows and undertakings they made on my behalf. Regrettably, there are very few children today in the twenty-first century who can even say the Lord's Prayer, let alone the rest of the Catechism!

Outstanding events at St Paul's School included Maypole dancing on May Day; special talks and demonstrations concerning the countries and peoples of the British Empire on Empire Day and the Christmas end-of-term concert.

On Empire Day, a child would hold up the Union Jack and then everyone would file past and salute the flag.

My best subjects were English and Composition. All the best pupils were encouraged to enter a Safety First competition, organised by the Chief Constable of Cambridge. This followed a showing of a Safety First film. Entries were submitted from all the schools in the town and when the results were announced, I had come top and received the Chief Constable's prize, a book.

Before the war, very few primary schools had their own cinematographic equipment so any film of an educational nature was screened at a local cinema in the morning and children from various schools were taken to see it. One such showing was at the Tivoli Cinema in Chesterton Road and the film was Frank Buck's jungle safari *Bring 'Em Back Alive*. It was made in 1932 and was an account of how an animal hunter scoured Malaysian jungles for specimens to stock world zoos. The film was introduced by an explorer dressed in tropical kit and toupée.

I took part in school plays and end-of-term concerts and during my last year at St Paul's, when I was aged eleven, I persuaded Miss Chandler to let me put on my own show consisting of short sketches and turns.

A friend of my Father's at the Pye Radio Works in Cambridge provided us with our first wireless set. They built it between them in a Pye Radio case, with its distinctive rising sun speaker front. It was worked by coils and valves which had to be changed every time you wanted a different station.

Each day, I would listen to the five o'clock Children's Hour and my favourite programmes included *Toytown* by Hulme Beaman where a stuffy Mr Mayor and a very slow Ernest the Policeman tried to govern a cast of unruly citizens. The chief troublemaker was Larry the Lamb (played by Uncle Mac, Derek McCulloch) who used to bleat 'I'm only a little lamb' as his excuse, accompanied by Dennis the Dachshound. Other characters were Mr Magician and Mr Inventor and there were over thirty episodes broadcast from 1929.

I also enjoyed the historic plays such as *The Castles of England* featuring Richard Goolden (known as the Funny Man because of his voice) and the current affairs talks by Commander Stephen King-Hall, who always ended his broadcast with the words: 'Be good, but not so frightfully good that someone asks "and what mischief have you been up to?".'

CHAPTER FIVE

Christmas Festivities

At Christmas, play and make good cheer,
For Christmas comes but once a year.

Thomas Turner, 1524–1580
Five Hundred Points of Good Husbandry

I AM NOT CERTAIN when I learnt the truth about Father Christmas. One year, I was determined to keep awake all night and catch him filling my stocking (Mother's stocking in fact because that held more!). I told my parents of my intention. But in spite of waking up periodically, I slept through most of the night. At daybreak, I got out of bed and went to my stocking. It was empty! I rushed out of the bedroom, calling to my parents that Santa Claus had not been and tripped over a pile of parcels stacked outside the door.

'That will teach you not to stay awake next time. Father Christmas only comes if children are asleep' they told me.

Every Christmas Day was spent at Merry Cottage. Unless the weather was very bad, we would walk there, a distance of about one-and-a-half miles. One year, there was deep snow everywhere and where the roads had been swept, it was piled over four feet high on either side of the road. We had to get a taxi to Grandmother's.

Only members of Grandfather's second marriage ever joined in our Christmas Day party, with the exception of Uncle Bill and Aunt Kate from Nottingham. There were Uncle Ben and Aunt Gladys with cousins Charles and Arthur, Uncle Wall and Aunt Ivy with cousins Audrey and Pauline (Gordon and Brenda were not born then) and Aunt Esther, Grandfather and Grandmother besides my parents and sister Eileen, seventeen persons in all, squeezing into two small rooms!

There was the traditional turkey and all the trimmings and plum pudding. To cook such a large bird, it had to be taken to the nearby baker's shop and there it was cooked in the baker's oven, together with other neighbours' birds. The brothers made certain there was a silver threepenny piece in everybody's portion of Christmas pudding but purposely omitted one from Grandfather's plate.

'I've got one!' Father would say. 'So have I' said Uncle Bill. 'And I've got one as well' from Uncles Ben and Wall.

Grandfather would search frantically through his pudding, grumbling all the time because he could not find a coin. Eventually, he was given a second helping and a coin was inserted into it. After dinner, we children were confined to the front room to make our own amusements whilst the adults played cards – Sevens and Rummy – for halfpennies in the dining room. Later, the older children were allowed to join them.

The same routine followed on Boxing Day and the following two Sundays, going to Uncles Ben and Wall and then our house in turn.

At the end of Christmas Day, everyone with the exception of our family stayed the night at Grandmother's. There were only two bedrooms and a box room in the house; some slept on the sofa or on the floor, whilst five slept crossways on a double bed! Father and Mother would never stay overnight – they preferred to sleep in comfort in their own bed.

Compared to children today, we did not receive large presents. Our stocking would contain an orange, an apple, some sweets, a book and one or two toys, such as a meccano set or some conjuring tricks. Eileen, of course, would have a doll.

Some years' later, when I was about ten, father became friendly with a family named Forman who had a small dance studio adjoining their house in Russell Street. Mother and Father joined their dancing class to learn ballroom dancing and we were invited to their New Year's party. This was a much livelier affair than Grandmother's with games, charades, dressing up and sketches. One person would play the piano, another a saxophone and a third a drum kit. About five families attended and there would be dancing, forfeits and a conjuror.

On the Sunday following, Mother had been busy all day baking and preparing food. Then about 8 o'clock in the evening, Eileen and I were bundled, protesting, off to bed. Half an hour later, we heard a lot of noise downstairs, so we crept down and found that the Formans and the other families had arrived for a reciprocal party, complete with musical instruments and drums! That put paid to our parents' idea of getting us off to bed!

CHAPTER SIX

Holidays and Outings

Hence, home, you idle creatures, get home,
Is this a holiday?

William Shakespeare,
Julius Caesar – Act 1, Scene 1

W E SELDOM WENT AWAY on holidays. My father preferred day trips and going home to his own bed. But being a railwayman, he got free passes and reduced fares for himself and the family.

Hunstanton on the Wash, in Norfolk, was our nearest seaside resort (fifty-two miles) and we went there frequently for a day or even half a day. Father was always much too early for the train but we never went on the first one. He would pick the latest possible and come home on the earliest! To avoid the crowds, he would say! Neither of my parents were keen on the seaside. They could not swim and did not like water. They complained about wasps and said they got sand in their sandwiches. They bought me an ice cream cornet and I was about to lick it when a wasp started buzzing round me. I shook my arm to ward it off but unfortunately, it was the arm which was holding my ice cream. One flick and the whole contents of my cornet flew out!

As a boy, Father fell into the dock at Grimsby (he alleged one of his half brothers pushed him in) and he nearly drowned. He later suffered from rheumatic fever which he blamed on the incident and the doctor sent him up to Scotland for treatment and convalescence.

Occasionally, we would stay a few days in a boarding house in Skegness, Great Yarmouth, Clacton or Lowestoft. In later years, Skegness was to become the turning point of my life! All will be revealed in a later chapter!

Father was very lucky at games and in the amusement park at Clacton, he kept winning prize after prize at one of the stalls. Eventually, the stallholder told him he had won enough and could have no more goes. So Father bent down to pick up his prizes and lo and behold, someone had nicked them! He swears it was an accomplice of the stallholder.

Another unfortunate incident took place when we went to London Zoo. We were watching the polar bears in their enclosure on Mappin Terrace when Father spotted a large rat in the gully separating the bears and the safety barrier.

'Watch me hit that rat!' he exclaimed and pulled out a penny from his pocket. His aim was good and he hit the rat but when his penny stopped rolling, we saw it was not a penny but a half-crown, a fortune in those days!

Father called the keeper over and asked him if it was possible to retrieve it.

'I'm sorry, sir,' he replied, 'we never go down there, it's too dangerous.' But half an hour later, when we returned to the Terrace, both the coin and the keeper had disappeared. I wonder what the polar bears spent it on!

As young children, we were told what to do if we ever went astray or got separated from our parents.

'Don't run around, stay where you are and we will come and find you.'

This happened to me on a crowded promenade, so I did as I was told and sat down on a nearby box and waited. Unfortunately, the box was behind a large notice board and I was completely hidden from passers-by. My parents passed the spot at least six times before they eventually spotted me.

'I did as you told me – I stayed put!' I said.

One of my Sunday School teachers went round to various farms in Cambridgeshire to collect boxes of newly-laid eggs and take them to the packing station. He would do this on Saturdays and I often went with him in his car. Another teacher drove a laundry van and in the holidays, I would go with him to collect the large laundry baskets from the big houses.

At the age of eight, my parents, Eileen and I went on a holiday to Clacton-on-Sea. On the pier was a children's entertainer, Clown Bertram. During the show, he invited children who could do a turn to come up on to the stage. I always fancied myself as a performer so I accepted the invitation and went forward.

'And what are you going to do?' asked Clown Bertram.

'A clown dance,' I replied.

'Clowns don't dance, they drink,' he quipped.

Then he asked if I wanted any special music. 'No', I replied so the pianist played the tune 'Carolina Moon' and I jigged up and down in a comic dance which received laughter and loud applause. Clown Bertram presented me with a Carolina Moon badge for my effort.

CHAPTER SEVEN

Grammar School Days

If every day in the life of a school could be the last but one,
there would be little fault to find with it.

Stephen Butler Leacock, 1869–1944
College Days – Memories and Miseries of a Schoolmaster

IN MY LAST TERM at St Paul's Junior School, just after my eleventh birthday, I sat the entrance examinations for secondary education (subsequently called the Eleven Plus). Miss Chandler had given me and about half a dozen other pupils extra tuition in her home in Tennison Avenue. When the results came through, I was one of only four pupils from the school who had sat the exam and all four of us had passed. No girls had sat that year. I was offered a free scholarship to the Perse Grammar School or to the Cambridge and County High School. If I had chosen the Perse School, my parents would have had to sign an undertaking to keep me there until my eighteenth birthday. Father said he was not going to keep me until that age and so I opted for the County School where I could leave at sixteen. My reward for gaining the scholarship was my first bicycle.

Before term commenced in September 1934, I had to undergo a medical examination at County Hall where it was discovered I was long sighted and needed to wear glasses. The first form at the County was for prep school fee-paying boys so I entered Form 2A. Form 2B was for boys moving up from form one and boys who had not gained a scholarship and so had to pay for their tuition.

There were four houses in the school, each named after a river – Cam and Granta (Cambridge rivers) and Cherwell and Isis (Oxford rivers). I was placed in Isis house.

Forms 1, 2A and 2B were housed in temporary wooden huts with connecting doors between the three classrooms. There were frequent battles between these classes, using ammunition according to season, ranging from conkers and apple windfalls from the school orchard in the autumn (strictly out of bounds) and snowballs in winter. The boys would bring snow into class in their satchels and when the master was not present, battle commenced. In spring and summer terms, the ammunition was usually balls of wet newspaper or blotting paper. Inevitably, detention was metered out to everyone to clean up the mess.

On one occasion, boys were creating a rumpus during the luncheon break. The master suddenly entered the room and shouted 'Everybody outside. The last one out gets detention.' There was a mad scramble for the door and in the melée, the master was pushed out as well, so in the end, he could not tell who was last!

Prefects were the natural enemies of everyone and were always on the receiving end of missiles.

Discipline and punishments varied with the different masters. The Latin master was very easy going as were the French and History masters. The Science master would throw the chalk at an inattentive pupil and one of the boys surreptitiously kept a book recording the number of direct hits. The master would also grab a boy by his hair and pull him to his feet before clouting him several times on the back of the head. These were recorded by our scribe as 'tweets' and clouts!

Only one master, the deputy head, and the headmaster used the cane. The former would call an offender out into the front of the class, make him bend over the desk and receive 'six of the best' on his rear anatomy. The headmaster was a mathemetician, Mr A. B. Maine, who had written several books on arithmetic, algebra, geometry and calculus. These were the text books we used (royalties going to the head!). His nickname was 'Tish', named after a racehorse I believe. One morning, when the whole school was assembled in the hall, we saw painted in large letters on the front of the balcony TISH. The head and the masters assembled on the stage had to face the balcony and the offending word. Whether the culprit was ever found I know not.

If a boy was sent to the headmaster, he knew he was going to get six of the best from him. He would have to stand in a line outside the master's study door with other victims, awaiting his turn. Those outside could hear the swish and the wack of the cane as each stroke was administered to the poor wretch inside.

I was that wretch on two occasions. The first was when I did badly in my examinations and the second occasion was the result of a complaint from the art master. Art classes were occasions for hilarity and misbehaviour. The master, who was a small man, spoke in a high pitched voice and when we were not drawing apples, bottles and other items of still life, we were allowed to draw anything we liked from memory, as long as it was not an aeroplane or a motor car. A live female model would have been wonderful but we could only dream!

During an exceptionally dull lantern slide lecture, someone threw a piece of chalk at me, so naturally, I picked it up and threw it back. As is always the case, the art master turned round at that precise moment, so off to the headmaster's study I had to go. After a severe lecture from the head, I was told to kneel on his armchair and bend forward, thus raising my posterior. My blazer was rolled up so as not to impede the target and then I was frisked to ensure I had no extra padding inside my trousers. Then, using both hands to hold a long cane, he measured the striking target and proceeded to deliver six strokes. It certainly stung and the red weals lasted for days.

Shortly after starting at the High School, my parents moved from Coronation Place to a new semi-detached house on Greville Road, Romsey Town, a few hundred yards from my grandmother's. It was a three bedroomed house, with lounge, dining room and kitchen and cost around £300. It had a large garden in which Father grew dahlias, chrysanthemums and vegetables.

During the following years, I progressed through the third and fourth forms and reached form five in the autumn of 1938. In the following summer term, I sat for the Cambridge University School Certificate Examination and gained a distinction in history, credits in English language, literature, Latin, biology and mathmatics and passes in French and chemistry. I had no failures.

I disliked chemistry and physics and was hopeless at woodwork. But I excelled in English and won the 1939 Headmaster's Essay Prize on the subject of church architecture! I was presented with a book prize (on architecture!) at Speech Day in the Cambridge Guildhall.

We did not have a swimming pool at school so we were taken to Sheep's Green where a part of the River Cam had been cleared of weeds and made into an open-air swimming 'pool'. When the water temperature reached sixty degrees or more, swimming was compulsory. Below sixty, it was voluntary. When we could swim thirty yards in the river, we gained a point for our house.

Games and sports were compulsory. In the autumn and spring terms, we played rugby football and in the summer cricket and athletics. I hated rugby and was not very good at cricket, always afraid of being hit with a hard ball. I always batted No. 11 and my highest score ever made was 12 not out! My average for my whole school career was 4.83 runs. My preferred fielding position was long-stop! I have never played association football or been to a football match. I am not a football supporter nor a fan! On the other hand, I love tennis, especially as it is a game in which you can play with members of the opposite sex! I joined St Paul's Church Young People's Tennis Club in my teens. We had two grass courts on the edge of the University Cricket Ground, Fenners.

During term time, I played a small part in our house dramatic competitions, and took part in the school debating society meetings. In 1974 the Cambridge High Schools became the Hills Road Sixth Form College and the girls' school the Long Road Sixth Form College.

CHAPTER EIGHT

Memories of Cambridge

Ye fields of Cambridge, our dear Cambridge, say
Have ye not seen us walking every day?
Was there a tree about which did not know
The love betwixt us two?

Abraham Cowley, 1618–67
On the death of Mr William Harvey

THERE WERE VERY FEW TREES that I had not seen when I was studying or doing my homework, for when the weather was fine, I used to take my books into the Cambridge Botanical Gardens and sit by the lake.

In springtime, too, I loved to walk through the Backs of the colleges and see the millions of crocuses among the trees. An American once asked how one could get a carpet of so many blooms and was told to plant the corms and leave them for fifty years.

There were always so many activities taking place in the town and I tried not to miss them. The University Boat Race was always eagerly followed on the wireless. I remember in 1949, John Snagge, the BBC commentator, describing the race, say:

'I can't see who's ahead – it's either Cambridge or Oxford!'

In town, undergraduates would sell light blue rosettes, ribbons and badges on race day. A dark blue favour was rarely seen.

As a boy, I would watch the University Bumps on the River Cam. These are races between crews of eight from the various colleges. The river is not wide enough for conventional rowing side by side, so lines of boats chase the one in front and bump it from behind. At the start of a race, the boats are lined up alongside the embankment above Baitsbite Lock, a length and a half space between each boat. With the firing of the one-minute gun, the eight crew members get into their boats and push out into mid-stream. On the firing of the starting gun, the crews start rowing furiously up-stream in an attempt to catch the boat in front. When a bump has been made, the one which has been bumped pulls into the side and is out of the race. The leading boat at the end of the day becomes the head of the river and sets off first on the following day. The races would last the whole week. They were part of the University's May Week Celebrations which take place every year in June to mark the end of the academic year. During this week, all the colleges hold their May Balls and huge marquees are erected in the college grounds and specially-sprung floors are laid inside over the grass. Chandeliers, colourful decorations and decks of flowers transfer the marquees into elegant ballrooms. The students and their lady friends wear evening dress and dancing proceeds throughout the night until dawn the following day. I would often see undergraduates in all their finery making their way back to their college rooms or digs as I was on my way to school the next morning.

Another May Week event takes place on the River Cam beside the great lawn of Trinity College when the madrigal singers gather in punts to entertain and at night, Chinese lanterns are lit along the river banks.

Also during this week at the A. D. C. Theatre, the University Footlights Society put on their 'Footlights Revue'. Many famous actors started their careers as a Footlight, including Jack Hulbert and his brother, Claude, Jimmy Edwards and Richard Murdoch.

Most universities have a Rag Day in aid of charity but Cambridge students stage theirs on 11 November, Remembrance or Poppy Day to collect money for the Royal British Legion's Earl Haig fund. There is no organised procession through the town; each college competes to raise the most money and each 'does its own thing'.

Some of the colleges aim to make a mile of pennies, requiring a total of 63,360 coins – the old penny measured one inch – inviting passers-by to add to the line. Other undergraduates go on raids in the town, hopping on to buses to collect contributions from passengers whilst others throw a cordon across a street and make motorists and pedestrians pay a toll before they are allowed to pass.

Decorated vehicles and tableaux wend their way through the streets; Aunt Sallys are set up on the pavement, brave undergrads would be put in the stocks and passers-by invited to 'buy' rotten tomatoes and shy at them. I remember one group of students proceeding down Hills Road carrying a long pole between two of them which was adorned with ladies' knickers and men's underpants. Other students would be carrying placards and collecting boxes demanding 'Your money or your pants!' Most pedestrians elected to give money.

Good Friday saw another old custom – skipping on the green. Each Good Friday morning, hundreds of children, young people and adults would gather on Parker's Piece, the large recreation ground behind Regent Street and start skipping, individually and *en masse*. The custom originated to mark the publicans' day out when they came for a game of bat and trap. Ropes which normally secured the the beer barrels were used for skipping. This custom ceased in 1948 but was revived again in 1987. Various stalls selling toys, sweets and refreshments would line the edge of the ground.

The famous Surrey and England cricketer, Jack Hobbs learnt to play cricket on Parker's Piece. Children would mark the wicket on a tree trunk.

Being a university town, there were always important people visiting Cambridge. Queen Mary was a frequent visitor, coming unannounced to visit the Fitzwilliam Museum in Trumpington Street and Woolston's antique shop. In 1934, *en route* to Cambridge, the Queen's car broke down at Waterbeach. Her chauffeur flagged down a passing motorist, a Mr Titmous, and to his great surprise, was asked to give the Queen a lift into town!

In the same year, the town was honoured with an official visit from King George V and Queen Mary to open the new University Library. The entire County High School, some 500 boys wearing their school caps and blazers, together with their masters, marched in threes from the school along Hills Road to the corner of Station Road and lined the pavement opposite the War Memorial to greet the King and Queen as they were driven from the railway station.

On 20 January 1936, George V died at his home in Sandringham. Two days' later, his body was brought by train to London. The railway line passed the end of our school playing field and we were allowed to leave our classes and watch the black-painted train carrying the King's coffin and members of the Royal family slowly pass by. The coffin was clearly seen on a raised dias.

For a treat, we would have afternoon tea at the Dorothy Café in Sidney Street or buy *real* sticky Chelsea buns from C. P. Hawkins, the confectioners, who were part of the Dorothy Café building. We have not found similar Chelsea buns anywhere in the country like those baked by Hawkins. The nearest we have discovered are being produced by Fitzbillies at 52 Trumpington Street by Mrs Penny Thomson. Real Chelsea buns are oozing with syrup, not the sugary rounds of dough you find in most establishments. The bun consists of six tightly rolled, overlapping ribbons of dough, permeated with butter, brown sugar, treacle and currants, guaranteed to add many calories to your diet!

Fitzbillies was established in the early 1920s by the Mason brothers and it soon became famous for its Chelsea buns. Dons, graduates and undergraduates, as well as the townsfolk of Cambridge would daily join the long queues for this delicacy. There have been only three subsequent owners and all have guarded the secret recipe and Mrs Thomson has kept the tradition alive. Tragedy struck the premises a few days before Christmas in 1998 when the premises in Trumpington Street were destroyed by fire.

The premises have since been rebuilt and once again, *real* Chelsea buns are being produced and sold in Trumpington Street.

In the late 1920s and early 1930s, most streets were illuminated by gas lamps and I was always on the lookout for the lamplighter. Each day before dusk, he would come into our street on his bicycle, carrying a long pole on his shoulder. Dismounting at each lamp post, he would raise his pole and insert it into an opening in the bottom of the lamp lantern. He would touch a lever with the end of the pole which would turn on the gas jet. At the other end of the pole was another lever which when pressed produced a spark which ignited the gas and lit the lamp. Later, the gas-lighter was replaced by a clockwork mechanism which turned the lamp on at a set hour. Occasionally, the lamplighter would allow me to switch on the lamp while he held the pole.

An eagerly awaited annual event was the Cambridge Midsummer Fair, held for four days commencing 22 June on Midsummer Common. The fair was opened by the mayor who would stand on the steps of one of Thurston's roundabouts whilst the Town Clerk read out the proclamation. The mayor would ring a bell and declare the fair open and then scatter handfuls of newly minted pennies to the crowd standing around. I was never fortunate to pick up a coin, there was too much pushing and shoving from the bigger boys.

I cannot remember when I saw my first circus but I'm sure my parents took me and that it was to see the famous Bertram Mills Circus. This show took three years to tour the major towns of Britain so it must have been 1929 when I was six years old.

The circus visited Cambridge in April in 1938. A week earlier, we heard on the radio that the founder of the circus, Mr Bertram Mills, had died on 16 April. He was a great showman, a perfect gentleman, and a loss which was felt throughout the land. Nevertheless, the show continued under the direction of Bertram's two sons, Cyril and Bernard, both of whom I came to know personally after the war, when I became editor of the Circus Fans' Association's magazine the *King Pole*. The king poles are the two (and later four) centre poles which hold up the Big Top. The poles round the edge of the tent are called side poles and midway between the king poles and the side poles are a row of longer ones called the queen poles.

The circus had arrived in Cambridge from Luton and after its week in Cambridge, continued to Nottingham and thence on to Scotland. It arrived in Cambridge on Sunday, 25 April and I cycled down to Midsummer Common to watch the build-up of the Big Top. The Mills' show used three trains to move from town to town and a relay of vehicles, caravans and equipment continued all morning from the railway station to the tobar (circus ground). Then came the horses in twos and threes with their grooms and finally, the procession of elephants through the town, each animal holding the tail of the one in front.

I went to see the show with girlfriend Phyllis. We queued for hours for the cheap seats at the back of the tier of benches. 'Move up closer' urged the attendants so as to squeeze more patrons on to the row. The 1938 programme included six Indian elephants with their trainer John Gindl, their act included a game of football. Horses always played a prominent role in the Mills' circus and trainer Charlie Mroczkowski performed a new liberty act with twelve Arab horses whilst the Baker troupe of ten males and females rode bareback on six horses.

Another essential ingredient of the circus is the clown and the Mills' resident funsters were headed by Coco (real name Nicolai Petrovich Poliakoff), the white-faced clown Percy Huxter, Alby Austin, Bob Beasey, and midgets Nikki and Little Billy. Although Coco is usually referred to as Coco the Clown, in correct terminology, he was an auguste. A clown is the white-faced man in the magnificent star-spangled costume who never gets the messy treatment handed out to the augustes such as buckets of water and custard pies.

In later life, I got to know several of these funsters personally and I was one of the last persons to visit Coco in Epsom Hospital just before he died. I also got to know his daughter, Tamara, who married Ali Hassani, a Moroccan tumbler, and together they formed the Hassani Circus which, for a number of years, became the resident circus in the Chessington World of Adventures.

On August Bank Holiday the same year, I went to the Conservative Party Summer Fête on the Gog and Magog Hills. I took another girl-friend with me on this occasion, Ella, who was a lady's maid in one of the big houses on Brooklands Avenue. One of the highlights at the fête was a display of television. The BBC had started its television service in 1936 and for most people, this was the first time they had seen it working.

My parents did not approve of me going to a Conservative function; they were strong Labour supporters and regular readers of the *Daily Herald* and the *Sunday People*. Both sets of their parents were Liberals before the Labour party came into being. Mother told me that Parliamentary elections were always occasions for fun. There were only two main parties – Tories and Liberals. The local Tory candidate would send horse-drawn carriages (and later, motor vehicles) round the streets to pick up voters and take them to the polling station. Everyone would crowd into them and get a ride to the polls. Then they would vote Liberal and sport their Liberal rosettes as they walked back to their homes. Genuine Tory voters would find they were crowded out as far as transport was concerned!

The cinema was at the height of its popularity in the 1930s. Cambridge had nine picture houses – the Victoria, Central, Playhouse, the Kinema (known as the 'flea pit') on Mill Road, the Tivoli on Chesterton Road, the Rendezvous (later renamed the Ritz), the New Theatre/Cinema, the Arts Cinema and the Regal.

When I was about ten, I discovered that all the cinemas tried out their films on Monday and Thursday mornings, the days their programmes changed. So, during the school holidays, every Monday and Thursday morning I would sneak into one of the cinemas through a side door and sit in a seat and watch a preview. Only the cleaning staff and the projectionist were on duty and they soon got to know me and did not object to my presence.

My mother and father very seldom went to the cinema – they preferred the live theatre. Mother would tell us about Nellie Wallace, Florrie Ford and George Robey and they both liked Gilbert and Sullivan. On one occasion, though, a friend had recommended they go and see the film *My Old Dutch*, a Gainsborough picture of 1934 with Gordon Harker, Betty Balfour, Michael Hogan, Florrie Ford, Finlay Currie and Felix Aylmer. It was a sentimental love story, built around the popular music-hall song of the same name.

So off they went into town and into the Central Cinema in Hobson Street. They watched the newsreel, a couple of shorts, a cartoon and the following week's trailers. Then came the interval and Father bought ice cream and then they settled down to watch *My Old Dutch*. But the projectionist must have got it wrong. The lights dimmed, the curtains opened and the captions and title came on the screen – *Alice in Wonderland*, American Paramount version.

My parents suddenly realised they had come to the *wrong* cinema! *My Old Dutch* was being shown in the Victoria Cinema on Market Hill. How much of *Alice* they watched they did not say, but when they left the Central, they went round to the Victoria and bought two more tickets! Never again did they patronise two cinemas in one day!

The Victoria Cinema closed and was demolished in 1988 and the Central Cinema no longer exists. We were in town shopping in 1934 when we saw the fire engines rushing along St Andrew's Street. We could see smoke rising further along the road and Father said, 'Look, there's a fire, let's go and see where it is.'

It turned out to be the Old Castle Hotel and it was completely destroyed. Three years' later, the Regal Cinema opened in its place.

We often went to the New Theatre to see variety shows and in 1933, it became the New Theatre Cinema. The programme consisted of four variety acts on the stage and then a screen was lowered and films were screened. I recall seeing the Western Brothers, Max Miller with his red and blue books, Stanelli and his hornchestra, Flotsom & Jetsom and other popular stars of the time. The theatre eventually closed and was demolished in 1962.

Adjoining the theatre were the offices of the *Cambridge Daily News*. My cousins Arthur and Charles both started their journalistic careers as reporters on that paper. These offices have now gone and my cousins subsequently became editors of regional newspapers.

Also in 1934, Marks and Spencer opened its store in Sidney Street, offering nothing over five shillings. A few doors away was Woolworths, with their threepenny and sixpenny store. They often sold goods costing more than this by splitting the item into two or three parts, each to the value of sixpence!

Father often came shopping with us. On one occasion, he wanted to buy a hat, so we went into town and entered a men's outfitters. The manager greeted us and offered Mother a chair, gave Eileen and I some sweets and Father a cigarette.

'You should offer the lady a chocolate,' said Father and immediately an assistant was despatched to purchase some. Then the manager asked Father what he wanted.

'Cap' said Father.

'What size?'

'Six and a half.'

'What colour?'

'Brown.'

With that, Father made his purchase in record time.

A remarkable event occured in 1930. One Saturday morning, Father who was working in the railway yard, suddenly came tearing home on his bicycle.

'Whatever's the matter?' Mother asked.

'You'll see in a few minutes' he replied.

We then heard a noise like a motor but it was no road vehicle. Suddenly, a giant cigar shape appeared in the sky and flew right over our house and garden. It was the airship R101 on a test flight from its base at Cardington. It was the largest airship built but, regrettably, after having flown the Atlantic in July, crashed at Beauvais, France, on 5 October 1930. The airship struck a hillside during a storm, exploded and burst into flames, killing forty-eight out of its complement of fifty-four crew and passengers. After this disaster and that of its predecessor, the R100, Britain gave up building airships. However, in 1989, my wife and I had a flight in the Fuji airship over Surrey.

In the 1930s, Britain was becoming more and more air minded and Father and I went to see Sir Alan Cobham's Flying Circus at Marshall's Aerodrome, Cambridge. During the day, we had our first flight in an aeroplane. It was a ten minute flight, costing five shillings in an open cockpit, two-seater biplane. It was extremely noisy and very cold. Among the display craft was a giroscope, a predecessor of the helicopter. The year was 1938.

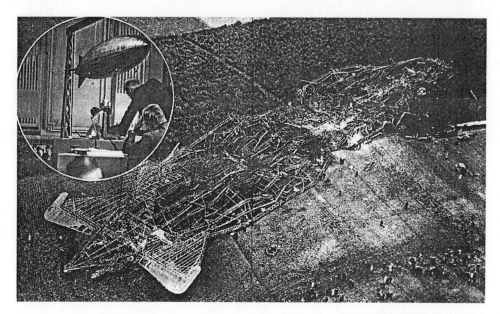

The burnt-out skeleton of the airship R101 in a field at Beauvais, France on 5 October 1930. Inset: a model of the airship.

CHAPTER NINE

Royal Occasions

Hurrah! Hurrah! we bring the Jubilee!
Hurrah! Hurrah! the flag that makes you free.

Henry Clay Work, 1832–84,
Marching through Georgia

I HAVE ALWAYS BEEN A MONARCHIST and been a follower of royal events from childhood. During my life, I have met several members of the Royal Family and witnessed numerous royal occasions.

Monday 6 May 1935 was the twenty-fifth anniversary of the reign of King George V and Queen Mary and Cambridge was bedecked with flags, bunting and flowers. The colleges, churches and civic buildings were floodlit at night and the town was a sea of red, white and blue. There was hardly a street which had no visible display of flags and bunting. The humblest homes and the most imposing business houses each conveyed its message of loyalty and thanksgiving.

The most colourful part of the town was the shopping centre in Sidney Street and St Andrew's Street where each premise had tried to do better than its neighbour. The colonnade at Sussex Street was enhanced by multi-coloured drapes of material. A grocer's shop had displayed in its window a large Union Jack made up of red, white and blue painted egg shells. Even Addenbrook's Hospital in Trumpington Street was transformed into a forest of colour with lines of bunting strung over the grounds from the front of the building to the fence facing the road.

Garden gates, window panes, door posts – all wore red, white and blue drapes and window boxes, tubs and gardens were ablaze with red carnations and geraniums and white and blue hydrangeas and other tricolour blooms.

It was an official holiday, a beautiful, sunny May Day, and the borough staged numerous events to mark the occasion. At 10 o'clock, a United Church Service of Thanksgiving was held in Great St Mary's Church, attended by the Mayor and Corporation the Vice-Chancellor and members of the University and other civic and commercial dignities. The address was given by the Lord Bishop of Ely. I was unable to gain admission to the church but took my place on the Market Hill where the service was relayed over loudspeakers.

Following the service, I made my way to St Andrew's Street to await the parade of horse-drawn vehicles, decorated motor cars and bicycles which toured the town before terminating on Midsummer Common.

The parade having passed me, I proceded to Jesus Green where the main celebrations were taking place, following a twenty-one-gun salute, fired by a battery of the Cambridge University Officers' Training Corps. The Green was thronged with tens of thousands of people watching the main events. These included a mounted gymkhana, a cricket match in fancy dress, a football match played in sacks, a giant push-ball contest and a daylight firework display. A magnificent more traditional firework display took place after dark, preceded by a torchlight procession.

More events took place on the river where a variety of water sports were carried out, including canoe racing, pillow fights and mop fights and walking on a greasy pole extended over the river. In the evening, celebrations continued with concert parties, band concerts, an old folks' tea party and open-air dancing. A pause at 8 o'clock brought everyone to a standstill to listen to a relay of the King's speech. Indeed, a day to remember!

Little did I realise that, forty-two years later, my future wife and I would be preparing and publishing the official souvenir brochures and programmes for the Borough of Elmbridge and the Mole Valley District Council to mark the Silver Jubilee of Her Majesty Queen Elizabeth II.

Royal Air Force Review

On Saturday, 6 July 1935, as part of the Silver Jubilee celebrations, the King carried out a review of the Royal Air Force at Mildenhall and Duxford Aerodromes. At Mildenhall, the King, accompanied by the Prince of Wales and the Duke of York, reviewed more than 350 aircraft from 38 squadrons lined up on the ground. This was, at the time, the largest number of aircraft ever brought together on one aerodrome in Britain.

After the inspection, the Royal party left by car for Duxford Aerodrome. I was determined not to miss this historic event and cycled from Cambridge to Duxford (about ten miles), arriving at the aerodrome some two hours before the King was due. I took up an advantageous position on the edge of the airfield, having been charged two pence to bring in my bicycle!

Promptly at 2.30, the fly-past of aircraft commenced, a total of twenty squadrons, including fighters, bombers and trainers taking part. One of them gave an exhibition of air drill while seventeen squadrons reformed to fly over in wings.

On 20 January 1936, we heard on the wireless that King George V had passed away. The nation went into mourning, radio programmes were cancelled and theatres and cinemas closed. On the following day, the Prince of Wales was proclaimed Edward VIII.

The year 1936 was historic. We had a new king and the rulers of Italy, Germany and Japan were making war-like threats. In March, Hitler re-occupied the demilitarized zone of the Rhineland. In May, the Italians captured the Abyssinian capital Addis Ababa and the Emperor Haile Selassie went into exile while King Victor Emmanuel II of Italy was proclaimed Emperor of Ethiopia.

On 18 July, a revolt by military commanders in Spanish Morocco set off the Spanish Civil War.

Towards the end of November, the country learned of the King's liaison with Mrs Wallis Simpson who had already divorced one husband and had secured a decree nisi from her second in October. Edward VIII planned to marry Mrs Simpson and this threw the country into crisis. The Government, led by the Prime Minister, Stanley Baldwin, was against the marriage as was the majority of public opinion. Schoolchildren were heard singing to the tune of the well-known carol:

> Hark the herald angels sing,
> Mrs Simpson stole our King,
> Peace on earth and mercy mild,
> She shall never have a child!

The King finally abdicated on 11 December and we all listened to his speech that evening on the radio in which he said he could not go on 'without the woman I love'.

On the following day, Saturday 12 December, I caught the train to London and made my way to St James's Palace where a huge crowd had gathered to hear the Royal Proclamation. By the time 3 o'clock arrived, I had wheedled my way to the front of the crowd.

The Coronation of King George VI and Queen Elizabeth took place on Wednesday 12 May 1937. It was an official holiday and again I attended the celebrations to mark the event in Cambridge. They followed very much the same programme as for the Silver Jubilee two years' previously.

This page and opposite: His Majesty King George V (in the car) reviewing aircraft at Mildenhall, 6 July 1935. *(Photograph Ref.: No.5517–3 Royal Air Force Museum)*

This page and opposite: Royal Airforce Review, 6 July 1935. *(Photograph Ref.: No.5517–15 Royal Air Force Museum)*

CHAPTER TEN

Railways – On and Off the Track

One should always have something sensational to read in the train.

Oscar Wilde, 1856–1900
Gwendolen Fairfax in *The Importance of Being Ernest*

IN CHAPTER ONE, I mentioned my father's occupation on the railways. At the beginning of 1939, he was offered promotion but this meant leaving the Great Eastern Section of the L. N. E. R. and moving to the Great Northern Section, based at Hitchin in Hertfordshire. He accepted the move and we left Cambridge on 13 February. We moved into a new three-bedroomed detached house in Strathmore Avenue which cost £499 freehold!

As I was sitting for my School Certificate examinations in the summer, Cambridgeshire County Council agreed to allow me to continue my education at the County High School and paid for a railway season ticket from Hitchin to Cambridge so that I could attend school each day. I had to catch the 6.45 a.m. train from Hitchin station but as this was not a through train, I had to change at Royston and catch another train to arrive in Cambridge at 8.55. It was always touch and go to get to the station in time and the station master would often stand at the station entrance and call me to hurry up as the train was waiting!

School finished each day at 3.15 and this meant a dash to the station to catch the 3.30 Garden Cities Express to Hitchin. I would take an unofficial short cut through the cattle market and across the railway goods yard and tracks. The journey took only thirty-five minutes and I would be back home before many of my fellow pupils had left school.

One of the stories my father told us concerned one of his fellow workmates. Railwaymen took their refreshments in a meal box and would eat them in their rest room. There was a stove in there on which they could heat up dishes or have a 'fry-up'. When on the footplate, they would often put a sausage on the coal shovel and cook it in the firebox of the cab.

On this occasion, though, my father's mate was going to cook his string of sausages on the rest room stove. He was about to put them in the pan when they slipped out of his hand and landed on the floor. As railwaymen were usually covered in coal dust and grime, the floor was likewise not the cleanest of surfaces. So he picked them up and went over to the sink to wash them. But sausages are slippery customers and popped out of his hands and disappeared down the large plug-hole. He expressed his dismay in the usual workmen's language but was determined not to be deprived of his repast. Running the tap, he went outside the hut and waited until his sausages were flushed into the drain. Getting a long stick, he tied a fork on the end and eventually fished them out. Triumphantly, he took them back to the rest room, popped them into the pan and fried them.

Author's father, Jack Sharp on the footplate

'The best sausages I have ever tasted!' was his verdict.

On one journey from Cambridge to King's Cross, a passenger walked up to his cab at the end of the journey and thanked Father for a smooth and comfortable journey and gave him a tip. The person was the black singer and film star, Paul Robeson. It was the only occasion in his forty-six years' service on the railways that he had been tipped by a passenger.

'If passengers can collect for coach drivers, why not for engineer drivers and firemen?' he would say.

Father was prone to explosive sneezes, especially when exposed to dust and sunlight. Mother always said he liked to make a meal of it when he sneezed! On a warm sunny day in August 1960, Father was in charge of the Cambridge-Garden Cities Buffet Express to King's Cross. Just outside Brookmans Park, about three miles on the London side of Hatfield, when he was leaning out of his Gresley V2 2-6-2 locomotive, he gave one of his gigantic sneezes, not a normal gentle 'atishoo'.

In so doing, his false teeth shot out of his mouth and disappeared along the line. He immediately applied the brakes and made an emergency stop.

'What on earth is the matter, Jack?' enquired his startled fireman.

'It's my false teeth,' he spluttered, 'they're down the line and I'm going to look for them. I'm jolly well not going to lose them!'

So saying, he climbed down from the cab and walked back along the track and eventually found them about half a mile back, undamaged. Returning to his engine and ignoring the puzzled passengers hanging out of the lowered windows and the shouts of an irate guard, Father re-started the train and arrived at King's Cross some fifteen minutes late, where he found an inspector waiting for him.

'You wouldn't expect me to arrive in London minus my teeth, would you?' was his explanantion.

This episode is related in Kenneth Westcott Jones' book, *Rail Tales of the Unexpected* under a chapter entitled The Big Sneeze, published in 1992.

In later life when I was married, we had some very exciting rail journeys, including on the Venice-Simplon Oriental Express. These are described later in the book.

Roy and Margaret on the Venice – Simplon Oriental Express

CHAPTER ELEVEN

'Born Again'

Behold, I stand at the door and knock.
If anyone hears my voice and opens the door,
I will come in and eat with him and he with Me.

Book of Revelation, chapter 3, verse 20

THE YEAR 1933 was the most significant year of my life, the year I became a Christian. My family were not religious but they married in a church and I was christened, though I do not know when or where. My godmother was Mother's friend, Winnie Bird. I believe Father's family were Baptists because occasionally, they went to St Andrew's Baptist Church in St Andrew's Street. Mother and Father insisted Eileen and I went to Sunday School every Sunday afternoon, first to St Andrew's and then to St Paul's C of E which was held in the day school we attended in Russell Street.

In 1933, Miss Chandler, our head teacher, gave each pupil an invitation card for a series of special talks for children which were to take place in Wellington Street. They were to be given by a well-known children's evangelist, Mr R. Hudson Pope of the CSSM, the Children's Special Service Mission and Scripture Union. The invitation said there would be models, illustrations, stories, chorus singing and free gifts for everyone with an extra prize for all those who attended every meeting throughout the week. It was the last items which induced me to go along. Mr Pope was a gifted speaker and held everybody's attention, His talks were based on the Bible and the need to come to Christ and accept Him as your own personal saviour.

On the third evening, 2 June, Mr Pope displayed a large painting by Holman Hunt, depicting a door overgrown with weeds and creepers and the figure of Christ, holding a lantern and knocking on the door. The text was from Revelation chapter three, with which I have prefaced this chapter. Mr Pope explained that the Lord Jesus, the Son of God, wanted to enter the lives of everyone, men, women, boys and girls. In the picture, the door is the door of one's heart and Jesus is knocking, wanting to

The Light Of The World

William Holman Hunt (1827–1910)

(By permission of the Warden and Fellows of Keble College Oxford)

enter. But there is no handle on the outside of the door and Jesus will not force His way in where He is not wanted. Only the person inside can open the door. When the door is opened and Christ enters, one's life becomes completely changed, you are no longer an unforgiven sinner but a forgiven sinner, whose sins have already been punished by God through His Son on the Cross. Jesus had died instead of me and if I accepted Him, I would be born again.

At the end of the meeting, Mr Pope asked if any boy or girl would like to open the door of their heart and invite the Lord Jesus to come in, he should remain behind in his seat when the others left. It was that moment I knew I had to stay behind. I wanted the Lord Jesus to come into my life. I was not alone, some dozen or so other children also remained behind and Mr Pope gathered us around him and he explained in simple terms what it meant to be a Christian. Then he asked each one of us to pray and ask the Lord Jesus to come into our lives. This was a tremendous decision and one which I have never regretted. Throughout all the following years – adolescence, military service, marriage, career and old age, Christ has been with me all the way, even when I have let Him down, gone my own way and not kept to the straight and narrow path. Mr Pope gave me a personal text card, quoting St John's Gospel, chapter 6, verse 37: 'All that the Father giveth me shall come to me and him that cometh to me I will in no wise cast out.' With that assurance, I knew that I had been accepted as a member of Christ's kingdom.

A few years' later, I attended St Paul's Church Young People's Bible Class on Sunday afternoons. St Paul's had acquired a new vicar, the Reverend Gerald W. J. Gregson, a dedicated and enthusiastic evangelical. Shortly after his induction, he took over the running of the Bible class and invited young people in the parish to attend and have tea with him afterwards in the vicarage. I went along and thus

Reverend Gerald Gregson with Roy and Margaret

began a great friendship with Gerald and his curate, the Reverend William G. Lee.

More and more of my spare time was spent on church activities. On Sundays, I would go to morning and evening service; in the afternoon, the Bible Class in the vicarage, followed by tea and after the evening service, the young people would meet again in the church hall for fellowship, chorus singing and refreshments.

Tuesday evenings was another social occasion at St Paul's. Officially, it was a meeting of the Band of Hope, a branch of the Church of England Temperance Society. It was run by the sister of my school headmistress, Miss Winnifred Chandler, and the Church Sister, Miss Corbyn. For the first hour and a half, we had games, quizzes, competitions and country dancing. After refreshments, the evening would close with a Bible reading and a prayer.

It was here I started having my first romances. There were a number of very attractive girls in the Bible Class and at the Band of Hope and at weekends, we would go cycling in the country. But none of these flights of fancy seem to last more than a month.

Two weeks before Christmas, the Bible Class would go carol singing round the parish. There would be thirty or more of us and we had a different itinerary each evening. A harmonium was fitted to a trolley and trundled round with us to provide the music and we would move from lamp post to lamp post. Money raised went to a local children's home. At the end of each evening, we would arrive at a particular large house and we would all be invited in for refreshments.

In August, 1937, Gerald Gregson invited me to accompany him on a tour of the CSSM seaside holiday missions. Each summer, parties of young people, mostly students and undergraduates, would form a houseparty at various seaside resorts around the country, led by an experienced children's evangelist. Mr Hudson Pope used to lead the mission at Criccieth, north Wales each summer. The party would take over a large house in the resort for the month of August and each day they organised a programme of activities for children on holiday. The CSSM was an interdenominational organisation which had been working for over 130 years among boys and girls in public and private schools with the object of leading them to a saving knowledge of Jesus Christ and teach them to value the Bible in daily life. Today, it is known as the Scripture Union.

Each morning, weather permitting, the party would proceed down to the beach and build a huge sand pulpit. A short service was held on the sands with an illustrated talk and then the rest of the day was taken up with games, treasure hunts, sports, picnics, sand modelling, etc. Over the years, these holiday activities have been a huge success and many families made a point of planning their holidays at a resort where there would be a CSSM party.

Gerald was the guest speaker at three resorts in 1937 and we stayed two days at each – Overstrand near Cromer, Sheringham and Hunstanton, all on the east coast. Jumping ahead, in 1947, my wife, Margaret and I spent August as a member of the CSSM houseparty at Cromer, Norfolk.

On 5th April, 1938, I was confirmed by Bishop Price in St Philip's Church and on 14 April, I celebrated my first Holy Communion.

To conclude this chapter, here is the Biblical text given to me by Bishop Price at my Confirmation:

I am crucified with Christ: nevertheless, I live, yet not I but Christ liveth in me and the life I now live in the flesh, I live by the faith of the son of God, who loved me and gave Himself for me.

(Galatians, 2, verse 20).

Members of St Paul's Young People's Bible Class, Cambridge, in 1938.

CHAPTER TWELVE

Darkening Days

Let him who desires peace prepare for war.

Vegetius, fourth century
De Re mil, 3, prologue

A S A STUDENT OF HISTORY, I was an ardent follower of world events. In 1938 the clouds of conflict crept ever closer and darker. On 12 March, German troops entered Austria and that country came under Nazi rule. The threat of war grew ominously, with German demands for the Sudetenland from Czechoslovakia

'This is the last territorial claim I have to make in Europe,' declared Adolf Hitler. Our prime minister, Neville Chamberlain, flew to Germany on 15 September to meet Hitler, the German Chancellor at Berchtesgaden. Two subsequent meetings resulted in the signing of the Munich Agreement which allowed Germany to annex German-speaking areas of Bohemia. Everyone in Britain was relieved when Mr Chamberlain returned and on the steps of the aircraft waived a piece of paper in the air on which, he said, was the signature of Adolf Hitler, stating 'the desire of our two peoples never to go to war with one another again.' During the crisis, everyone in Britain was issued with a gas mask and trenches were dug in the parks.

With the threat of war imminent, I joined the school's Officer Training Corps, much against my parents' wishes.

My father's promotion and move to Hitchin in February 1939 meant leaving St Paul's Church, the Bible Class, Young People's Fellowship and all my girlfriends! I could not find an active evangelical church in Hitchin but eventually met Pastor Morris of the Albert Street Baptist Church in Stevenage, four miles from Hitchin. He lived in a village called St Ippolytes, a mile from Hitchin, and I would cycle to his house on Sundays and he took me to his church in his car. I became a teacher in his Sunday School and in August, gave two addresses on Christ's Second Coming in the evening service in his church. Mr Morris had two daughters, Lucy and Poppy, who also taught in the Sunday School.

Events in Europe were rapidly reaching crisis point. German troops invaded Bohemia and Moravia in Czechoslovakia, in spite of Hitler's solemn pledge at Munich the previous year.

At the end of that month, the Spanish Civil War came to an end with General Franco and his fascists as the victors. Two pacts were signed by Germany with foreign powers – in May an alliance with Mussolini and Italy and in August, a non-aggression pact with the Soviet Union.

With the threat of war more and more imminent, my father thought I should leave school and get a job. I was now sixteen and a half years of age and I wanted to stay on for my Higher Certificate but my parents insisted I leave. My last day at school was, officially, 31 July but during the next five months, I continued to go to Cambridge and attend some classes, including the school's Officer Training Corps. It held a field day on the Gog and Magog Hills at Madingley where we took part in rifle shooting and manoeuvres. In November, I passed the OTC Certificate 'A' examination.

Outbreak of War

The Caravan Mission to Village Children, a branch of the Children's Special Service Mission (CSSM), aimed to take the gospel to the villages and hamlets in England, using a caravan, tent and a county missioner. Mr F. T. Varney was the evangelist for Cambridgeshire and in August 1939, he invited me to spend three weeks with him and his wife in the 'mission field'. I joined him on the 14th, the final day of his campaign in the village of Caxton. The closing meeting filled the single pole 'big top' with about 200 villagers, both children and adults. It was a very moving meeting and, in view of the international situation, they were very worried and were turning to God.

The next day was moving day and I helped to take down the tents. A local contractor came with his lorry to transport the tents, seating and all the other props and paraphernalia used in the mission. A shire horse was hired from a farm and hitched to the caravan and Mrs Varney and I slowly wended our way alongside the horse sixteen miles to our next village venue, Gamblingay. Mr Varney had already gone ahead in his car to prepare the site where we were to encamp.

On our arrival in Gamblingay, near Sandy, Bedfordshire, a small village with eighteen public houses, the contractor's lorry had arrived and discharged its cargo. Our first task was to erect our living and sleeping tents in the field, near the village centre and then all hands were required to raise the big top. My next task was to visit every house in the village, leaving leaflets and inviting the children and their parents to the meetings planned for the following two weeks.

Our first meeting was on 20 August and we had quite a good attendance. I gave several illustrated talks to the children. Meanwhile, events were coming to a head in Europe. The *Times* of the 28th spoke of 'this eleventh hour of the gathering storm'. Three days later, Hitler's troops invaded Poland. On the same day, evacuee children from London arrived in the village.

'Cor, look,' a little boy exclaimed on seeing our camp, 'a circus!' That night we had a full tent for the children's meeting which I conducted and gave a talk entitled 'The envelope'.

Mr Chamberlain, on behalf of the Government, had sent a message to Hitler, stating that, unless operations in Poland were suspended and that Germany was preparing promptly to withdraw, His Majesty's Government would, without hesitation, fulfil their obligation to Poland.

During the night, it started to rain and we had to leave our beds and loosen all the guy ropes because if they shrank when wet, they could pull out the stakes and cause the tents to collapse.

The next day, Saturday 2 September, Mr and Mrs Varney took their children home to Stapleford, leaving me in charge of the camp for the night. More evacuees and mothers with small children arrived from London. Mr Varney returned to Gamblingay on Sunday morning, 3 September and at 11.15 a.m. we listened to Mr Chamberlain's broadcast to the nation in the home of one of the villagers. He said that the Government had told Germany that if a satisfactory assurance was not received by 11 a.m. that she was suspending her advance into Poland, a state of war would exist between our two countries. He went on:

'No such satisfactory assurance has been received. Consequently, this country is now at war with Germany.'

Shortly afterwards, the air raid sirens sounded. The family in whose house we were put on their gas masks and squatted under the dining room table. The all clear sounded shortly afterwards and it transpired that it was just a test of the equipment and not a German raid!

The next morning, just after breakfast, the village air raid warden (a typical Warden Hodges in the TV series *Dad's Army*) came storming into our camp and demanded we took down our tents immediately. From the air, he told us, we look like a military encampment and would be bombed!

We lowered the Big Top and living tents and arranged for their storage. Mr Varney hoped to continue his mission in the church hall and it was decided I should return home to Hitchin.

CHAPTER THIRTEEN

The Waiting Game

We are waiting for the long-promised invasion. So are the fishes!

Sir Winston Churchill, 21 October 1940

M Y SCHOOL CERTIFICATE results arrived in the post on 6 September 1939 – a distinction in History, credits in English composition, French, Latin, biology and botany and mathmatics, passes in English literature and chemistry and no failures. I was also granted London University Matriculation Exemption. Father decided I should leave school and get a job. However, as my train season ticket to Cambridge was valid until 31 December, I continued to make daily trips to my school and attend OTC training classes.

A month had passed and no war-like action had so far taken place, so on 30 September, I went to London for the day. I observed all the defence precautions which had taken place – sandbags in front of Government and other important buildings, criss-cross strips of paper across windows, trenches in Hyde Park and St James's Park, barrage balloons in the air and shutters and black-out materials ready to be put into place after nightfall. I then went to the Victoria Palace theatre to see Lupino Lane and Teddy St Dennis in the famous musical comedy *Me & My Girl*, featuring the hit song *The Lambeth Walk*. This subsequently became one of my most favourite shows and saw it numerous times after the war.

I was still without a job, although I had several interviews. One was with the Post Office in Hitchin and another with the De Havilland Aircraft Company at Hatfield, neither of which was successful, seeing that I could be called up for military service within a couple of years. In the meantime, I had registered at the local Labour Exchange and was attending evening classes for shorthand, typewriting and book-keeping.

My school speech day took place in Cambridge Guildhall on 13 November and I received the Headmaster's Essay Prize from the Master of Selwyn College. Ten days later, I was successful in the Officers' Training Corps Certificate 'A' examinations.

Just before Christmas, I had an interview with Mr John Bennett, the Master of Chalkdell House Public Assistance Institute & Emergency

Hospital in Hitchin and was offered the post of Master's Clerk at a weekly wage of £1 10s. I started work on Boxing Day and my hours were 9.00 to 1.15 and 2.30 to 5.00, Monday to Friday and 9.00 to 12.30 on Saturdays, but these hours were later changed, reducing my lunch hour by fifteen minutes and working until 6 p.m. in the evenings. I also had to start at 8.30 instead of 9.00. My duties involved entering admissions and discharges to the hospital and manning the switchboard. Sometimes, I would get the lines crossed or pulled out plugs by mistake, much to the annoyance of the matron (Mrs Bennett) and the assistant matron, the latter a real spitfire and a pain in the neck! She subsequently married one of the doctors.

The year 1940 began peacefully. In Turkey, over 30,000 people perished in a series of earthquakes and floods. At home, Christmas was celebrated in the usual way with turkey, plum pudding and mincepies. A few weeks' later, however, bacon rationing was introduced at 4 oz. per person per week, together with 12 oz. sugar and 4 oz. butter.

Since Christmas, Britain, like the rest of Europe, had been shivering as temperatures dropped to 25 degrees Fahrenheit, (minus 12 degrees Centigrade), the coldest spell since 1895. The River Thames was frozen for eight miles between Teddington and Sunbury and ice covered stretches of the Humber, Mersey and Severn. The sea froze along the shoreline near Bognor Regis and Folkestone harbour and Southampton docks iced over. In Kent, there were snowdrifts twelve feet deep!

My Sundays were spent mostly in Stevenage where I assisted with the services at the Albert Street Baptist Church and in the Sunday School. I went up to London to attend the annual meeting of the China Inland Mission, after which a visit to the London Palladium to see the Crazy Gang in George Black's revue *The Little Dog Laughed*.

Although no German bombs had fallen on London so far, an IRA bomb exploded at Euston Station, injuring four people. In Birmingham, five bombs were by the IRA. In April, Germany invaded Denmark and Norway and in the following month, the Nazis launched their 'Blitzkrieg' on Holland and Belgium. Neville Chamberlain resigned as Prime Minister on 8 May and Winston Churchill formed a coalition war cabinet on the 10th.

The 'phoney war' had definitely ended with German forces sweeping all before them in Holland and Belgium and then into France Winston Churchill made his famous speech in the House of Commons on 13 May when he said, 'I have nothing to offer but blood, toil and sweat!'

Life in Hitchin carried on as usual. I continued working at the Chalkdell Hospital for the same wage – thirty shillings per week, from which was deducted my National Insurance levy. I gave my mother one pound and, with my remaining money, I had just sufficient to pay a visit to the cinema (ninepence, double if I went with a girlfriend), a haircut eightpence, church one shilling, plus train fares when I went up to London or to Cambridge. I continued attending evening classes, eventually taking and passing the Royal Society of Arts book-keeping and typewriting examinations and Pitman's shorthand.

The war across the Channel was reaching crisis point as the Germans drove our troops back to the coast of France. Boulogne was captured on 25 May and the situation was now desperate. A National Day of Prayer for our forces was held throughout the country on Sunday, 26th. The nation's intercessions were heard and God provided a miraculous evacuation of our soldiers from Dunkirk. My future brother-in-law, John Bamford who was to marry Margaret's eldest sister, Winnie, and was with the British Expeditionary Force, was one of those fortunate ones who managed to reach England. He was in a filthy state when he arrived home in Nottingham, completely exhausted. He was allowed only a couple of days' leave before being recalled to his unit. Subsequently, he was posted to North Africa to join the Eighth Army.

With the collapse and surrender of France, Britain stood alone against Hitler. Things looked very bleak indeed and Britain braced itself for invasion. This is the only occasion I ever saw my mother in tears. Father was exempt from military service as an engine driver but he organised fire-watching in Hitchin and became local organiser for the National Savings movement to raise funds for the war. When hostilities eventually ceased in 1945, he was invited to a Buckingham Palace Garden Party and was presented to Queen Elizabeth (the late Queen Mother).

Britain now entered a state of siege. Railings and iron gates from public and private properties were removed, together with all scrap metal, to be melted down for armaments. All signposts were removed from roads, town names were obliterated from shop fronts, churches, public buildings and railway stations around the country, so as to hinder and confuse any invader.

Petrol prices were increased to one shilling and eleven and a half pence a gallon (equivalent to ten pence today). Because of the blackout, travelling by road at night became a hazardous operation. Car headlights were reduced to a mere horizontal slit by means of a mask and, for the first time, a white line was painted down the middle of the road to help motorists. There was even a popular song written entitled *Follow the White Line*. Pedestrians were urged to wear something white at night and to carry a torch. Every window in private and public buildings had to have a black-out curtain or blind and a familiar cry was often heard from an air raid warden 'Put out that light!'

By mid-August, the Battle of Britain had truly begun. As a prelude to the invasion of Britain by Germany, code-name Operation Sealion, the

German Luftwaffe was ordered to destroy the Royal Air Force. Air battles took place all over southern England and along the east coast, the targets being RAF airfields. These were followed by air-raids on British towns and cities, in particular Portsmouth, Cardiff, Swansea and areas around London. In Hitchin, we had our first air raid warning on 24 August. It lasted fifty minutes but no raid took place. We had two more alerts a week later. Up to the end of 1940, I recorded no fewer than 324 air raid alerts in Hitchin, but fortunately, we were not bombed. These alerts continued throughout the first half of 1941. Bombs were dropped on the Letchworth Golf Course and in a field on Great Offley Hill. One morning, whilst on duty at the hospital, the alarm went and shortly afterwards, we heard the drone of aircraft. The assistant master and I looked out of our office and saw a large formation of German bombers flying overhead. They disappeared from sight and a short time later, we heard the sound of explosions. It transpired that their target was the Vauxhall Motor Works at Luton. After work, I cycled to Luton (seven miles away) to see what had happened. A whole street of houses adjoining the Vauxhall Works had been demolished but the public was not allowed to approach the works themselves so I do not know whether they had been hit or not.

On 31 August, I went on 'holiday' to my Uncle Frank and Aunt Annie's home at Huyton, Liverpool. Three days earlier, Liverpool had experienced its first air raid and on the night of my arrival, there were two attacks – the first from 9.30 to 10.15 in the evening, followed by a prolonged raid from 10.30 until 4 o'clock the next morning. We spent the night in the next door neighbour's Anderson shelter in their back yard. Searchlights swept the sky and continuous gunfire from the anti-aircraft batteries was heard throughout the night with spasmotic dull thuds as bombs exploded somewhere in the city. The following day, I took the tram into the City to see the damage caused by the previous night's raids. This included direct hits on the overhead railway.

During my nine days in Liverpool, in spite of 24 air raids and alerts, I managed to visit the museum, saw shows in the Shakespeare, Empire and Pavilion Theatres, took tram rides to various Liverpool suburbs, the ferry across the River Mersey to New Brighton, travelled on the undamaged section of the overhead railway along the docks to Bootle and attended a Valedictory Service for missionaries about to leave for the Far East with the China Inland Mission. Little did they know what events were to take place in the Far East in two years' time.

Whilst in the City centre, the sirens sounded and I made my way down into an air raid shelter. Seating ran along the side of the walls and a rather attractive girl sat down beside me. As we heard anti-aircraft fire, she put her arms round me and clung tightly. An air raid is not all that bad after all! A similar situation prevailed in my aunt's neighbour's

Anderson shelter when sitting next to the daughter of the house, a girl named Edna.

I left Liverpool and returned to Hitchin on Sunday 8 September, another National Day of Prayer. Four air raid alerts were sounded that night. These became regular occurances with up to six alerts a day. In London, the Blitz had begun in earnest with day and night raids on Docklands and the City. Buckingham Palace was twice hit by bombs, causing damage in the quadrangle and forecourt and wrecking the Royal Chapel. But the King and Queen refused to be driven from London. At the height of the Battle of Britain, over 2,000 German aircraft were claimed to have been shot down by RAF Fighter Command and anti-aircraft (ack-ack) batteries between 17 August and 28 September.

But the RAF suffered grievous losses – 915 Spitfires and Hurricanes, according to official figures and among the Battle of Britain pilots lost was my wife's cousin, Bob Barton, aged twenty-one years, who had just qualified as a pilot at the RAF College, Cranwell.

Throughout September, October and November 1940, the sirens in Hitchin were sounding every few hours, although no bombs were dropped. December was somewhat quieter and we actually had ten days during the month without an air raid alert.

Meanwhile, Hitler's plans to invade Britain – Operation Sealion – planned for 17 September, were postponed until April 1941 as the result of the RAF's gallant and successful fight to deny the Luftwaffe air supremacy over the south of England and the English Channel.

The city of Coventry was bombed on 14 November by 449 bombers, reducing the cathedral into a mound of smoking rubble and many factories and homes were destroyed or damaged. As many as 568 people were killed in the raid and 863 seriously injured.

CHAPTER FOURTEEN

'On with the Motley'

There's no business like show business ...

Irving Berlin

THE YEAR 1941 began comparatively quietly. We still had our daily air raid alerts in Hitchin and we had our first snow of winter. The bread ration was cut to 10 oz a day and the import of bananas was stopped to save shipping space. Fire-watching had become compulsory and men and women between the ages of sixteen and sixty had to register for part-time Civil Defence service and were required to do forty-eight hours of

The cast of Roy Sharp's wartime revue 'Saving High', produced in aid of the War Savings Campaign, 1941

fire-watching duties a month. Besides fire-watching on a rota at the Town Hall, I also had to take turns in our civil defence post on our road, Strathmore Avenue.

In North Africa, our troops were having some successes against the Italians in Libya and captured Tobruk. The Luftwaffe continued its bombing raids on British cities – Liverpool, Southampton, Portsmouth, Birmingham, Sheffield, Plymouth, Nottingham, Swansea and, of course, London.

I was now seventeen years of age and would be eighteen in April and the prospects of being called up for military service before long was a certainty. I had no wish to join the army, so on 3 February, I joined the Air Training Corps which I hoped would eventually get me into the Royal Air Force.

To help the war effort, the National Savings Movement set up street savings groups and I was responsible for the Strathmore Avenue group and six other streets. I was also a member of the Hitchin War Finance Committee which organised the various fund-raising activities associated with National Savings Weeks. These were called War Weapons Week, Warships Week and similar campaigns.

In February, at a meeting of the committee, I offered to stage and produce a show for War Weapons Week. The committee accepted my offer and booked the Town Hall for the show. But at the time, I had no show – no script, no players, no singers, dancers or musicians. So I sat down and wrote three sketches.

With the script complete and the actors picked, I wanted a chorus of dancers and an orchestra. I approached a local dancing school and the principal, Miss Gladys Ingram, readily agreed to join the cast and choreographed an opening chorus and a number of dances and brought in eight of her senior girls and eleven juveniles. Next, I looked for a musical director and found a local dance band leader, Ray Turner, who agreed to provide an orchestra and be the conductor. Tony Barker, an electrician, undertook the lighting and amplification.

I called the show *Saving High* and wrote the words of the opening chorus to the tune of the RAF song *It's in the Air*.

The show opened on Tuesday 15 April 1941 and long before the doors were open, a queue had formed outside. Before long, the house was full and people were standing at the back and sides of the hall. Among those unable to get a seat was my boss, the master of Chalkdell Hospital and the matron.

The show went off without a hitch and was enthusiastically received by the large audience. The local newspapers, the *Hitchin Pictorial* and the *Hertfordshire Express*, which had been lukewarm before the show and had given it little publicity, were full of praise. 'Roy Sharp – Hitchin's Showman of the Week' said one headline.

Roy Sharp with his HI-CHIN Concert Party, 1941–42

Such was the success of this show and the demand for tickets that we had to put on a repeat performance.

After the final curtain, the cast and I discussed as what we should do next and decided to form a concert party to raise money for the war effort and help local charlties. We called ourselves the Hi-Chin Concert Party, young people from Hitchin who were keeping their chins up.

CHAPTER FIFTEEN

A Call to Arms

Your country needs you!

A war poster in 1915

SUNDAY, 7 December 1941 was a day of infamy when 184 Japanese aircraft came plunging out of a sunny Hawaiian sky at 7.55 a.m. and attacked the American Pacific fleet in Pearl Harbour. At one blow, they sank four battleships, sank or disabled fifteen other warships, destroyed 188 military aircraft and damaged 159 and killed 2,403 Americans. One thousand of these were on the battleship *Arizona*, which blew up and sank at her moorings. As a result of this unprovoked attack, the United States of America declared war on Japan and also on Germany and Italy.

In the meantime, the war in Europe went on. I was promoted to corporal in the Air Training Corps and later acting Flight Sergeant.

On the Continent, Germany invaded Greece and crossed the Danube into Bulgaria and Yugoslavia and Romania was 'persuaded' to join the Axis powers. Italian forces occupied Albania. The to and fro battles continued in North Africa. The British advanced eastwards and captured Tobruk and Benghazi and took tens of thousands Italian prisoners-of-war. In consequence, Germany appointed General Erwin Rommel commander of the Afrika Korps who hit back and recaptured Benghazi, Tripoli and other outposts in the Libyan desert.

In Britain, the German air force continued to bomb London and other British cities mercilessly. Civilians had to 'make and mend' as clothing rationing was introduced and coal was limited to one ton a month.

On 22 June 1941, German troops invaded the Soviet Union and Russia became our ally. For the rest of the year, Germany advanced into that country; Leningrad was under siege and the Nazis were on the outskirts of Moscow, when bad weather forced them to call a halt.

The Japanese invaded Thailand, Burma, Borneo, Malaysia, the Philippines and a number of islands in the Pacific. Three days after Pearl Harbour, the British battleship, HMS *Prince of Wales*, and the battle cruiser

HMS *Repulse* were sunk by Japanese torpedo planes. On Christmas Day, Hong Kong surrendered.

Regrettably, I have lost my diary for the year 1942, a momentous year in my life. I must, therefore, rely on my memory and letters I wrote for relating the important happenings. I was still a civilian and had changed my job. Leaving Chalkdell Hospital, I commenced work as a temporary junior clerk in the Sanitary Inspector's office in the Public Health Department of Hitchin Urban District Council in the New Town Hall on 14 July 1941 at a salary of £1 8s. 10d. per week, 1s. 2d. less than I had been earning. I continued my commercial studies at night school and my Hi-Chin Concert Party entertained around the district. At night, I would be on regular fire-watching duties in Strathmore Avenue and at the Town Hall, but no incidents occurred during these watches.

Meanwhile, the war in the Far East was going from bad to worse with Japanese forces capturing territories throughout the Pacific area. Singapore surrendered on 15 February. The situation appeared to be desperate and there was only one thing Winston Churchill could do. I received a printed letter from the Ministry of Labour and National Service requiring me to submit myself to a medical examination by a medical board in St Albans. A railway warrant was enclosed, together with a subsistence allowance of 1s. 6d. I duly reported and was given a glass and told to give a specimen. A specimen of what? Should I spit in it? The medical officer told me to lower my pants. He placed his hand under an intimate part of my anatomy and told me to cough!

Nothing more was heard until I received another notice to report to the Royal Air Force station at Cardington, Bedfordshire on 9 July for military service. Even more restrictions were placed on the civilian population. Soap was rationed and a Government decree said that no lace, embroidery or appliqué work could be used on ladies' undies! The Board of Trade urged women not to wear stockings in the summer so that there would be enough for winter wear. Some women reverted to staining their legs with suntan lotion and onion skins to resemble stockings and drawing a seam down the back with eyebrow pencil. In July, the rationing of sweets and chocolate came into force.

On 21 June 1942, Rommel's Afrika Korps entered Tobruk, capturing 35,000 allied soldiers and seventy tanks. He then pushed on into Egypt, captured Mersa Matruk and advanced towards El Alamein. On 7 August, a relatively unknown soldier, Lt General Bernard Law Montgomery was appointed commander of the British Eighth Army in North Africa in place of General Auchinleck.

I caught the train from Hitchin to Bedford, passing the RAF station at Henlow to disembark at RAF Cardington, the stop before Bedford. Cardington was famous before the war as the base for the ill-fated British airships R100 and R101 and their giant hangers were now housing barrage balloons. Having reported at the camp, I proceeded to the stores to be issued with uniform and kit; the medical centre for inspection by the medical officer, who again made me cough! Then to the camp barber's shop for a haircut.

'But I had a haircut two days ago,' I protested.

'Get your hair *cut*,' bellowed the sergeant and we recruits were duly marched to the hairdresser's who swiftly reduced my wavy locks to regulation trim!

My stay at Cardington lasted only a few days and then I was transferred by train to the Lincolnshire seaside resort, Skegness. Here, I was billeted with several other 'erks' in a private boarding house. The following eight weeks consisted of 'square bashing' (drill), marching, rifle drill, lec-

AC2 Roy Sharp, 1632576,
Royal Air Force

tures and general instruction on life, rules and regulations in the Royal Air Force

My arrival in Skegness had not escaped the notice of the German Luftwaffe who sent an aircraft to Skegness in a determined attempt to get me. I had just collected my lunch in the dining hall and taken a seat at the bench table when a burst of cannon fire sent everyone diving under the tables, still clutching their luncheon trays. Fortunately, Jerry missed our block and so I escaped to live another day. No airmen was injured during the attack and we resumed our initial training.

'Skegness is so bracing!' so the pre-war holiday posters proclaimed. Clean sandy beach and safe bathing but not on 3 September 1942. The beach was neither clean nor safe. Barbed wire extended along the water's edge and large sections of the sands were fenced off and out of bounds to civilians. I would not have been surprised if mines had not been laid along the shoreline. However, a small 100-yard stretch near the Clock Tower had been left open for public use. It was here that small units of the RAF recruits trained.

Another National Day of Prayer had been called for this day, the third anniversary of the outbreak of the war. The whole country was urged to go to church on this day to pray for victory over fascism, and the RAF units in Skegness were to take part in a church parade that afternoon.

In the meantime, on that morning, my unit marched down to the open section of the beach and told to sit down in a circle for a lecture on firearms. We were dressed in battle uniform and tin hats – not a pretty sight!

There were very few civilians about but sitting on the beach and watching us was a very pretty young girl in a bright summer dress. Naturally, I could not take my eyes off her and she gave me a smile. Half way through our instruction, the sergeant in charge told us to take a ten-minute break for a smoke. As I did not smoke, I walked across to the girl and sat down beside her.

'Hello,' I said, 'are you on holiday?'

'Yes,' she replied, 'but I go home later today.'

'A pity,' I replied. 'Where is your home?'

'Nottingham,' came the answer.

'Oh, I have an uncle and aunt who live in the Meadows in Nottingham. Do you know it?'

'Yes, we used to live in Arkwright Street in the Meadows where my father owned a brass foundry. When he died, we sold the business and moved to Mapperley.'

'Oh I know Mapperley,' I told her. 'I liked to take tram B to Mapperley when I came to Nottingham during my school holidays, just for the ride.'

'I am afraid the trams have stopped running and have been replaced by trolley buses' she told me.

'What a shame! I love trams. By the way, my name is Roy – what's yours?'

'Margaret, Margaret Holmes.'

'A nice name. Do you have a boyfriend?'

'Not a regular one. I used to go out with the bandmaster of the Irish Guards but we were not really tuned in to one another. He said I was too young for him and it is now finished.'

'My girlfriend stopped writing to me when I joined this mob,' I told her. 'My home is in Hitchin in Hertfordshire and my father is a train driver.'

Just then, the sergeant walked over to us.

'Come along, airman, stop annoying the civilians. Get back to the squad, the corporal is ready to resume his demonstration.'

Saying 'Cheerio' to Margaret, I rejoined the other recruits. The sergeant, though, sat down beside Margaret and proceeded to chat her up.

Miss Margaret Holmes, later to become Mrs Sharp

'How about you and me meeting for a drink later today?' he asked her.

'No thank you,' came her answer. 'I don't drink and I'm going home this afternoon.'

'Well, give me your address and I will write to you,' he said.

'Sorry, I must go,' replied Margaret and with that, she got up and left the beach.

Later that afternoon, we were marching along Marine Parade to join the rest of the units for the church parade when a thunderstorm broke out.

'Take shelter, lads,' said the corporal. 'It won't last long and we will wait until the rain eases off. We don't want to get our nice new uniforms wet, do we?'

We broke ranks and most of the squad sought shelter in doorways and under shop canopies. To avoid the crush, I ran across the road to a bus shelter. To my surprise, Margaret, the girl on the beach, was there waiting for a bus.

'Hello again, Margaret. Where are you off to now?' I asked her.

'To the station,' she replied 'and here comes my bus.'

Quickly, I put my hand inside my pocket and pulled out one of my father's visiting cards which I had previously amended to give my name and service address. Taking my fountain pen, I wrote on it, 'Please write to me,' and thrust it into Margaret's hand as she boarded the bus.

Within a few days, to my great delight, a letter arrived from Margaret, the first which was eventually followed by over 300 others from her.

Skegness Skipper. Since 1908, Skegness's jolly fisherman has skipped across this classic of poster art created by John Halsall.

CHAPTER SIXTEEN

Chores, Cycling and Courting

How a little love and good company improves a (wo) man!

George Farquhar, 1678–1707,
The Beaux Strategem

WITHIN A FEW DAYS of receiving my first letter from Margaret, I was posted to RAF Valley on the Isle of Anglesey, North Wales, to await a training course. When I was called up, I was asked what were my qualifications. I said I was a local government officer and had passed examinations in typewriting, shorthand and book-keeping. I was asked what I knew about radio. 'Nothing' I replied.

Was I interested in electronics? Again, I replied in the negative.

The interview concluded with me being assigned to be a radio-telephony operator, an RTO.

RAF Valley was an operational station, within sight of the sea, valleys, lakes and mountains. A flight of Beaufighters was based here which patrolled the Irish Sea.

Nobody on camp could tell me anything about the proposed RTO course and so, in the meantime, I was put in charge of the washing-up machine in the cookhouse and on general duties in the stores and dining room. The bonus was I was never to go hungry. Other recruits were put on latrine duties, so I considered myself lucky.

I was due to take my first leave in November and I decided to spend it with Margaret in Nottingham. I had written to my Aunt Kate to ask if I could stay with her during my leave. She readily agreed but my mother was furious. She said it was my duty to come home.

Friday 20 November arrived at last, the day I went on my first leave, the day I met Margaret again. She was waiting for me at the barrier on the Midland Station, a wonderful sight! After a fond embrace (our first), Margaret suggested we had a cup of coffee at the milk bar next to the station. Then came an embarrassing moment. The bar stools were very high and Margaret is only five feet tall. Attempting to sit on one, she slipped and ended up on the floor. Fortunately, she sustained no physical damage except to her dignity. She did have a nice pair of legs, though!

We caught a bus to Margaret's home in Mapperley and there I met her mother and her four sisters – Winnie the eldest, Iris a civil servant, Florence who was engaged on war work and her youngest sister, Renée, a land-girl in the Women's Land Army. She had to work on a farm and she was terrified of cows! Margaret at this time was twenty-two years of age and I was nineteen. She worked as a typist in the Ministry of Labour and National Service, a reserved occupation.

The next few days simply flew by. We spent the week together and I reluctantly had to walk back to my aunt's house at night (the buses stopped running at 9 o'clock). After tea on Sunday, everyone started to get ready for church. At the last minute, I said to Margaret, 'Do you think we could miss church and stay in the house?' Margaret agreed at once to the consternation of the rest of the family.

We spent the evening on the settee in the lounge.

'Darling,' I said to her. 'I love you. When all this trouble is over, will you marry me?' After a short pause, the answer I wanted to hear came from her.

'Yes,' she said, 'if you do not think our three year age difference is a drawback.'

'Of course not,' I replied and so we became engaged.

A few days later, we visited a jeweller's shop in the city to buy an engagement ring. Diamonds, it seemed, were in very short supply and diamond engagement rings were far too expensive and beyond my budget. However, the jeweller produced a very attractive blue zircon ring and this we purchased. At least Margaret did, as I did not have enough money for it. I agreed to send her instalments each pay day until it was paid for.

The days following my return to Valley found me floating on air. The excitement of those days spent with Margaret and her consent to marry me seemed like an impossible dream, a dream though which had become true. How we longed for my next leave.

In the meantime, there was some good news on the war front. The Eighth Army under General Montgomery had scored a notable victory at El Alamein and had driven Rommel and his Panzers out of Egypt. At the other end of the Mediterranean, American, British and Allied troops had landed in Morocco and had advanced through Algeria into Tunisia.

Prime Minister Winston Churchill authorised the ringing of church bells on Sunday 8 November to mark the successes in North Africa and had declared: 'This is not the end. It is not even the beginning of the end. But it is, perhaps, the end of the beginning.'

CHAPTER SEVENTEEN

Wedding Bells

*With this ring I thee wed, with my body I thee worship and
with all my worldly goods I thee endow.*

Wedding vows at the Solemnization of Matrimony

THE YEAR 1943 began with news of the Russians fighting back on the
Eastern Front. In North Africa, the Eighth Army under General
Montgomery had captured Tobruk and continued westwards through
Libya. On 7 May the Allies entered Tunis. U-boats continued to play
havoc with Allied shipping in the Battle of the Atlantic and in Burma and
the Far East, things were not going so well.

On 7 January 1943, I left RAF Valley for RAF Station Cranwell, in
Lincolnshire to join No. 1 Radio School. Here, I underwent instruction
in Morse Code, signalling, wiring and soldering, radio-telephony and
science. Good fortune enabled me to spend six weekends with Margaret,
travelling from Grantham to Nottingham by bus and train.

At the end of February, I sat my Radio Telephony Operators' examinations and obtained an overall mark of 69 per cent. As a result, I received
my 'sparks' badge and was promoted to Aircraftsman First Class (AC1).
My pay was increased to thirty shillings per two weeks. Whilst at Cranwell,
we underwent a medical examination to see if we were fit for service
overseas. The MD just listened to my chest with his stethoscope and that
was that – less than one minute and I was told I was A1. Providing you
are breathing, you are fit for overseas!

At the end of the course, I had fourteen days' embarkation leave. I
caught the train to Nottingham where Margaret joined me and we took
the train to Hitchin via King's Cross. My parents' reception of Margaret
was lukewarm!

On 10 March, Margaret and I returned to Nottingham. Margaret had
no more leave so I did not see her until after office hours. On Tuesday
16th, I said goodbye and returned to Hitchin and on the following day,
caught the train to Morecambe to await embarkation instructions. I was
billetted in a private boarding house, whose owner, an ex-military type,

laid down the rules and said, 'You play ball with me and I will play ball with you!'

On 1 May, I was posted to No. 219 Squadron at Catterick, Yorkshire, a fighter squadron preparing to go overseas to the Far East. After being fitted out with tropical kit, I was informed that as I had not yet had any practical experience as a Radio Telephony Operator, I was to be taken off the draft and told to return to Morecambe. I was not sorry.

I was then posted to No. 63 Squadron at RAF station, Macmerry, in East Lothian, Scotland, overlooking the Firth of Forth.

On 23 June came another overseas draft and another fifteen days embarkation leave. I asked Margaret to marry me now but she replied 'No, not yet'. But the next day, Friday, after being chivvied by her workmates at her office, she changed her mind and when she came home, said she was willing to go ahead on two conditions: one – that we got married in her church, the Bridgeway Hall Methodist Mission in Arkwright Street; two – that we take precautions not to have a baby before I went abroad. I agreed to both conditions unconditionally.

Margaret's mother agreed to our wedding but what would my parents say? A hectic round of activities followed and we set the date – Saturday 3 July, just one week ahead. We went to see the minister at Bridgeway Hall, the Rev. William Bollom, to fix the ceremony and to Gilbert's Tea Gardens at Mapperley to book the reception and order the cake. Then Margaret compiled a list of guests to be invited. War-time restrictions meant we could not have more than fifty. We were also limited to one taxi, so we hired a Nottingham Corporation double-decker bus to convey guests to and from the church and the reception.

On Sunday, I went alone to Hitchin to break the news to my parents and obtain their consent, as I was still only twenty years of age and this was required by law. My mother's first greeting was 'Where's Margaret? I told you it wouldn't last!' Then came the bombshell.

'She's very busy,' I told her, 'we want to get married next Saturday.'

'*You fool*!' she exclaimed, 'you don't know what you are doing.' Then she went into the garden where Father was tending to his dahlias and told him.

'The boy must be out of his mind!' was his comment.

Mother's next shock came when I told her we would like her to make four bridesmaids' dresses for her sisters Iris, Florence and Renée and one for my sister Eileen. They had managed somehow to obtain clothing coupons for the material and a girl in Margaret's office had sold her an unused white wedding dress for £5 as her own wedding had been called off.

The next day, I went to the Registrar's Office to obtain a Special Wedding Licence – it cost me 17s. 6d.! – and a consent form for my parents to sign. Back in Nottingham, I bought Margaret a gold wedding ring, costing £2 5s. (a fortune in those days and two weeks' RAF pay!). Margaret ordered her bouquet and posies for the bridesmaids and we attended a rehearsal at the church. We also visited Margaret's family doctor to discuss contraceptives.

Four days before the great day, a telegram arrived from the RAF, recalling me to my unit. We were devastated. I wired back, informing them I was getting married on Saturday and requesting a forty-eight-hour extension. This was granted but I had to return to Scotland on 5 July, two days after we had tied the knot.

The day before the wedding, Friday, my Aunt Doll (mother's sister) arrived from Cambridge, followed by my mother, father and sister from Hitchin. Except for Eileen, they were all staying with Uncle Bill and Aunt Kate in their two-bedroomed terrace house in Newcastle Road in the Meadows. Aunt Doll slept in the front room (drawing room), the first time I can ever remember anyone even sitting in there, let alone sleeping! Mother and Father slept in the second bedroom and I bedded down on the couch in the dining room.

Having settled them in at Aunt Kate's, Eileen and I *walked* all the way to Margaret's house in Mapperley (no buses after 9 p.m.) and I could not afford a taxi!

By now, it was nearly midnight and Margaret's mother and sisters would not allow me into the house. 'It is unlucky for the groom to see his bride on their wedding day before they meet in church.' I borrowed Margaret's bicycle and cycled back to Aunt Kate's and a restless night on the couch.

Saturday, 3 July 1943

The great day had arrived. Bridgeway Hall was only a short walking distance from my aunt's and we all set off together for the church. It was a beautiful sunny summer's day – we could not have asked for better – and I was dressed in my RAF uniform, carefully ironed and pressed with buttons polished bright. Outside the church I met my best man, Corporal James Lodge, who was the fiancé of Margaret's friend, Josie, and he was stationed at RAF Newark. We waited a while and a church official came and asked us if we were guests at the wedding. 'I think so,' I replied, 'I'm the groom!' We entered the church to await the arrival of the bride.

In the meantime, our one and only taxi, arrived with Margaret, her mother and sisters at the church. 'We're too early,' Margaret exclaimed, so the driver drove round the block before they eventually drew up at the church door and entered.

Margaret looked radiant in her white satin gown with a head-dress of

Our wedding group – 3 July 1943

From left to right: Florence and Renée Holmes, Jim Lodge, Roy and
Margaret. Mr Bamford, Snr who gave the bride away, Iris Holmes and
Eileen Sharp

3rd July 1943

orange blossom and she carried a bouquet of pink roses and trailing fern. She was escorted on the arm of Mr Fred Bamford, her sister Winnie's father-in-law, as Margaret's father was dead. Behind them came the four bridesmaids. My mother had worked a miracle and in four days had made their dresses – two in blue taffeta and two in pink and each carried a posy of mixed sweet peas.

Accompanied by Mr F. Shepherd on the organ, two hymns were sung during the ceremony – 'Lead us, Heavenly Father, lead us' and 'Oh, Perfect Love'. The resident minister of Bridgeway Hall, the Rev. William Bollom, officiated and pronounced us 'man and wife'.

We left the church in the one taxi cab, followed by the double-decker bus which had been draped with white ribbon, and made our way to Gilbert's Tea Gardens on Woodborough Road for the reception. As both our families are teetotallers, all the toasts were drunk in non-alcoholic beverages. The cake, unfortunately, was a disappointment. War-time restrictions meant only two eggs could be used, very little dried fruit and *no icing sugar*! Even the frill did not meet! But we were married, the happiest day of our lives up to then.

We caught the 4.30 p.m. train to Liverpool where we were to spend our abbreviated honeymoon at the home of Aunt Annie and Uncle Frank. Those forty-eight hours simply flew.

The next day, Monday 5 July, we wandered together in the city centre and toured Lewis's department store, envisaging all the things we would need when setting up home together. Margaret had already started to fill her 'bottom drawer' but there were lots of other things we would need when I came home. Home? We wondered where that would be.

It was now time for our last meal and we went for lunch at the Queensway Restaurant in London Road. More wartime restrictions decreed that no restaurant meal was to exceed five shillings. The *pièce de resistance* on the menu was roast duckling, costing just five shillings, so this is what we had. We enquired about a dessert – Margaret has always been fond of her desserts! – but being told this was our last meal before I went overseas, the manager served us with ice cream.

At 2.40 p.m., we parted at the Exchange Station and I took the train back to Edinburgh. A flight-lieutenant passed me on the road back to camp and so I got a lift to Macmerry.

The next day was hectic. I had to get my clearance certificate signed, attend pay parade (£4 18s.), fill up forms to get Margaret her marriage allowance and hand our marriage certificate over to the accountant officer. Then it was back to Morecambe and the now familiar routine of kit and clothing parades, innoculations, gas equipment inspection, lectures and the issue of a rifle and a deep-sea kitbag. I also received a pith helmet and tropical kit and shorts, so it looked like the real thing this time.

Confirmation of this came with a full dress rehearsal on Saturday evening and on Sunday 18 July (fifteen days after my marriage), we were marched with full kit and kitbag to the station and boarded a train to Glasgow, Greenock and Gourock on the River Clyde, where we boarded the Orient Lines troopship, the former luxury liner SS *Orion* (24,000 tons).

CHAPTER EIGHTEEN

All at Sea

... on such a full sea are we now afloat.

William Shakespeare, *Julius Caesar*

A T 8.00 p.m. ON MONDAY, 19 July 1943, our ship weighed anchor and set sail from the River Clyde. The sea was calm and the next day, we joined a convoy of other ships, together with Royal Navy escort vessels, and sailed through the Irish Sea and out into the Atlantic Ocean.

Accommodation for other ranks (that's me) was well down in the ship – it could be below the water-line as there were no portholes. It was just an open deck with fixed tables and benches. All our meals were eaten here and at night, hammocks were slung above the tables whilst other men chose to sleep on the tables and benches. There must have been several hundred of us packed down in this 'Black Hole of Calcutta'.

I tried a hammock but no way could I manage to sleep in it, so I gave up and arranged my blankets on the table to form a bed. No coverings were needed as it was so hot and stuffy down there. I had to crawl over a dozen bodies to get to my space on the table. We had to carry our life-jacket at all times and did not undress at night.

On the second day at sea, we had an action stations alarm – whether it was real or not we were not told. We had three alarms the next day and one of the escorting destroyers dropped depth charges, so we assumed there was a submarine lurking near us. We must have been sailing west in the Atlantic because our clocks were retarded two hours.

On board our ship was the famous trumpeter and band leader, Nat Gonella (Nat Gonella and his Georgians) with his signature tune 'Georgia on my mind'. He was a gunner in the Royal Artillery and at night, he gave a concert, accompanied by the Dance Band of the Royal Tank Corps.

On the fourth day at sea, we were told to change into tropical kit (khaki shirt and shorts). The Navy who were in charge of the ship seem to have a good racket going. They were selling oranges, apples and tins of fruit which they had picked up on a previous voyage from South Africa. A tin of pears cost fifteen pence and had to be shared between three of us. But

Author's abode on the Rock –
Hut 32, New Camp Gibraltar.

they did taste delicious. On Sunday, Holy Communion was celebrated on board and there were C. of E. and interdenominational services.

We must have altered course during the night as our clocks were advanced one hour. We were forbidden to throw anything overboard but during the night, all rubbish and debris was discarded at a certain hour. This was to prevent any enemy craft following on our trail. The sea was still very blue and calm, the sun was shining and it was getting warmer.

On the evening of the seventh day at sea, we sailed through the Straits of Gibraltar and into the Mediterranean. We saw the lights of Tangier, Spain, Spanish Morocco and Gibraltar in the distance. Day Eight was wash day. We were issued with some Rinso and allowed extra cold water. Then we spread our smalls out to dry on deck and sat and watched them. Anything left unattended was pinched! During the day, a school of porpoises accompanied us, racing ahead and then diving underneath the ship and leaping out of the water. We also saw lots of flying fish jumping out of the sea just in front of the ship.

At 12.30 p.m. on day nine, we anchored in the port of Algiers in French North Africa where many of the army units disembarked. Crowds of Arabs lined the quayside, a really scruffy lot. Their clothes were torn and in ribbons, whilst others wore robes covered with multi-coloured patches. All of them looked filthy dirty with grisly beards and most of them were bare-footed. They were supposed to be helping to unload supplies from the ship. Their 'foreman', in less patched clothes, and wearing a dirty white topee marched up and down, brandishing a stick and telling the men to get on with the work.

Some of the troops aboard threw cigarettes on to the quay and there was a mad scramble to retrieve them. Old torn and dirty clothes which some of the troops had discarded were tossed overboard, only to be fiercely fought over by the Arabs.

The following day, we were allowed ashore for seven hours. For most of that time, I walked! Algiers is built on a hillside, starting from sea-level. It is a city of boulevards, each one higher than the previous one, and you wend your way along each, getting higher up the hill at each turn. Small Arab boys followed me continuously, trying to persuade me to have a shoe shine.

I changed five shillings into French francs at the rate of 200 to the pound. But goods in the shops were very expensive. There was a shortage of most things, especially food and clothes, with the exception of fruit. The Germans had commandeered and shipped most of the stocks to Germany before they retreated and what goods there were in the shops had been brought in by the Allies. Surprisingly, there seemed to be an abundance of packets of English-made Kotex sanitary towels!

Back on the ship, we sailed westwards, hugging the African coast. On board, I discovered I could earn a little extra money. Being a dab hand at sewing, I undertook stitching badges, stripes and flashes on fellows' tropical tunics at one shilling a time. In one day, I made nearly ten shillings!

On 2 August 1943, we anchored in Oran Bay where some more soldiers were taken off in tenders. Here, we stayed overnight but were not allowed to leave the ship. Then west again until we sighted the Spanish coast on our starboard side and at 10 p.m., we saw the Rock of Gibraltar.

At 9.45 the next morning on Wednesday 4 August, we left the SS *Orion* for the last time and was transported to RAF New Camp for a 'Welcome to Gibraltar' briefing. As one of the new arrivals remarked, 'If this is New Camp, what the hell was the old camp like?' After our pep talk, I was posted to Air Headquarters, deep inside the Rock. My quarters was a Nissen hut at Europa Point, the southern tip of the colony, overlooking the Straits towards North Africa.

CHAPTER NINETEEN

Life on the Rock

Rock of Ages, cleft for me,
Let me hide myself in thee.

Augustus Montague Toplady, 1740–78

FOR THE NEXT TWO and a half years, Gibraltar was my home. Looking back on it, I fared very well and there were many other places to which I am glad I was not sent.

Being at Europa Point, I was away from the main RAF camps. We were a small unit consisting of two Nissen huts and a dining hut and most days, we could see right across the Straits to the Atlas Mountains in Morocco. Adjoining our hut was a small Catholic chapel, the Shrine of our Lady of Europa. It was formerly a mosque until Gibraltar was captured by the Spaniards in 1482. At night, we could see the lights of Tetuan in Spanish Morocco. Looking across the Bay of Gibraltar is the Spanish town and port of Algeciras, four miles across by ferry, and adjoining the colony is La Linea de la Fronteria and the Spanish border.

Each day, hundreds of Spaniards entered Gibraltar to work in the dockyard, shops and cafes but they had to return to Spain by the evening curfew. Many goods could be bought here which were unobtainable in Spain and the Spanish workers would stock up each evening before returning home. Cigarettes in particular were in demand – one hundred Players cost 3s. 4d. Before crossing the frontier, you could see men and women hiding cigarettes, soap and other goods in their underwear, but they always kept one or two packets of cigarettes to give to the Spanish custom official and the police.

Among the strange attractions for me after three years' wartime restrictions in the UK were very white bread, fresh bananas and no black-out at night. This was to make it more difficult for enemy aircraft to identify Gibraltar from 'neutral' Spain. The roads around and up the Rock are very narrow and steep and most of the traffic consisted of military vehicles. The Royal Engineers were busy every day blasting and excavating fresh tunnels inside the Rock. All the stones and rocks which they dug out were transported by lorries down to North Front to be deposited into the sea to form the extension to the runway. The aerodrome had been built parallel to the Spanish frontier on what was formerly the Calpé race course and on so-called 'no man's land'. The lengthening of the runway was vital to enable large aircraft to land. At one time, some 7,500 tons of rock were excavated and dumped into the sea each day.

Motor vehicles were not allowed to use their horns because they could interfere with radio communications so it was customary for the drivers to extend their hand out of the window of their cab and bang the sides of the door to warn pedestrians of their approach. There were very few vehicles on the Rock without dented doors!

Once a week, the Ceremony of the Keys took place. Led by mounted military police, a band marched along Main Street and paraded outside The Convent, the residence of the Governor-General. With an escort of motorcycle police, the Governor would arrive and take the salute. A squad of retiring guards would emerge from the guard house and would be immediately challenged.

'Halt! Who goes there?'

'The keys,' would come the reply from the retiring guards.

'Whose keys?'

'King George's keys.'

'Pass, keys.'

A B-17 Fortress at readiness beneath the low Levanter cloud

The airfield photographed by the RAF on 16 November 1943, from 7,000ft. *(Crown Copyright)*

The squad would then approach the Governor and hand him a big bunch of keys to the fortress, which he then hands over to the new guard. After an inspection, the Governor would depart, the keys would be returned to the guard house and the new guard would take up sentry duty. This Ceremony of the Keys is still carried on in Gibraltar today.

Gibraltar was vital to Britain's war effort. It was a major naval base, guarding the entrance into the Mediterranean, a stopover for troops proceeding to North Africa and the Middle East, a base for Coastal Command Catalinas and Sunderland flying boats searching for U-boats and German and Italian shipping and a fortress against an attack from Spain.

At the outbreak of the war, the Spanish occupied the neutral ground between the Rock and La Linea and erected concrete 'dragon's teeth' and pillboxes on it.

Hitler's original intention was to capture Gibraltar through Spain. He set up a network of spies and observers in the Hotel Reina Cristina in Algeciras, in a number of villas along the coastal road of the bay, in La Linea and on a hilltop at San Roque. Extensive plans were drawn up; troops trained for the assault but all depended on General Franco. But the Spanish dictator withstood all the pressures and rejected every bribe and inducement from Hitler and Mussolini so the plan was finally abandoned.

Fearing Spanish intervention in the war on the side of the Axis powers and an attack on the Rock, over 16,000 Gibraltarians, including all the women and children of the colony were evacuated to Madeira, the Canary Islands, Jamaica and Northern Ireland and some to England. Male Gibraltarians who remained were employed by the Forces and worked in the dockyard or joined the Gibraltar Defence Force.

Many famous regiments were stationed on the Rock for varying spells of duty, as well as the Royal Engineers, Royal Artillery, the Royal Navy and the RAF.

As far as the war went, the Russians had begun to fight back on the Eastern front and Stalingrad was re-captured. In North Africa, the Eighth Army captured Tobruk and continued to push westwards, capturing Tunis on 7 May 1943. The Battle of the Atlantic assumed alarming proportions with attacks on Allied convoys by packs of German U-boats. Things were not going too well, either, in the Far East and Burma. But good news came on the 13 May with the announcement that the North Africa campaign was over with victory for the Allies.

Back in Gibraltar, life was full of interest. I worked on shift duty in the Operations Room, deep in a tunnel inside the Rock at Europa Point. Later, I was transferred to New Camp and worked in the Watch Tower, listening out for incoming aircraft. In 1944, I was 'posted' to a listening post at the western end of the runway (a dangerous position) and finally, in the Air Traffic Control in the tower by the runway. This was sited on the south side of the runway adjacent to the road to Spain which crossed the runway and had to be closed every time an aircraft landed or took off. When the claxon sounded, pedestrians would scamper across to safety. On one occasion, a donkey pulling a cart refused to move and had to be pushed across by the RAF police. Landings and take-offs were always tricky as the pilots had to avoid over-flying Spanish waters and territory. Aircraft were always liable to be hit by cross-winds as they took off to the east or landed from that direction. The Polish commander-in-chief, General Sikorski, was killed when his aircraft plunged into the sea off the eastern end of the runway when taking-off on 4 July 1943. A buoy anchored in the sea marks the spot.

Just before D-Day in 1944, we had a most distinguished visitor, General Montgomery. Actually, it was not *the* General but Monty's double, Lieutenant Clifton James.

He was sent to the Rock to be seen by the Spanish and Hitler's spies to give the impression the general was planning a Mediterranean invasion of Europe.

Being on shift work meant I had plenty of free time in the day and evenings and there were lots of activities for those keen enough to participate. But there were always men who constantly complained about life on the Rock. But for some, such as the tunnellers, life was sheer hell. But we had a fine climate, good food augmented with fresh fruit and supplies from Spain and a wide range of entertainments and sports. There 0were several cinemas, a garrison theatre staging plays and concerts, the Theatre Royal which ENSA companies visited on a regular basis and numerous clubs and societies catering for all tastes.

Particularly popular with the troops were the pub entertainers. The bars along the Main Street all had open fronts and each had a Spanish band and dancers performing for the customers. But these performers had to be back over the frontier by curfew.

Whenever I was off-duty during the summer months, I went swimming. Eastern Beach and Catalan Bay were for other ranks whilst the better Sandy Bay was reserved for officers, WRENS and Royal Naval Nursing Sisters exclusively. Officers were mostly accommodated in the Rock and Bristol Hotels, not in the camps.

Of the numerous societies on the Rock and one of the most popular was the Gibraltar Literary and Debating Society which I joined. Open to all ranks and all members of the forces as well as any civilians, it provided a wide range of cultural activities. We even had a Mock Parliament to debate important issues and a Mock General Election, which was won by Labour with a large majority, a foretaste of what was to happen in the real General Election in 1945. Runners-up were the Communists and there were two Conservatives! The new Common Wealth Party formed by Sir Richard Acland had a number of supporters. One debate was on the motion: 'That this house is of the opinion that the future of mankind depends upon the moral rather than on economical change.' It was carried by forty-five votes to thirty-three. The same opinion holds good today.

We also published a monthly *Rock Magazine*, comprising short stories, anecdotes, cartoons and news from home. A regular feature was entitled 'Pepys Diary on the Rock' which recorded events and entertainments in Gibraltar during the previous month. It was written by the editor, Reg Cudlipp and when he was repatriated, I took over his column and entitled it after another famous diarist, John Evelyn. I eventually became joint editor of the magazine until I returned to the UK. This was the beginning of my journalistic career.

Another lively group was the RAF New Camp Thursday Club, which held discussions and talks on all sorts of topics. We also had a social studies group, a music group and educational lectures as well as evening classes for Spanish and other subjects.

The *Rock Magazine* was printed for us by the *Gibraltar Chronicle*, the colony's daily newspaper which was founded in 1801. It was the first newspaper to report Nelson's victory at Trafalgar. His damaged ship *Victory* was towed into Gibraltar for repairs after the battle, carrying the body of the admiral in a barrel of rum. In the Trafalgar Cemetery at the southern end of the Main Street are the tombs of sailors killed in the battle, including that of two sailors killed by the same cannon ball.

Mention must be made of the famous Rock Apes which roam freely on the Upper Rock. They are part of the tradition which says that as long as they remain, the Rock will be British. But during the war, their numbers dwindled to seven. When Winston Churchill heard this, he sent a telegram to the Governor saying that every effort must be made to bring the number up to a minimum of twenty-four. Embassy officials were sent to North Africa to catch some Barbary apes and bring them back to the Rock. An officer and a corporal of the Royal Artillery were assigned to care for the apes who became part of the garrison force. Since the war, the Gibraltar Regiment is responsible for the apes' welfare. Each birth and death is officially recorded in Fortress Orders and each new baby's name must be submitted to the Governor for his approval.

Off-duty, troops were permitted to cross into Spain, either over the border to La Linea or by ferry across the bay to Algeciras. You had to wear civilian clothes and carry no weapon. We were warned not to pick a fight with any Germans we may meet in Spain. An enterprising RAF corporal bought six civilian suits and hired them out to other servicemen for their Spanish trips. The ladies of Spain soon recognised the suits when their wearers crossed the border and knew they were British servicemen.

On my first visit to Algeciras, I was returning to the boat when two young girls standing in the doorway of a house asked me for a cigarette. Although I do not smoke, I did have a packet in my pocket so I offered them one. Immediately, three or four other girls emerged from the house and so I soon emptied the packet. The girls wanted me to come inside the house and invited me to make love to senoritas. I realised then that this was a brothel, so making the excuse that I had no 'dinero', I extricated myself from their clutches and caught the ferry back to Gibraltar.

Several times a year, the Spanish hold fiestas and I was able to cross the border to witness the festivities. All the towns would be decorated and the streets festooned with electric illuminations. But these created a problem. When, for instance, it was La Linea's fiesta, in order to be able to switch on the illuminations, lights in San Roque, Algeciras and other neighbouring communities were turned off so that La Linea had sufficient electricity! Similar extinguishing of lights would take place when it was the turn of the other towns to hold their fiestas. One of the events common to most towns was the staging of bullfights. A number of servicemen would attend these but would annoy the locals when they cheered the bull instead of the matador!

Along the eastern shore of La Linea, I saw families living in 'houses' constructed from petrol cans and large corned beef tins filled with sand or concrete. They still bore their original labels, indicating that the containers were ex-War Department and had come from Gibraltar.

Overlooking the Rock and some five or six miles away is the mountain village of San Roque, Here, on top of the mountain was a German observation post and it was obvious that they were logging all shipping and aircraft movements of the Allies.

Our spiritual needs were not neglected. As a Christian, I regularly attended church services. Sometimes, it would be in the Anglican cathedral, others at the Methodist Church or the Salvation Army. Gibraltar has two cathedrals – Anglican and Roman Catholic. The Anglican bishop has one of the most extensive diocese in the Church of England, covering the entire Mediterranean area from Asia Minor to the Canary Islands. At Christmas, carol services were held and Handel's *Messiah* was performed in the cathedral with a choir made up of servicemen. There was also a non-conformist church and a Toc H mission hall.

The Governor's official residence is known as The Convent. Adjoining it is the King's Chapel, a former Franciscan convent and is the oldest British garrison church. Inside are the remains of the wife of the Spanish governor of 1648.

I frequently attended the Salvation Army services – they provided excellent suppers afterwards! – and occasionally, I would beat the drum for them. On one occasion, it was my turn to serve in the canteen and to make the tea. I duly put the tea in the urn (no tea-bags in those days), boiled the water and served the canteen customers. Suddenly, loud protests were heard – the tea was undrinkable! It transpired that I had filled the urn with water from the wrong tap. Most establishments have two taps – fresh water from one for drinking purposes and one with salt water for washing. My tea was somewhat salty! I was not very popular that night.

With a few other Christian servicemen, I started a Scripture Union Bible Class. We met once a week at the house of Mr Foggett, the Army Scripture Reader. We had quite a good attendance.

On 3 April 1944, I celebrated my twenty-first birthday (two days late) with a dinner party for four of my pals – Ron Elbon and John Clarke, both of whom were from Cambridge and had been members of St Paul's Church and Gerald Gregson's Bible Class, AC1 Ken Palmer and Private Douglas Bryan. Ron was in the RAF and John in the army. We arranged with Major Ashley of the Salvation Army to hold the dinner in his dining room adjoining the canteen and to use their cooking facilities. Ken and

Over 150 aircraft flew into Gibraltar in July, 1944, prior to the Allied invasion of Southern France

I spent the day purchasing the various ingredients and preparing them and Major Ashley obtained for us a joint of beef from Spain.

We started off with mock turtle soup (canned), followed by a salad of eggs, lettuce, radishes, tomatoes, onions, sardines and salad cream. Next came the main course – roast beef, Yorkshire pudding, spring cabbage, roast potatoes and fresh peas and beans. For dessert, we had a trifle, fruit salad, blancmange and cream. Regrettably, we could not manage the cheese and biscuits. We only consumed half a dish of trifle and a third of the blancmange so we gave the remainder to Major Ashley and his colleagues. The meal over, we went to the Theatre Royal to see a film, *Henry Aldrich, Editor* with Jimmy Lydon and Rita Quigley.

The following date was 4 April. I had been waiting eleven years to write 4-4-44 'all the fours' in my diary. I recalled sitting at my desk in Standard four at St Paul's Junior School in Cambridge and writing in my exercise book the date, 3-3-33. I wondered what I would be doing when 9-9-99 came around.

A birthday present was notification that I had been promoted to Leading Aircraftsman (LAC) and my weekly pay increased from twelve shillings to fourteen. To mark my birthday, the BBC in its 'Calling Gibraltar' broadcast, brought Margaret, sister Eileen and my mother to the microphone. Their brief message over the air was – Margaret: 'Here's wishing you fond greetings, Roy, on your birthday. Best wishes from everybody. Love always, dearest.' My sister said: 'Wishing you a happy birthday. Hope you'll be home again soon' and my mother simply added 'Good luck, Roy'.

I myself took to the air on 6th April, 1945 when I presented a forty-five minute programme of recorded music on Gibraltar Radio Redifusion *This is my choice*. It consisted of ten pieces, which included the overture to Offenbach's *Orpheus in the Underworld*, and a selection from Gilbert and Sullivan's *Iolanthe*.

The turning point in the war came in 1944. Italy had surrendered unconditionally the previous September and on 4 June 1944, the Allies had entered Rome. On D-Day, 6 June, the Allies landed on the Normandy beaches.

In Gibraltar, we sensed that something else was afoot. We had seen the Swedish liner *Gripsholme* carrying repatriated British prisoners-of-war from the exchange port of Barcelona pass through the Straits on its way to the UK, arriving in Belfast on 27 May.

Our air mail service was suspended the following month and we could not send letters home but we were not told the reason why. Then one morning in July, on arriving for duty in the Flying Control Tower at North Front, I was told to listen out for arriving aircraft. Then they came, over 150, one after the other – Dakotas, Hudsons, Halifaxes, Hurricanes and Spitfires – a continuous stream. No sooner had one touched down than another was approaching from the west.

'Keep rolling, keep rolling' we told the pilots as they turned off the runway at the eastern end to park in rows on the north side of the airfield. It turned out to be the advance air force for the invasion of southern France. Two days later, the aircraft took off again for North Africa and on 15 August 1944, the Allies landed on the south coast of France between Toulon and Nice.

In Algeciras Bay were hundreds of ships of all kinds, getting ready to sail for the invasion.

Meanwhile, the invasion on the western front was proceeding and on the 19 September, the Allies crossed the German frontier north of Trier. Paris was liberated on 23 August and in October, Field Marshall Rommel was reported dead; Athens and Belgrade were freed and the Russians captured Riga, the capital of Latvia. In Britain, the end of full black-out was announced and Romania capitulated.

Above and below: pupils in Author's class at the RAF Emergency
Secondary School, Plata Villa, Gibraltar, 1944

Back in Gibraltar, the first of the Gibraltarian women and children returned to the colony from Madeira and the Canary Islands with more following later from Northern Ireland and the United Kingdom.

The government of Gibraltar was now faced with a crisis – hundreds of children of school age but no school. The teachers had left the Rock with the general evacuation of civilians and they had not yet returned. So the RAF was asked to set up an emergency secondary school in Plata Villa, formerly run by the Catholic Christian Brothers. Ex-school teachers in the Force were invited to run the school and as I was due to take up teacher training on my release, I volunteered and was accepted.

The classes consisted of about thirty boys and girls from the age of eleven upwards. All of them spoke English but babbled away behind my back in Gibraltarian Spanish. I taught a variety of subjects, including English and history and I was temporarily relieved of my RAF duties.

In December, I was transferred to the Sacred Heart Boys Secondary School. In my spare time, I undertook some private tuition for a number of local children, thus supplementing my service pay.

At the end of the year, I was granted seven days' leave in French Morocco. The RAF had taken over a large French villa at Ain Sebba, near Rabat and sixteen airmen at a time from Gibraltar were able to spend their leave there. We had some attractive French ladies to look after the cooking and keep the place tidy. During the week, I was able to visit Casablanca, Rabat and Port Lyauty.

Members of the RAF who acted as schoolmasters at the Plata Villa School in Gibraltar.

CHAPTER TWENTY

1945 – The Year of Victory

*With malice toward none; with charity for all; with
firmness in the right, as God gives us to see the right –
let us strive on to finish the work we are in: to bind up
the nation's wounds; to care for him who shall have
borne the battle and for his widow and his orphan; to do
all which may achieve and cherish a just and lasting
peace among ourselves and with all nations.*

Abraham Lincoln
Second Inaugural Address, 1865

THE NEW YEAR began with mixed feelings. Would this be the last year of the war? In the Belgian Ardennes, the Germans had mounted a powerful counter-attack, the Battle of the Bulge, and United States troops were surrounded in the town of Bastogne.

But on Christmas Day 1944, the Allies began a counter-offensive and the Germans were finally driven back. On 1 January 1945, the Germans launched an overnight offensive against Allied positions along a 50-mile front between Saarbrucken and Strasbourg.

In Gibraltar, it was business as usual. I went to the Theatre Royal to see a burlesque pantomime *Babes in the Wood*, staged by the troops, and the following day, I had a tooth filled by the RAF dentist. I was now attending lectures by the colony's Education Officer, Dr Howe on education and teacher training; teaching in the Sacred Heart School during the day and on Sundays, I took a Sunday School class in the Anglican cathedral.

Having served on the Rock for eighteen months, I was offered the chance of staying on in Gibraltar for a further unspecified term of duty or to be posted to another theatre of war. This could be on the European mainland, the Middle East or even the Far East. I certainly did not want to go to the last-name sphere so I opted to remain in Gibraltar. My colleague, Ken Palmer, chose to move on and he left RAF New Camp on 7 April. It turned out that he was posted to Malta.

In Europe, the war was rapidly moving to its climax. The Russians had taken Warsaw and crossed the German frontier whilst the British and US troops had crossed the River Rhine. In the Far East, the US Marines landed in the Philippines and over 80,000 people are said to have been killed in an air raid on Tokyo by US B29 Superfortress bombers.

On 11 February, the 'Big Three' – President Roosevelt, Winston Churchill and Marshal Stalin – met at Yalta and decided the fates of Germany and Japan. Little did I know that fifty-six years later, I would be standing in the same room and at the same table as the 'Big Three' in the Livadia Palace, in Yalta, the former home of Czar Nicholas II.

Now the end was near. Hungary and Austria were both liberated and Hitler's 'Thousand-year Reich' was being attacked on all sides. More than 100,000 German soldiers surrendered in the Ruhr and after occupying Vienna, the Russians advanced on Berlin.

On 12 April 1945, President Roosevelt died and Harry S. Truman became president of the United States of America. The US troops and the Russians reached the River Elbe simultaneously whilst in the west, the Battle of the Ruhr ended with another 325,000 prisoners in Allied hands, including thirty generals and an admiral. After three weeks of tense negotiations, the German garrison in Italy surrendered unconditionally on 29 April.

On the following day, the final battle for Berlin was over. The Red Flag flew over the ruins of the Reichstag and in the afternoon, Herr Hitler committed suicide by shooting himself in the mouth. His mistress and wife for thirty-six hours, Eva Braun, took poison. Two days previously, Benito Mussolini – Il Duce – and his mistress, Clara Petacci, were captured by Italian partisans and shot. Their bodies were suspended upside down in a garage forecourt in Milan.

Josef Goebbels, the Nazi propaganda minister was the next to die. He gave lethal injections to his six children, aged three to twelve years, before he and his wife were shot at their own request on 1 May by an SS orderly.

All German forces in north west Germany, the Netherlands and Denmark surrendered on the 4th and Innsbruck and Salzburg were occupied by units of the US Third Army.

VE-DAY – Victory in Europe – 8 May 1945. Norway was liberated and Field Marshal Hermann Goering was arrested by US troops. At 3 o'clock in the afternoon, the Prime Minister, Winston Churchill broadcast to the nation.

'The German war is at an end,' he said. 'Advance Britannia! Long live the cause of freedom! God Save the King!'

This was followed by a broadcast on Gibraltar Radio by His Excellency the Governor, after which a twenty-one-gun salute was fired. I went to the Anglican Cathedral at four o'clock for a thanksgiving service, had tea with a Gibraltarian lady, Mrs Saunders, and then proceeded to Alameda Gardens where a funfair from Spain had been erected. In the evening, the speech by the King was relayed throughout the Rock and then every big gun and piece of artillery was fired in a tremendous barrage. All the searchlights swept the sky, after which, the Royal Navy put on a terrific firework display from the detached mole. The combined show of fire power must have scared the life out of the Spanish in La Linea and Algeciras!

The next day was a public holiday and the RAF put on a Victory dinner in New Camp and at North Front. The menu featured vegetable soup, roast pork and apple sauce, vegetables, steamed Victory pudding with brandy sauce and mince pies and cheese, biscuits, oranges and bananas. A huge Victory bonfire was lit in the Governor's Meadow on Rosia Road. A Victory parade of all units marched through the town with the Governor and all the Service chiefs taking the salute.

On the 4 June, I went to Tangier on seven days' leave, staying at the Ville de France Hotel. We dined at the famous four-star El Minzah Hotel and during the week, I visited all the town's major attractions. Tangier has a beautiful sandy beach, so soft like talcum powder but so hot it burns your feet. Seven days later, I went down to the quayside for the return trip to Gibraltar in the RAF Air Sea Rescue launch but the sea was so rough that the skipper decided to stay put. This meant another twenty-four hours' leave in Tangier! The next day, we set sail in the Royal Naval pinnance *Tender Heart*.

It was back to routine duties in the Flying Control Tower, so I had quite a lot of free time and days off. I continued to give tuition to two Gibraltarian boys; attended meetings of the Literary and Debating Society; went to the cinema and the theatre; swam in Catalan Bay and went to the fiesta in Algeciras. Another 778 women and children were repatriated to the Rock from Northern Ireland.

Back in the UK, Mr Churchill resigned as Prime Minister and a General Election was held on 5 July. On Gibraltar, the forces cast their vote by post and I voted for Mrs Florence Paton, the Labour candidate for the Rushcliffe Division of Nottingham. I was on duty in the tower when the election results were being announced. I kept switching my radio receiver over to the BBC, much to the annoyance of the duty sergeant who was a staunch Conservative and for him the results were bad news.

Labour won with a massive 146 seat majority and Clement Attlee became Prime Minister. He took Winston Churchill's seat at the Potsdam Peace Conference at which the Big Three – Britain, the USA and Russia – decided on German disarmament and reparations. On 26 June, fifty countries signed the Charter of the United Nations. The lights of London went on again on 15 July, officially ending the black-out.

On the Rock, the two topics of conversation and concern were – will we be transferred to the Far East and fight the Japs and how soon would we be demobilised and return home to civvy street? My plan when demobbed was to become a school teacher. The RAF had started an EVT course (Education & Vocational Training), which I joined. Its purpose was to provide instructors to lead discussion groups on national and international topics and to prepare servicemen for life as a civilian. Current affairs were also discussed at our New Camp Thursday Club.

The annual fiesta in La Linea was held in June and I crossed the border to witness the celebrations. They lasted several days and ended with a massive firework display. Whilst in Spain, I took the opportunity of seeing the Gran Circo Corzana.

The famous St Michael's Caves were being opened and I was privileged to be allowed to accompany a small party to explore them. Life in the colony was rapidly returning to normal. The Rock's Cage Bird Society held its first show since the outbreak of hostilities and local orchestral, operatic and dramatic societies put on shows in the Theatre Royal.

In the Far East, the war against Japan was hotting up with heavy bombings on the Japanese mainland. On 6 August 1945, the USA Air Force dropped the first atom bomb on Hiroshima. Three days later, a second bomb was dropped over Nagasaki. This proved to be the last straw and Japan surrendered unconditionally on 14 August. 'VE-J Day' was celebrated on the Rock the next day with a twenty-one-gun salute, a thanksgiving service in the cathedral, victory concerts and entertainments and a special Victory breakfast in New Camp.

The Spanish fascist general and Governor of Algeciras paid an official ceremonial visit to Gibraltar at the invitation of our Governor and Commander-in-Chief, Lieut. General Eastwood. British troops were ordered to show him respect customarily accorded to honoured guests. Members of the forces were disgusted at the way one of General Franco's governors was entertained and I took the initiative of writing to my Member of Parliament, Mrs Paton. In my letter, I described how the Spanish general was given a guard of honour and entertained by the Governor at Government House and enclosed photographs and cuttings from the *Gibraltar Chronicle*. I went on to say,

> On the last occasion, he [the General] was provided with an escort of RAF Ventura aircraft and Royal Naval launches as he crossed the Bay and a salute of 21 guns was fired as he landed. Troops had to line both sides of the streets leading to Government House. We feel most strongly that anyone connected with Fascist Spain should not be entertained on British territory by representatives appointed by His Majesty's Government at the taxpayers' expense.

Mr Tom Driberg, MP for Maldon, raised the subject in the House of Commons on 24 August and read out my letter to Mrs Paton (see *Hansard*, Vol. 413, No. 11 cols 1092 & 1093). Not long afterwards, the Governor of Gibraltar was replaced! A word in the right quarters can achieve miracles!

As the editor of the *Rock Magazine* had now left for England, I took over as joint editor until it ceased publication a few months later. I had taken over Pepy's 'Diary on the Rock' and continued describing life and entertainments in the colony, writing as 'John Evelyn II on the Rock'. Life was certainly not boring!

I was due to take another seven days' leave in Tangier in November but on the 6th, I was informed I was to return to England the following day. I spent all night packing my books and kit and at 8 a.m. the next morning, I was taken by tender to board HM Troopship *Highland Princess* (Royal Mail Line, 15,000 tons). We set sail at 1.15 p.m. and two hours later, passed by Tangiers and then rounded Cape Trafalgar and entered the Atlantic. On day three, we sighted Lizard Point in Cornwall and sailed into the English Channel. Late afternoon, we passed the Needles on the Isle of Wight and entered the Solent, finally arriving in Southampton at 5 p.m. Also in port were the *Queen Elizabeth* and the *Orion*, the latter being the ship on which I sailed to Gibraltar in 1943.

That night, I was detailed for Boat Guard duties from midnight to 2.00 a.m. and from 6.00 to 8.00 a.m. Having come from the warmth of Gibraltar to a cold, foggy English November night was not my idea of fun and I was not sure what I was supposed to be guarding. Perhaps it was to stop any serviceman jumping ship before time!

At 11.15 the following morning, we disembarked and set foot once more on dear old England's shore. A train was awaiting us to whisk us off to Blackpool. The date was Remembrance Day, 11 November.

CHAPTER TWENTY-ONE

Back in 'Blighty'

England, with all thy faults, I love thee still.

William Cowper, 1731–1800,
The Task 2 – The Timepiece

MONDAY 12 NOVEMBER 1945 – Two years, four months after leaving Blackpool for overseas, I was back in Britain's 'playground of the north'. I was billeted with a Mrs Thompson at 30 Lytham Road and that evening, I went to the New Opera House to see Johann Straus' operetta *The Gipsy Baron*.

The following day, the 13th, I left the seaside resort for twenty-three days' disembarkation leave. I arrived in Nottingham at 1.30 the next morning, so I went to the YMCA hostel in Broad Street until daybreak. Then, at 8.30, I waited in the Market Square at the No. 31 bus stop. The bus arrived from Mapperley and as Margaret stepped off, I grabbed her and held her in my arms. When she had got over her surprise, she called to her colleague to tell them in her office at the Ministry of Labour in Clifton Boulevard that she would not be coming to work today.

The next three weeks were the most exciting, really the first weeks of wedded bliss, our real honeymoon. I stayed at Margaret's home at 438 Westdale Lane and we visited relatives and friends in Nottingham. Two days later, we went together to my parents' home in Hitchin. When we arrived at Hitchin station, we bumped into my sister Eileen. She was somewhat tearful, not because of my return but because her boyfriend, Eric, who was also in the RAF had just left to return to camp.

After visiting friends and relatives in my former home town, Cambridge, and my junior school headmistress, Miss Margaret Chandler at St Paul's School, we spent four days in London, staying at the Tuscan Hotel, Shaftesbury Avenue. This cost us £6 1s. 0d. bed and breakfast! We visited all the well-known sights, including Regent's Park Zoo; saw the vast amount of bomb damage, especially in the City around St Paul's and ate knickerbocker glories at Lyons Corner House.

On our return to Nottingham, Margaret had to go back to work but in the evenings, we continued our visits and attended services at the

Bridgeway Hall Methodist Church, where we were married two and a half years' previously.

At 4.00 a.m. on 1 December 1945, my grandfather, Arthur Sharp, whose exploits I described in chapter one, died at Cambridge, aged ninety-six years.

During the following week, my parents came to Nottingham for a few days and we went to look at a new housing estate off Plains Road, Mapperley. We were interested in a new three-bedroomed detached house which was being built at No. 12 Pateley Road. It had a front and back garden, lounge, separate dining room and kitchen and the cost was £1,140 freehold. With my father's advice and approval, we signed the contract and, during the following months, watched our house being built. We obtained a loan from the Co-operative Building Society.

During my leave, I had an interview with the deputy head of the department of education at Nottingham University College for a teacher's training course.

My leave came to an end on 7 December and I left Nottingham for my new posting at RAF Station, Welford in Berkshire. Here, I was transferred from Signals and became a full-time EVT instructor. My first lecture was on the working of Parliament and subsequent topics included the United Nations and the Security Council.

Off-duty, I tried my hand at making a bookcase – not very successfully – and when I tried to take it on the train to Nottingham, the guard shouted 'Put that crate in the guard's van!' What an insult to my handiwork!

Christmas and the New Year was spent on leave with Margaret and her family at Westdale Lane. Her mother was none too pleased when I decorated the mirrors and picture frames in the house with cotton wool, stuck on with glue which was very difficult to remove. My leave was regrettably cut short when I received a recall telegram from the RAF and I returned to Newbury on New Year's Day 1946. On the following day, I caught the train to No. 9 Educational & Vocational Training School at Bourn, Cambridgeshire. Here, I commenced a course on the Principles of Teaching. In the evenings, I was able to go into Cambridge where I met once more the Rev. Gerald Gregson, now a Wing Commander and a Chaplain-in-Chief, RAF, and other friends from St Paul's Church.

The course ended on 22 January and I was promoted to Acting (paid) EVT Sergeant. I received £3 16s. (two weeks' pay) and I was now having my meals in the Sergeants' Mess. In the meantime, Margaret had been temporarily transferred to the Ministry of Labour office in London and she stayed at my mother's house in Hitchin. I received a posting to RAF Station, Wymeswold in Leicestershire and my pay was increased to £2 a week!

Margaret's brother-in-law, Leslie, the husband of Florence, was demo-bilised from the army on 10 April. He was fortunate that he did not have to serve overseas but remained as an instructor in the UK all through the war.

After her spell of duty in London, Margaret was now back in her Nottingham office, so I obtained permission from the RAF to live out at 438 Westdale Lane, commuting each day to Wymeswold. Progress on our new house was moving quickly and in the evenings and at weekends, I was able to make a start on digging the rear garden. My service pay went up again to £2 12s. 6d. per week!

On 8 May we attended the Children's Special Service Mission and Scripture Union Anniversary Rally in Nottingham and met once again the evangelist, Mr Hudson Pope who had led me to Christ in 1933. The 16 July 1946 was a great day for us, the day we moved into our very first home, 12 Pateley Road, Mapperley, Nottingham. But this was not the only reason for celebrating for Margaret announced that she was pregnant! Finally, I received my discharge papers from the Royal Air Force and together, we went to 100 PDC Unit, RAF Uxbridge on 10 September, received my demob suit and overcoat and re-entered civvy street! I had been given priority release to attend Nottingham University College, although the effective date of my demobilisation was 28 October 1946.

Our first home – 12 Pately Road, Mapperley, Nottingham, bedecked for the Queen's Coronation, 1953.

CHAPTER TWENTY-TWO

Student Days

Learning makes a good man better and an ill man worse.

Seventeenth-century proverb

EVENTS MOVED QUICKLY after leaving the Air Force. We met the Rev. Gerald Gregson in London; attended a CSSM Reunion in the Central Hall, Westminster; visited my parents in Hitchin and went to the Nottingham Forest Recreation Ground to see the famous Bertram Mills' Circus, now resuming its first tour of Britain since hostilities started in 1939.

I registered at the University College on 2 September 1946 and started life as a full-time student the following day. My studies consisted of history, Latin, French and theology. My extra-mural activities consisted of membership of the college Christian Union and making Margaret pregnant!

We went to the Theatre Royal, Nottingham on 13 November to see Bruce Trent and Cherry Lind in Sigmund Romberg's musical *The Student Prince*. On the following day, as Margaret was going outside our door, she slipped on the iron shoe grating and sat down heavily on the path. Although feeling bruised, she still accompanied me to college for a meeting but in the afternoon, she said she did not feel well so we returned home and she went to bed. Our GP, Dr Bradbury called to see her the next day and gave her some medicine. In the evening, labour pains started. I telephoned the doctor who referred me to the midwife. She did not think they were labour pains as Margaret was not due to give birth for several more weeks. Nevertheless, she said she would come and see her.

The pains became more frequent and at 7.15 p.m., Margaret said the baby was coming. Still no midwife, so I had to act on my own. A head appeared and a few minutes later, the whole body shot out into my hands. Just then, the midwife arrived. Our house was three-quarters of the way up a steep hill and the road was very icy. She had to push her bicycle all the way from Arnold. Luckily, she was in time to receive the afterbirth. But then came the bad news – our child, a boy, was still-born. Apparently, it was the result of Margaret's fall the previous day.

On the same day, 15 November, my sister Eileen married her boyfriend,

Eric Keith, in Hitchin. Margaret's mother came to stay for a few days and insisted I did not sleep in the same bed as Margaret for the next couple of nights (we could not understand why) and then my mother came from Hitchin and took over.

My second term at college saw me taking part in various meetings of the Christian Union. I was having some difficulty in coming to terms with my theology tutor whom I gathered was not an evangelical Christian. I had always thought of God as being God and it seemed strange to call Him *Yahweh*. On the four Sundays in February (1946), I conducted a children's mission at Bridgeway Hall Methodist Church, assisted by members of the college Christian Union. An average of fifty boys and girls attended each meeting.

February 1947 was a month of hardships in the UK. It was very cold, temperatures down to 17 degrees Fahrenheit and we had snow. This lasted until 7 March when a thaw set in, resulting in the River Trent overflowing and inundating the Trent Bridge and Meadows area. Food rationing was still in force, there was a fuel shortage and there were widespread cuts in electricity. In contrast, we had a heatwave in June with the temperature in the nineties.

At the end of the summer term, I worked for a month as a temporary civil servant at the Ministry of Labour office in Castle Gate. On 2 August Margaret and I travelled to Cromer in Norfolk and joined the Children's Special Service Mission houseparty, led by Mr and Mrs F. C. R. Dye. The party was made up principally of university and college students and several of the girls were from Nottingham. The mission ran for four weeks until 30 August and the sun shone the whole month. Each day, a service for children was held on the beach and the children helped us to build a huge sand pulpit. We each took it in turns to give an illustrated talk and, during the rest of the day, we organised games, sports, treasure hunts, 'sausage sizzles', sand modelling and bathing parties. For the last-named activity, Margaret wore a nylon bathing costume with a bare midriff which was disapproved of by the house leader, Mrs Dye!

During the month, our friend Rev. Gerald Gregson, now CSSM and Scripture Union general secretary for Canada, joined us at Cromer as guest speaker at our beach service and we accompanied him the following day to another CSSM houseparty at Sheringham, a few miles farther along the coast where he was again the guest speaker. After saying 'goodbye' to him, we returned to Cromer and Gerald continued his tour of other seaside missions. After our final meetings at the end of the month, we returned home and back to college.

During the autumn, Margaret and I held 'open house' at our home and a series of tea 'squashes' at which we invited friends and relatives and a number of keen Christians to give us a talk. We had up to twenty-five

Members of the CSSM house party with their sand pulpit on Cromer
Beach – August, 1947

young people at our home 'squashes'. Our church attendances were divided
between the Bridgeway Hall Methodist, St Ann's C of E on St Anne's
Well Road (Rev. R. T. Little) and St Jude's C of E at Mapperley (Rev.
Woodhams). I ran a young people's Bible Class and taught in the Sunday
School and at college became a committee member of the Christian Union.

The year 1948 began with a trip to London to see the Bertram Mills'
Circus at Olympia and to view the wedding presents of Princess Elizabeth
and the Duke of Edinburgh in St James's Palace. We also attended a
Labour Party rally in Nottingham to hear the Rt. Hon. Emmanuel
Shinwell, Secretary of State for War, and Sir Richard Acland, MP for
Gravesend.

On 12 February I was delegated to meet Lieutenant General Sir William
Dobbie, GCMG, KCB, CB, CMG, DSO, Ll.D, Governor of Malta from
1940–42 during the months of heavy bombardment by both the Germans
and the Italians. I escorted him from the Midland Station to the University
where he gave a talk on 'Lessons from the Siege of Malta'.

In June, we went to the Trent Bridge Cricket Ground to watch the
third day's play in the First Test Match against Australia and to see the
great Don Bradman in action. He scored 138 runs and Australia won by

eight wickets in spite of Dennis Compton's 184, Len Hutton's 74, Godfrey Evans' 53 and Nottingham's Joe Hardstaff's 43 in the second innings.

On 17 July 1948 I became an uncle as my sister, Eileen gave birth to a daughter, Hazel.

At the end of the following month, we made our first trip abroad together. We took the ferry SS *Arnheim* from Harwich to the Hook of Holland and for the next fourteen days we stayed with Miss Ardien de Louwere, a pen-friend for a number of years, and her family in Amstelveen, a suburb of Amsterdam. Ardien had several brothers and the family had suffered hardship during the Nazi occupation. Our experience of living with a Dutch family was 'educational'. The house was kept spotlessly clean and Ardien was in hot water one day because she fried some potato chips when her mother was out and contaminated the air! As soon as a member of the family got up in the morning, around seven o'clock, he or she would make a large pot of tea and then leave it stewing on the hot stove until breakfast time at nine o'clock! You could say the tea was well brewed! Another unusual custom at meal times was to turn one's plate over after the first course and use the other side for the entrée! It saved washing-up!

Our visit to Holland coincided with the Golden Jubilee celebrations for the Dutch Queen Wilhelmina. These were immediately followed by her abdication in favour of her daughter, Princess (and subsequently Queen) Juliana. Her coronation took place a week later on 6 September. We watched the Royal procession but just before it was due to pass by, a tram pulled up and stopped almost in front of us.

'Why haven't they stopped the traffic?' I asked.

'Business must carry on, even on a Royal occasion,' was the reply.

Bad news reached me on my return. I had failed my BA examination. I had passed in English and European history, Latin and religious knowledge but had failed in French, the one compulsory subject. I knew I had done badly in French. I had to write an essay in French on the subject of the novel. I had misinterpreted the word *le roman* for *romance* and wrote a love story. Still, it was a novel! The government was not prepared to give me another chance and extend my grant for a further year, so I left college and went to look for a job.

Having previously worked in local government before I joined the RAF, I was able to get an appointment as a clerk in the Public Health Department of Nottinghamshire County Council at County Hall, Trent Bridge. I started in the Maternity and Child Welfare Department on Monday, 27 September 1948. My first salary cheque was for £23 6*s.* for one month!

After six months at County Hall, I obtained the post of chief clerk in the Public Health Department of Basford (Nottingham) Rural District Council at a starting salary of £395, rising to £440 per annum. I worked with the Medical Officer of Health, the chief sanitary inspector, three district inspectors and the rodent officer. I was assisted by a clerk/typist, Mrs Withers. The offices were situated at Rock House, Basford.

Among my duties was to compile the monthy infectious disease returns, send out appointments for children to be immunised, prepare the monthly reports on the work of the Department for the Council meetings and once a year, prepare the annual report of the Medical Officer of Health.

Although I had failed to get my degree, I was determined to gain some qualification and joined the Rapid Results Correspondence College, Wimbledon and studied for the Corporation of Secretaries examinations in Public Administration, the General Principles of Law and Local Government Law. I also took a correspondence course in journalism and freelance writing and succeeded in getting some articles and short stories published in the *Nottingham Evening Post* and one or two monthly journals.

CHAPTER TWENTY-THREE

Back to the Rock

One of the pleasantest things in the world is going a journey.

William Hazlitt, 1778–1830,
On Going a Journey

AFTER LEAVING COLLEGE, I was invited by the Rev. Charles F. Grose, vicar of St Paul's C of E Church, Lenton Abbey, Nottingham, to conduct a children's gospel mission in his church. I agreed and we held a week of prayer, preparation and devotion in the Church House. Children's meetings were held each evening and attendance ranged from sixty to 119. I used models, pictures and other visual aids in my talks and at the end of the week, a number of children came forward to accept Jesus Christ as their personal Saviour. A follow-up 'tea squash' two weeks later was attended by no fewer than seventy-four children plus adults.

On the political front, we attended another Labour Party rally in the Nottingham Albert Hall at which the principal speaker was the Rt. Hon. Aneurin Bevan, Minister of Health.

At the end of June 1949, the City of Nottingham began a week of celebrations to mark the 500th anniversary of the city's foundation. These included a Civil Thanksgiving Service in St Mary's Church with an address by Dr Garbitt, Archbishop of York; a Sea Cadets show on the river Trent, an historical pageant, speedboat races, exhibitions, illuminations and fireworks.

Whilst in the RAF, I promised Margaret that I would take her one day to some of the places I went to during the war. The opportunity came on 3 September 1949, the anniversary of our first meeting in 1942. We caught the train to Newhaven and then the ferry across the Channel to Dieppe where we boarded a train for Paris. From there, we caught the train for Hendaye on the Franco-Spanish border and crossed over to Irun, in Spain.

We were travelling second class and were the first to take our seats in the carriage by the window facing each other. A few minutes later, a man entered carrying a large piece of machinery. 'This is my seat', he said, indicating my window seat and unceremoniously lifted my bag from the rack above me and dumped it further along, installing his machine in its place. The remaining seats in the carriage were then occupied and as soon as we were all settled, a pompous French lady got up and slammed shut the window, which I had previously opened. A fine start to *entente cordiale*!

As this was a night journey, seats on both sides of the carriage pulled out to meet in the gangway and form some sort of bed. For the rest of the night through France, we all laid down facing each other like sardines in a tin.

Having entered Spain, we had half a day to explore Irun until we boarded the Spanish train at 6.30 p.m. for our journey to Madrid. As we did not expect a very high standard of comfort on the Spanish trains, we travelled first class for this part of our trip, a wise move as it turned out to be. We had pre-booked accommodation in Madrid at the Hotel Londres, a medium class establishment, and the male attendants obviously had not shaved for several days.

Through the Scripture Union, we had been in correspondence with a Spanish Baptist minister, Senor Francisco Fernandez Garcia. He invited us to his house to meet his wife and family, consisting of several boys and girls. They had very little income and were constantly threatened and persecuted by the Roman Catholic Church and the authorities. They were forbidden to hold public services and met secretly in the homes of other non-Catholics for spiritual communion. They entertained us to an evening meal – a modest affair which included eggs. As we ate, we were conscious of the envious looks of the younger children for whom, apparently, eggs were a luxury seldom enjoyed.

We returned to our hotel just before midnight and were met in the foyer by the manager who greeted us and said they had kept the restaurant open for us and would now serve us dinner. We did not have the heart to tell him we had already eaten so we sat down to a full-course meal!

The next day, we toured the city and met three retired English missionaries, with whom we had tea. But Madrid was stifling hot and extremely smelly. There was a water shortage; it was only available for an hour in the morning and the same in the evening. In consequence, the whole city smelt like a vast cesspit. We had intended to stay in Madrid for a few more days but the aroma was so overpowering, it proved too much for us, so we boarded a train that evening for Algeciras.

The locomotive, a steam engine, used wood in its furnace and belched forth thick smoke as it chugged up the steep inclines. At some points, it went so slowly that small boys ran alongside it, offering *aqua fria* – cold water.

We eventually arrived at Algeciras at 2.30 in the afternoon and took a taxi to La Linea via San Roque to arrive at the Spanish-Gibraltar border.

We entered British territory and booked into the Bristol Hotel. The first thing to greet us was a huge beetle in the bathroom. Having removed the offending beast, we made this our abode for the next five days.

I guided Margaret around and up the Rock, walking from one end to the other, taking in Europa Point and my old war-time billet, Catalan Bay, Rosea Bay, Little Bay, Alameida Gardens, Sandy Bay, the Moorish castle and the den of the Rock Apes. We met some of my war-time acquaintances – Mr and Mrs Fogell of the Church Army, Padre Brown of the Methodist Church and the English lady Mrs Sanders, the widow of an army officer, whom I originally met on her return from evacuation.

Mrs Sanders took us in her car across the border into Spain to Tarifa Point, overlooking the Straits of Gibraltar. A terrific thunderstorm broke out on our return journey, with four inches of rain falling in an hour. We suddenly found ourselves in flood water on the coastal road between Algeciras and La Linea and our car stalled. Fortunately, a group of small boys waded out to us and helped us to push the car through the water to higher ground. Eventually, we got the engine to start and went on our way. But as we passed several people, they pointed to our car, so at last, Mrs Sanders brought it to a halt and we got out and inspected it. The bonnet was completely covered with vegetation and debris from the flood.

Arriving back in Gibraltar, we decided to take a walk to the top of the Rock. Little did we realise the devastation caused by the storm and no sooner had we passed one road turning than it was closed behind us. We made it to the top, however, and down again in safety.

On 12 September we took a boat, the SS *Rescue* and sailed through the Straits to Tangiers. On disembarkation, we were surrounded by Moroccan taxi drivers, all seeking a fare. We therefore announced our destination – the North Africa Mission at Hope House, situated on Mount Charf. Immediately, the drivers attempted to outbid each other on the cost of the journey and we finally settled for the lowest but one as his vehicle looked in better condition.

For the next seven days, we stayed with the English missionaries, Miss Bradbury and Miss Roberts, at Hope House. Adjoining the Mission was the British Tullock Memorial Hospital, run by Dr St. John, a missionary doctor. Tangiers was still an International Zone, jointly administered by Britain, France and Spain and, in consequence, each power was responsible for running the city on different days.

Whilst we were there, there was a road accident and a member of a Moroccan family was admitted to the British hospital. Dr St. John treated him but he died shortly afterwards. The next day, the doctor took us in his car to the Caves of Hercules on the Atlantic coast, as it was his day off. After a swim in the sea, we sat down on the beach for a picnic lunch. Almost at once, a large crowd of Moroccans approached us. We were a little scared as they seemed to be hostile and we did not know what were their intentions. But it soon became clear that they were friendly. They were the family and friends of the man involved in the road accident who had died the previous day in the British hospital. They had followed us to the beach and wished to thank the doctor for his care of their deceased relative; and to show their gratitude, they presented us with a basket of freshly caught and cooked shrimps. They tasted delicious with our picnic lunch.

During the week, we went by bus to Tetuan in Spanish Morocco, accompanied by the Misses Bradbury and Roberts, and lunched at the Tetuan mission house, after which we met the British vice-consul who took us in his car to the Rio Martin. Whilst in Tetuan, we called on a former pupil of mine from Gibraltar, Kishin Tarachand, who was now helping to run his family's bazaar in the town.

Returning to Tangiers, we saw the missionaries at work, running a Spanish Bible Class and Sunday School and preaching the Gospel whenever they could. They invited me to give the address at the children's service on the Sunday at Hope House. My subject was 'Stronger than the Rock of Gibraltar'. Back home, I illustrated my children's talks with a flannelgraph. I cut out words, pictures and drawings of people and objects and stuck pieces of cotton wool on the back of them. I then pinned a piece of flannel or similar material on to a blackboard and the cut-out pieces would adhere to it. I asked my hosts in the hospital for some cotton wool. They were aghast. Cotton wool was scarce and worth its weight in gold. So I had to give my talk without a flannelgraph and to resort to holding my illustrations in my hand.

We flew back to Gibraltar on 19 September in a De Havilland Rapide of Gibraltar Airways and proceeded to Algeciras where we caught the Maroc Express for Madrid. After an hour's stop, the Express continued its journey to Irun, where we left the train and crossed the frontier into France. We resumed our journey five hours' later and arrived in Paris at 11.30 p.m.

As we had not pre-booked any accommodation in Paris, I went off in search of an hotel for the night, leaving Margaret with the luggage. But all the rooms near the station were fully booked. However, at one hotel, the hall porter agreed to let us recline on a settee in the lounge until the morning.

At 10 o'clock the next day, we caught the train from St Nazaire station to Dieppe and the cross-Channel ferry to Newhaven and our train home to Nottingham, arriving around midnight. Thus ended our first overseas tour together.

CHAPTER TWENTY-FOUR

The Festival of Britain

Where Britain, modestly, lets down her hair,
You've seen, besides the shores of Waterloo,
What seldom things the local natives do,
Here, in our quaint, uncontinental way,
We aim at Beauty and pursue the gay.
Here shall we see, despite the fumes of Power,
That foggy London can produce a flower.
Here shall the birds appropriately sing
Among the flags of Britain and the Spring.
There may be little, as the sad folk shout,
For anybody to be glad about.
The planet's blue, the firmament is dun –
But that was so in 1851.
In fact, since paper first emerged from wood,
The news could seldom be described as good,
One tyrant falls, another takes his place,
It's one long worry for the Island Race.
...
Think what you will, we hoist the Flag of Fun,
We bid you welcome – and we pray for sun.

A. P. Herbert, 1951
Reprinted from the official Festival of Britain programme

A GENERAL ELECTION WAS HELD in 1950 and we went to hear the Prime Minister, the Rt. Hon. Clement Attlee speak at the Robert Mellors School in Arnold, Nottingham. The election was held on 23 February and Margaret and I acted as polling clerks in Mapperley. Labour just scraped home with a majority of just five seats!

In April, we bought our first television set, a twelve-inch black and white Murphy table top model, costing £54. In the same month, we had the pleasure of once again meeting Mr Hudson Pope, the CSSM children's evangelist who was the guest speaker at the CSSM 71st Anniversary rally of the Scripture Union in Nottingham. You will recall that it was through

Mr Pope that I was led to Christ and became a Christian in 1933. After the Nottingham rally, we were delighted when Mr Pope accepted our invitation to spend the night in our home. We met him again the following year when he conducted a children's mission in the Queensbury Street Baptist Church, Nottingham.

I still worked for Basford Rural District Council and continued with my correspondence course studies for the Corporation of Secretaries examinations and my writing course. I also enrolled for a course on the general principles of English Law at the Nottingham Technical College.

After our stillborn child in 1946, we tried again but Margaret had several miscarriages. In July, she was admitted to the Women's Hospital in Nottingham for a D & C operation (dilation and curettage). She was discharged after four days and thereafter had to receive a series of twelve injections.

Another welcome visitor to our home in March 1951 was our old friend, the Rev. Gerald Gregson. On the Sunday, he spoke at our Bible Class and at the evening service in St Ann's Church.

The Festival of Britain was held in 1951 and the Nottinghamshire village of Trowell was chosen as Britain's Festival Village, much to the astonishment of everyone, not least the villagers themselves. In London, an imposing new skyline took shape alongside the River Thames. A bombsite on the South Bank between Westminster and Waterloo Bridges was laid out with new buildings and terraces as an exhibition. It told the story of the British people at work and at play, in industry, transport, the farm, at home, on the seas, in sport, at leisure and in the boundless fields of exploration and discovery in which British scientists were helping to build the world of tomorrow.

The centre of the Exhibition was the Dome of Discovery, telling the story of British discovery in all spheres, from the extremes of outer space down into the depth of the earth itself; from Francis Drake and Captain Cook to the men of today.

Other parts of the South Bank Exhibition included the Shot Tower, the Skylon, a telecinema, an 1851 Pavilion, restaurants and a new permanent building, the Festival Concert Hall.

A short journey upstream in Battersea Park was the Festival Pleasure Gardens. Here, in a beautiful setting of trees, lawns and flower beds were spacious courtyards and terraces, fountains and ornamental lakes. Among the many attractions were open-air theatres, concerts, beer gardens, a dance hall, shopping centre, a funfair extending over six acres, a tree-top walk, boating lake, a children's zoo, restaurants, cafés and bars. By night, the gardens were illuminated and there were displays of fireworks. We visited the South Bank Exhibition on two occasions and the Pleasure Gardens several times.

The Festival extended throughout Britain, not just in London. Nottingham's festivities took place between 15 September and 6 October. In Wollaton Park, there were open-air concerts, the *Ballet of the Enchanted Lake*, shows and displays by the army, the Royal Air Force, youth organisations and the Civil Defence. The park was illuminated at night and there were firework displays. There was a Trades Exhibition on Queen's Drive Recreation Ground, an art exhibition in the Castle Museum, historical exhibitions in the Guildhall and in the Police Assembly Rooms and a Social History of the People of Nottingham in the Albert Hall.

Touring the country was the Festival Land Travelling Exhibition and this was sited on Broad Marsh, Nottingham. The main theme was the British people and the things they made and used, their past and present achievements in technology and industry and how they aimed to enrich our daily lives.

Lt General Sir William Dobbie, former Governor of Malta spoke at a Bible Rally in the Nottingham Albert Hall and an open-air Christian Rally took place on the Forest Recreation Ground.

On 16 June 1951, we embarked on our first cruise aboard the P & O Liner SS *Chusan*. The previous month, we had travelled to London to pay in cash for this cruise – £62 each for fourteen days. In those days, there were two classes on board most cruise ships – first and tourist. We travelled tourist. Seventy-five per cent of the passengers were in the tourist class but were only allowed to use a quarter of the ship. At first, all passengers were permitted to exercise by walking all round the ship but after a couple of days, first class passengers complained, saying people looked in their cabin windows as they went by, so this promenade round the decks was restricted and the first class section was now out of bounds to tourists! The two classes also had separate dining rooms and separate menus.

Moral attitudes in the latter half of the century have changed considerably. But in 1951, if you were not married, you were not permitted to share a cabin with a member of the opposite sex! Furthermore, two married couples could not share a four berth cabin. The men were split up so that four men were in one cabin and four women in another! You probably did not know your fellow cabin bedmates! We were lucky as we had a double cabin with a lower and upper berth – no good for honeymoon couples! This was a most enjoyable cruise, the first of many to come. Our ship called in at Funchal (Madeira), Casablanca and Rabat in Morocco and at Lisbon. We fell in love with Madeira and thought we would like to have a villa here. They were on sale for about £1,000, including maid service. We took the sledge ride down from the mountain to the town and then transferred to a bullock conveyance along the main street. Whilst in Casablanca, we met a missionary friend, Miss Winifred Sellwood of the North Africa Mission, with whom we had previously made an acquaintance in Nottingham.

In August, we joined the CSSM houseparty at Sutton-on-Sea, Lincolnshire for three days, which was led by Major Oliver Wright Holmes (no relation) and his wife. At the end of the month, Margaret had another miscarriage.

Another General Election took place in October and the Labour Government was defeated. Winston Churchill became Prime Minister again at the head of the Conservative Party. Their first act in gaining power was to raise the duty on petrol by one penny a gallon and to reduce the meat ration to one shilling and fivepence per person per week!

I sat for the Intermediate examination Section A of the Corporation of Secretaries in December, the subjects being Public Administration, the general principles of law and local government law. Early in the new year, I learnt that I had been successful.

The South Bank, Waterloo, London Festival of Britain Exhibition.

CHAPTER TWENTY-FIVE

Bring on the Clowns

I've just signed an agreement to run a circus at
Olympia next winter!

Bertram W. Mills, February 1920

A S READERS MAY HAVE GATHERED from previous chapters, Margaret and I are admirers of the circus. My first visit to Bertram Mills' was as a schoolboy and ever since, whenever a show rode into town, I would go down to the tobar (circus ground) and watch the erection and build-up of the Big Top.

As soon as Bertram Mills resumed his annual show at London's Olympia in December and January 1946–47, we went up to town to see it. This became an annual treat for us and the circus was immensely popular with post-war audiences. Impressario Tom Arnold staged a rival show in Harringay Arena in the winter of 1947–48 and continued to do so until 1958 when Harringay Arena was sold and converted into a food store. We came up to London to see these shows as well. They were spectacular and featured such stars as Sabu, the elephant boy and Pinito del Oro, a brilliant trapeze artiste who actually dubbed for Betty Hutton in the film *The Greatest Show on Earth*. In 1952 and 1953, a virtual circus 'war' took place with three Christmas circuses in London – Bertram Mills in Olympia; Tom Arnold in Harringay and dance band leader Jack Hilton staged a circus in Earls Court.

Rivalry extended during the tenting season which came to a head in September, 1954 in Salisbury. Both Mills and Chipperfields booked for the same week and there were circus road signs 'To the Circus' pointing in opposite directions. Later, in Nottingham, both Chipperfields and Billy Smarts booked to play on the Forest Recreation Ground, one in the spring and the other in the autumn but both circuses advertised their shows on hoardings and on posters at the same time, each claiming to be the bigger and better show.

Margaret and I joined the Circus Fans' Association of Great Britain and attended rallies and circus performances in various parts of the country. Members would meet before the show for refreshments, attend the performance and afterwards, meet the artistes and enjoy a meal with them in the circus ring. I was appointed editor (unpaid) of their circus magazine the *King Pole*.

Animal rights groups have always opposed the use of animals in circuses, alleging cruelty in their training. But in my capacity as editor, I was permitted to attend training sessions unannounced and no cruelty whatsoever was observed. Animal tamer is a misnomer – you cannot tame wild animals but you can train them by offering them rewards. An animal soon gets to know if it performs a certain act, it will receive a tasty titbit. People train their dogs to perform all sorts of tricks and learn obedience but they cannot achieve this by beating them!

During the subsequent years, we have seen dozens of different shows. Besides the 'big three' – Bertram Mills, Chipperfields and Billy Smarts – these have included Robert Brothers, Gerry Cottle, Gilbert's, the Moscow State Circus, Austen Brothers and the Chinese State Circus. The Moscow State Circus is one of the world's best shows and we have seen it in Russia as well as on each of its tours of Great Britain.

Perhaps the most memorable of these was its show in Wembley Arena. The entire first half of the show consisted of human acts – acrobatics, cycling, balancing, etc. After the interval, almost all of these acts were repeated but this time not by humans but by bears – even to riding a motor cycle and driving a car. One of the greatest circus clowns was the Russian Popov.

Mills' star clown was Coco. His real name was Nicolai Poliakoff and originally came from Russia. Strictly speaking, he was not a clown but an auguste. A clown is one with a white face and spangled costume who does not get wet or receive custard pies in the face. Coco performed hilarious entrées with other augustes Alby Austin, midgets Little Billy Merchant and Nikki and white clown Percy Huxter in which buckets of water were thrown at each other; custard pies and billposter's paste were in frequent use. In 1973, Coco was awarded the OBE by Her Majesty the Queen in recognition of his services to road safety. He would give talks to children in schools on the subject and visited schools in the towns in which the circus played since 1947.

When performing with another circus in Epsom, Surrey in 1974, he was taken ill and admitted to Epsom Hospital. I went to see him there just before he died on 25 September, one of the last people to see him. He was buried in the churchyard in the village of Woodnewton, Northamptonshire, where he lived after semi-retirement.

In 1952, I learnt that the Bertram Mills' Circus was coming to Nottingham from 16–28 June and it dawned on me that the circus 'Big Top' would make an ideal venue for an interdenominational church service. I wrote to the circus directors, Cyril and Bernard Mills, sons of the late founder, Bertram Mills, with the suggestion and they were very enthusiastic about the idea. Their press officer, Mr Bob Aylwin, came to Nottingham in February to discuss the project with me and I approached church leaders of all denominations in the city for their support. I formed an organising committee comprising representatives of the Church of England, the Baptist and Methodist churches and the Salvation Army.

During the following weeks, special meetings for prayer for the service were held in the participating churches and it was agreed to invite a well-known Christian speaker, Major William F. Batt, MBE, DL, JP of East Beckham, Norfolk to give the address. A former officer of the Coldstream Guards, Major Batt was deputy lieutenant of the County of Norfolk, a farmer, a member of the Officers' Christian Union and of the Norwich Diocesan Conference. To conduct the service, we invited Dr Richard B.Dobson, MA, MB, ChB of Matlock, Derbyshire and Councillor Arthur E. Foster, JP of Woodborough, Nottinghamshire, to give a personal testimony. The singing was led by the band of the William Booth Memorial Hall of the Salvation Army and massed choirs from seven churches and five Salvation Army corps.

When the circus arrived in Nottingham, thousands of posters and notices were displayed in the buses, public notice boards and hoardings. The circus directors had printed full details of the service on the reverse side of all their handbills and the local newspapers gave full publicity to the event. As was to be expected, there were protests from so-called animal rights organisations and threats were made to interrupt the service. To prevent this, the police turned up in force to ensure there were no violent demonstrations.

The big top held approximately 5,000 people and it was packed solid. Director Bernard Mills read the lesson and clowns, acrobats and other members of the circus were in the congregation. The band occupied the ring with the choir lined up behind it in the front rows of seats. The service was relayed by loud speaker to the crowds outside the tent who could not be accommodated inside. One of the stars of the circus this year was Borra, the international pickpocket, who sat with Coco the Clown, Percy Huxter, Alby Austin, Little Billy and Nikki.

Following the event, I received a congratulatory letter from Mr Stanley Bird, manager of the circus, on behalf of the directors. Henceforth, Margaret and I received a personal invitation to attend the opening performances as their guests at each of the succeeding Olympia seasons.

Three years later, we repeated the process when Billy Smarts' Circus visited Nottingham in May 1955. On this occasion, the service was conducted by Rev. T. J. Hamer, BA, BD, minister of the Derby Road Baptist Church, Nottingham, the address was given by John Williamson, CBE, Chief Constable of Northampton and chairman of the International

Christian Police Fellowship. A personal testimony was given by Sergeant Alec Catto of the Metropolitan Police, and the lesson was read by the Rev. Professor R. R. Turner, MA of the Paton Congregational College and Nottingham President of the Free Church Federation Council.

Attending the service was the 'Guvnor', Mr Billy Smart senior, his son Ronald Smart, other members of the family and the circus artistes. Used for the first time was a new four-pole big top and an act of dedication and blessing was performed by Rev. Canon J. Lowndes, MA, vicar of St Leodegarius, Old Basford.

I offered to hold a similar service in the big top of Chipperfields' Circus when they came to Nottingham but they were not interested. However, they did invite me to ride on one of their vehicles in the big circus parade from the Midland Station to the Forest tobar. The streets were lined with people all the way.

During the years, we saw some really outstanding acts in the circus. There were the giraffe-necked women from Upper Burma with their myriad brass rings round their necks; Rudy Horn, the unicycling juggler with cups and saucers on his head; Cavallini's crazy car; the Norwegian Fjord and golden palomino horses; the superb horsemanship of Max, Albert and Paulina Schumann; Rudi Lenz and his chimpanzees, imitating The Beatles; Alex Kerr with his gentle handling of his cage of tigers and Koringa with her snakes and crocodiles.

The Bertram Mills' Circus was the only one in Britain to tour the country by trains and not by road vehicles. They required four trains to carry their big top, the vehicles, caravans, animals and artistes. These were loaded onto flats (sideless trucks) and the circus vehicles, caravans, horse boxes and tractors were loaded on to them. At the end of the train were the baggage wagons and the sleeping cars for the artistes and staff.

On the final day in a town, the first performance ended with the big cats – lions or tigers in the ring. The ring cage was not dismantled so that the second and last performance began with the cage act. As soon as this was over, the cage was dismantled and the animals were then ready to be taken to the station and loaded on the train. By the time the interval came, some of the horses had already made their way to the station and various parts of 'circus town' had been taken down and removed. Before the performance was finally over, all the side walls of the big top had gone and much of the other equipment.

The first train departed with the kitchen wagons and staff, offices and the wild animals wagons. The second train departed an hour later with wardrobes, small tents, canvas and poles and seating, almost immediately after the show had ended. The third train departed as soon as the pull down had been completed with the big top canvas, king poles and quarter poles, side poles, stakes and the sleepers.

The fourth train left at 8 o'clock the next morning with all the horse boxes, elephant wagon and passenger coaches for staff and artistes. Such was the efficient organisation of the railway companies in those days – the big four and then British Railways after 1948, that the trains always departed and arrived more or less on time. But when Lord Beeching started to axe many of the lines, plus the steep rise in charges, the Mills brothers decided to revert to road transport.

But things were not going so well and the circus sustained losses in 1963 and 1964 and it was reluctantly decided to cease touring. The last tenting show was held in Liverpool at the end of October, 1964. Most of the animals were sold to other circuses. The Olympia show continued with hired acts in 1964 and 1965 but poor financial results decreed that the 1965–66 season would be the last.

We attended what was to be the final performance and demise of Bertram Mills' Circus at Olympia when it was announced that the hotel and newspaper tycoon, Maxwell Joseph, had purchased the shares of Cyril and Bernard Mills and that he proposed to run one more Olympia circus. Cyril Mills relinquished his chairmanship and declined to run the 1966–67 season. His brother Bernard took over the show as sole managing director. This was indeed the very last Olympia show and the end of Bertram Mills' Circus. A few years later, Cyril Mills did produce a circus for one season in the Brighton Centre but it was not a great success.

I continued to edit the *King Pole* and contribute to *The World's Fair* and we visited the permanent indoor circuses at the Tower, Blackpool and in the Hippodrome, Great Yarmouth. On one occasion, when I was trying to photograph Blackpool's famous clown, Charlie Cairoli, my camera jammed. Charlie said to me, 'Who's the clown in this outfit?'

Coco the clown meets school children in Great Bookham.

CHAPTER TWENTY-SIX

Ladies from Spain

The French are wiser than they seem and the Spaniards seem wiser than they are.

Francis Bacon, 1561–1626, *Of Seeming Wise*

HAVING PASSED the first part of the Corporation of Secretaries Examination, I sat for the next section in June, 1952. The subjects were Local Government Secretarial Practice, Local Government Law, Constitutional Law and English.

In the same year we paid our first visit to Paris (apart from the few hours we spent *en route* to Spain). We flew from Blackbushe Aerodrome to Le Bourget and stayed in Citée Universitaire. This was 'budget' accommodation as were the meals. We were served steak for dinner but it was so tough, we could not cut it. We complained and shortly afterwards, a massive chef stormed into the restaurant, brandishing a large carving knife and steel and demanded why we were complaining. He attempted to cut the steak without success; then he sharpened the knife on the steel but the meat still resisted his efforts. In disgust, he stormed back into the kitchen, produced another steak and flopped it down on our plate. This proved to be equally tough but we dared not complain again, our lives were not worth it! For dessert, we were served peaches but oh so small and barely ripe – not a bit like the delicious fruits we had seen in the market.

During our holiday, we visited all the famous sights, including the Louvre, Fontainbleau, Versailles, the Zoo, Malmaison, the Latin Quarter and took a trip on the Bâteau Mouche. We also made a tour of the Parisian sewers! We met a young couple from Barking, Essex, Ron and Elsie, and we went with them to the theatre. We saw the Folies Bergère, the Casino de Paris revue with the famous Can-Can and the revue *Nus, 1952* at the Mayol Theatre. For Ron especially, these shows were an eye-opener, seeing topless and semi-nude dancers in the flesh.

We joined a party of students from the University on a lightning tour of *Paris by Night*. We later discovered that these tours were intended as 'warm-ups' for would-be patrons to see that the bars and show places were well patronised so that they would attend the proper shows and entertainments after the students (and us) had left.

Before going into the theatre, we bought a programme from a seller outside the building. It transpired that this was not the proper programme and that we should have purchased one inside the theatre. We also discovered that you were expected to give the girl selling programmes a tip and also to tip the usherette who showed you to your seat! The French are certainly wise to making money!

We enjoyed our first visit to Paris but decided next time, it would not be an economy one!

During our visit to Senor Garcia and his family in Madrid in 1949, we offered to have two of his child-

Margaret with Julita and Raquelita from Madrid, our temporary adoptees 1952–53

ren for six months to help them learn English and to give him financial relief. We had a letter from him this year to say he was taking up our offer and was sending us his two eldest girls – Julita, aged eleven years, eleven months, and Raquelita, aged ten. They were coming by train to England, accompanied by a friend and they would be arriving on 1 August 1952. This placed us in a quandary as we were not due back from our Paris trip until Saturday 3rd. We therefore asked my parents, who lived in Hitchin, if they would meet the girls on the steps of St Martin-in-the-Fields Church in Trafalgar Square. Reluctantly they agreed – they were not in favour of looking after these girls from Spain.

Somehow, the lines got crossed. My father waited several hours at the church without meeting them and eventually gave up and returned to Hitchin. Later that evening, he received a telephone call from the police to say they had two lonely and lost Spanish girls who could speak practically no English but had my father's name and address. Apparently, the 'friend' who had brought them to England had left them at Victoria Station and went on her way. Father had to return to London to collect the girls and bring them back to Hitchin. They were tired, hungry and bewildered.

On our arrival back in England, we went straight to Hitchin. The first thing Mother said to us, 'You're not going to keep them, are you?' We assured her that we were doing a good deed and that it was only a temporary arrangement. We took them home with us to Nottingham and began the task of introducing them to the English way of life. The girls were not equipped for our English weather. Their only clothes were thin cotton dresses, so Margaret had to buy them some warmer clothes, coats and raincoats for the coming winter months. Some friends helped us with some items.

Our next problem was to get them into an English school. Fortunately, the council school at the bottom of our road was prepared to take them and they commenced with the autumn term. They immediately became popular with the other pupils and rapidly learnt to speak English. They joined the local Brownies and the Sunday School.

On 13 August, the results came through for the CCS Intermediate Examinations Section B. I had passed in English and Local Government Secretarial Practice but deferred in Constitutional Law which I was required to take again.

A week later, we gave the girls a little tea party to celebrate Julita's twelfth birthday. For a treat, we took them to the Theatre Royal to see Ivor Novello's musical play *Gay's the Word*, a delightful show starring Cicely Courtneidge, Thorley Walters and Doreen Duke and produced by Cicely's husband, Jack Hulbert. It had been especially written by Ivor for Cicely and, in those days, the word 'gay' meant carefree and happy, not the sordid meaning used these days.

I was now due for some leave from work so we took Julita and Raquelita (we now called her Rachel) to Blackpool to see the illuminations. It rained heavily during the day but we were able to see the sights, visit the Pleasure Beach amusement park, the Tower Zoo and the Tower Circus. At the end of November, I took the CCS examination in the subject in which I had failed – Constitutional Law which I subsequently passed.

Christmas was celebrated in the traditional way with decorations and a tree and then we took the girls to Hitchin for three days, on one of which we all went up to London to see Tom Arnold's Circus in Harringay Arena. It was in this show that we saw Pinito del Oro balancing on her head on the swinging trapeze as seen in the film *The Greatest Show on Earth*.

After being with us eight months, it was time for Julita and Rachel to return home. We were unable to take them back ourselves so we arranged with Thomas Cook to provide an escort for them. They were to return by train on 27 March 1953. Three days previous, Her Majesty Queen Mary died.

We took the girls up to London the day before their journey was to begin and booked into the Denmark Court Hotel, Granville Place at the rear of Selfridges, at a cost of fifteen shillings each, bed and breakfast! This was the first time the girls had ever stayed in a hotel. For their last day in England, we took them all over London and for lunch, we went to the Quebec Café in the Marble Arch Corner House. We told them they could order anything they liked and they chose egg and chips! We all had a knickerbocker glory for dessert.

The next morning, we said goodbye to them at Victoria Station. After their eight months' stay with us, they could speak fluent English but had almost forgotten their Spanish. They were far more knowledgeable about world affairs and life in general. As a result of their stay with us, Julita subsequently obtained a good job as an interpreter and married a Swiss. Rachel also did well when she left school. Unfortunately, we lost touch with them in due course.

Whilst they were away, their mother, Mrs Garcia gave birth to yet another child. 'Would you like to take two more of our children?' Senor Garcia asked us but we politely declined.

Following their departure, we went to the Daily Mail Ideal Home Exhibition at Olympia and to the Victoria Palace to see the Crazy Gang in *Ring Out the Bells*.

Her Majesty Queen Elizabeth II was crowned in Westminster Abbey on 2 June 1953 and we watched the ceremony on our television. Nottingham had had its own Coronation procession and fireworks the previous day and we decorated the outside of our house with flag poles and bunting. (See illustration on page 101)

CHAPTER TWENTY-SEVEN

Adoption

*This child I myself will take; she will be mine and I will make a
lady of my own.*

William Wordsworth, 1770–1850,
Three years she grew

TUESDAY, 18 AUGUST 1953 was a day to change our lives forever. Margaret's brother-in-law, John Bamford, took us in his car to London. We had an appointment at the Mission of Hope at Birdhurst Lodge,

Our adopted daughter Rosalind

Croydon, a Christian adoption society. After numerous attempts and miscarriages, Margaret and I had decided to adopt a daughter and the Mission had found us a baby girl, born on 10 June 1953 by the name of Jacqueline Farey. Her mother was a teenager and the father had been killed in a road accident. We took the baby, who weighed 10lbs. 7 oz. and returned with her to Nottingham. On 13 September she was christened in St Jude's Church, Mapperley and renamed Rosalind Margaret Sharp. But not only was she christened but she wet the vicar as well! He was the Rev. Brian Woodhams and fourteen relatives and friends came to the christening party afterwards. Margaret's friend Josie Lodge and her husband, Jim (my best man at our wedding) were godparents, as well as the Rev. Gerald Gregson by proxy.

We had to attend the County Court in December and obtained the Adoption Order in respect of Rosalind who was now legally our daughter.

Also in December, I took the final part of the CCS examination in local government secretarial practice, the law and conduct of and procedure at meetings of public authorities, the law of contract and tort, constitutional law and practice and the law and practice relating to the National Health Service, including the public hospital service. The results came through in February 1954 and I had passed in all subjects. Subsequently, I received my Certificate as a Certified and Incorporated Secretary and was entitled to add the letters ACCS after my name.

An historic meeting took place on 15 January. Appearing in variety at the Empire Theatre, Nottingham were the famous film stars Stan Laurel and Oliver Hardy. I went along to the stage door and was able to meet the pair and interview them. I also obtained their autographs and I discovered that the businessman of the partnership was Stan Laurel, the thin one!

On 29 January, Rosalind, now six months old, said her first word 'Daddy'! She now weighed 21lbs and a week later, she was standing alone, holding on to a chair.

I was still very active in church affairs, teaching in Sunday School, taking a Bible Class and speaking at a number of different churches around Nottingham. I also spoke on several occasions at meetings of the RAF Watnall Christian Fellowship. Mr R. Hudson Pope came to Nottingham for the 75th Anniversary rallies of the Scripture Union and stayed the night with us. In London, Dr Billy Graham, the American evangelist, conducted his Greater London Crusade and we went to the Nottingham Albert Hall to listen to a direct relay of his final rally from Harringey Arena.

A different rally we attended in the Nottingham Albert Hall was addressed by the Rt. Hon. Clement Attlee, the former prime minister and now leader of Her Majesty's Opposition. Rosalind celebrated her first birthday with having her first tooth.

We went to Great Yarmouth for our summer holiday and attended the Circus Fans' Rally at Billy Russell's Hippodrome Circus, followed by supper with the artistes in the circus ring. Among the acts were Bertram Mills' Shetland ponies and Rosalind was permitted to ride on one of them, named Nigger, as they exercised along the promenade. By August, Rosalind was walking unaided and she now had three teeth.

We took our second holiday of the year in September – five days in Morecambe and three in Blackpool. It was illuminations time in both resorts and in Blackpool, there was another Circus Fans' Rally in the Tower Circus. We tried to get Rosalind to sleep before we went down to dinner in the hotel but she would have none of it so eventually, she had to come down with us.

The previous year, we had visited the Daily Mail Ideal Home Exhibition and admired the show houses exhibited by the Esher builders E. & L. Berg Ltd. I was now seeking a secretarial appointment in London and had attended several interviews. We therefore approached Bergs with regard to the houses they were building in Hinchley Wood, Surrey. We travelled to Esher at the end of October to see them and were told that all the Hinchley Wood houses had been sold. However, they had plans to build about forty detached houses and bungalows in Oxshott, halfway between Esher and Leatherhead in the 'stockbroker' belt.

We had never heard of Oxshott, so the builders' representative took us by car to view the site. It was raining hard at the time as we passed through woods on either side of the road. In Oxshott they showed us a field off the main road. This was where the houses were to be built and we agreed on plot seven and paid a deposit.

My search for employment in London was now desperate and one of the interviews I attended was for the secretaryship of the National Chamber of Trade and another for the Showmen's Guild of Great Britain, neither of them successful.

The new year (1955) brought forth many more interviews but none of the jobs materialised. The situation was getting critical as Berg's were about to start building their estate on Charlwood Drive, Oxshott.

In the meantime, I was busily organising two big Christian events in Nottingham. The first was the big top service in Billy Smarts' Circus, which I have already described in chapter twenty-five and the second, a united churches Nottingham Crusade for Christ, to be held in September. I was the organising secretary.

On 23 June 1955, I attended an interview in London with the committee of the National Caterers' Federation, a trade association for caterers, café owners, coffee and milk bar managers and other independent establishments. I was successful and offered the post of general secretary of the Federation, together with the editorship of their newspaper, the *Caterer's Record*, my first professional step in journalism. The appointment came none too soon for we were due to sign the final agreement to purchase the Berg house in Oxshott.

Events then moved very quickly. I had to give one month's notice to the Basford Rural District Council; we had to sell our house in Mapperley and I was still organising the great Nottingham Crusade for Christ. We also had to find temporary accommodation in or around London until our new house was completed.

The Royal Show was staged for the first time in Nottingham in Wollaton Park and this was visited by the Queen and the Duke of Edinburgh. Plans for the crusade were now well advanced. I had persuaded the BBC to broadcast its *Sunday Half-Hour* programme from the Salvation Army Hall in Nottingham on the first day of the crusade and Bishop A. Morris Gelsthorpe of Southwell Minster to take part in the broadcast, as well as the Salvation Army Band and Songsters and other persons taking part in the crusade.

The crusade was spread over two weeks at the end of September and the beginning of October in four districts of Nottingham. It was led by evangelist David Shepherd and a team of Young Life Campaigners. In addition to nightly meetings in various churches of all denominations, there were open-air services, a torchlight Procession of Witness and the screening in a city centre cinema of the Billy Graham Fact and Faith films. All the meetings were well attended and the crusade made a great impression on the city. It concluded with a great rally in the Albert Hall, preceded by torchlights from the Market Square to the hall.

CHAPTER TWENTY-EIGHT

A New Career

The old order changeth, yielding place to new,
and God fulfils Himself in many ways.

Lord Alfred Tennyson, 1809–92,
The Passing of Arthur

O N 5 AUGUST 1955, my career in local government came to an end with my resignation from the Basford Rural District Council. We put our house in Mapperley up for sale and coming home a few days later, we found a couple waiting on the doorstep. They told us they had decided they would like to buy the property even before they had been inside it. As our house in Oxshott was not yet finished, we had to place our furniture into store.

My parents arranged for us to stay temporarily with a widow, Mrs Gooding, further down Strathmore Avenue in Hitchin as they could not (or did not want to?) put us up in their house at No. 80. I commenced work in the office of the National Caterers' Federation at 84 Great Portland Street, London and became a commuter. Being close to All Souls' Church in Langham Place, next to Broadcasting House, I was able to attend their mid-week lunchtime services, conducted by the well-known evangelical minister, the Rev. John Stott.

My job as general secretary of the NCF was to look after the interests of its members, the café and small restaurant owners, advising them on legal and other problems and act as their spokesman. I was appointed one of their representatives on the Unlicensed Places of Refreshment Wages Board which determined the minimum wages of catering staff on the side of the employers. When negotiations took place between the employers and the union, the former always insisted on a lower rate of pay for waiters and waitresses because, they said, their money was made up with tips.

Margaret came up to London with me and assisted in the office, needless to say unpaid and unappreciated!

The committee members were a difficult bunch with whom I had to deal. They knew how to run their own establishments but had little idea of organisation and secretarial procedures. Being young in the profession, I did not assert myself as I should and I let them dominate me.

Part of my duties was to edit their newspaper the *Caterer's Record* and my first issue was published in September 1955. I enjoyed this work and strove to improve its quality and content. I received some criticism for introducing a religious note into the Christmas edition, although, as I pointed out, an innkeeper was involved at the time of Christ's birth! Some time later, I changed the *Record* from a newspaper tabloid format into a magazine. As editor, I attended numerous trade presentations and press conferences. At the end of January 1956, the Federation had a stand at Hotelympia, the Hotel and Catering Exhibition which was held in the National Hall at Olympia, London. Bertram Mills' Christmas Circus occupied the adjoining Grand Hall.

As I was now on familiar terms with the circus management, they agreed to 'loan' me two of their chimpanzees to grace our stand in the exhibition. We put chef's hats on their heads and they proved to be a sensation, with press coverage and photographs of their antics. Publicity-wise, this was a great success, though the committee did not appreciate the effort.

In February, my sister Eileen went into hospital for a major cancer operation, which, thankfully, was successful.

March 27th, 1956 was an exciting day for us. It was moving day to our new house on Charlwood Drive, Oxshott. We named it 'Rosaletta', a combination of Rosalind and Margaret's names.

We had a large garden, a third of an acre front and rear, and at the back, I laid out lawns, two pools, fruit trees, rockery and vegetable plots. The larger of the two pools was L-shaped and I constructed a wooden bridge over it which connected to the rockery. Rosalind was now three years old and in the autumn, she attended the church Sunday School for the first time.

In the summer, we went to the Circus Fans' Rally at Chessington Zoo and Circus. On the lawn outside Burnt Stub, the former mansion in the zoo grounds, the band of HM Irish Guards were playing. The conductor was Captain Michael Jaegar, Margaret's former boyfriend. When the concert was over, Margaret introduced me to him and he entertained us to afternoon tea in the Burnt Stub restaurant.

On 10 October 1956, Margaret and I attended a 'culinary breakfast' at 6 Stanhope Gate, London, to commemorate the 250th anniversary of the foundation of the food company, Crosse and Blackwell. It started at ten o'clock and by one o'clock, we were still eating! One of the guests was the chairman of the English Tourist Board who had to leave at mid-day because he had a luncheon appointment! The menu was a replica of the meal served when the firm was founded and was called 'As in bygone days'. The meal started with carp and pike in wine jelly, braised sturgeon, salmon trout, Cornish crayfish, conger eel in jelly sauce and turkey eggs.

The second course consisted of boar's head, roast swan (permission had to be obtained from the Queen for this item), peacock pattie, pickled ox tongue, roast suckling pig, marinated haunch of venison and beaver lamb in port sauce.

After all these delicacies, we were offered porcupine of beef, hare in coffin, sheep's tongues in jelly, mutton pie, roast grouse in game jelly, roast partridge in spiced jelly sauce, artichoke pie, stuffed hog's ears, Royale salade and Migandi salad.

To round off the breakfast were Maids of Honour, orange jelly, custard tarts and sylibubb. (The spellings are as those on the original menu card.)

In our own garden in Oxshott, I harvested 180lbs. of Majestic potatoes!

On the international stage, Colonel Nasser, President of Egypt, nationalized the Suez Canal Company whose shares were mainly held by the British Government and French investors. On 29 October 1956, Israel launched a surprise attack on Egypt, later to be known as the Six Day War.

Margaret was helping me most days now in the office (still unpaid). We would catch the train from Oxshott to Surbiton, take Rosalind along to a nursery school, then return to the station and continue our journey to Waterloo. The procedure was reversed at the end of the day. Rosalind was beginning to be a bit of a rebel. At nursery school, bread and butter pudding was a regular item on the menu. But Rosalind did not like this dish, nor did her friend sitting next to her, so they filled their spoons with pudding and flicked it over their shoulders. Inevitably, they were caught at it and were made to clean up the mess!

My relations with some members of the Committee of the National Caterers' Federation were not good and at the end of August 1957 I resigned as general secretary.

My sister, Eileen, was also in trouble and had to undergo another operation in July at the Chelsea Hospital for Women which put matters right.

Two of the Bertram Mills' chimpanzees on the National Caterer's Federation stand at Hotelympia catering Exhibition

CHAPTER TWENTY-NINE

A Full-time Journalist

*Three hours a day will produce as much as a man
ought to write.*

Anthony Trollope, 1815–82, *Autobiography*

ATTENDING EACH MEETING of the executive committee of the National Caterers' Federation was Mr Percy Binsted, editor/proprietor of the *Caterers' Journal*, a monthly magazine for the trade. He had noted the antagonism towards me of some committee members and, at the same time, was impressed with the way I had edited and produced the *Caterer's Record*. So immediately I left the NCF, he offered me the post of assistant editor of the *Caterer's Journal* on a full-time basis at a starting salary of £12 per week (£624 per annum) with effect from 30 August 1957, the day after leaving my previous post. My salary with the NCF had been £580 per annum.

This turned out to be valuable training in journalism for me and I gained a deep knowledge not only of the profession but also of the hotel and catering industry. After a month, Mr Binsted increased my salary by £3 per week, to £680 per annum.

Work on the *Caterer's Journal* was always full of interest and I rarely spent more than three hours a day writing. I visited hotels and restaurants and sampled their meals, writing up new establishments and attending press receptions.

The office of the *Caterer's Journal* was in Garrick Street, a few yards from Leicester Square tube station and in the heart of the West End. Many of the restaurants I visited were in Soho and each year was held the Soho Fair.

Among the events at the fair were waiters and waitresses races and the Perfect Coffee Girl contest. The last-named was to find the most beautiful waitress in a Soho coffee bar who was also expert in serving customers. I was invited to be one of the judges at this contest, together with Charles Forte (later Lord Forte). We were seated at a table on the stage and each of the contestants in turn had to serve us with coffee and cakes. We had to judge how well she did it, as well as admiring her figure and looks and general appearance and smartness.

Margaret and I were invited with the Binsteds to the opening of the new Talk of the Town Theatre Restaurant which had replaced the Hippodrome Theatre. This was another of Charles Forte's enterprises and it offered a three-course dinner and a two-hour spectacular revue. Among the stars performing was Judy Garland. We were also guests at the Carl-Alan Awards ceremony and dinner at the Lyceum Theatre. Among the recipients of an award was a young rock 'n' roll singer, Cliff Richard.

Talking of singers, a visit to the Windmill Theatre in Great Yarmouth, where we were attending a rally of the Circus Fans' Association at Peter Jay's Hippodrome, brought us into contact with Irish singer Ruby Murray and her husband Bernie. They were appearing in the Tommy Cooper Show. A little later, a new couple moved into the bungalow opposite our house in Charlwood Drive; they turned out to be Ruby Murray and her husband. For showbusiness personalities, they were a quiet couple and Ruby did not even have a car. I often gave her a lift into the village.

Another personality was our immediate next door neighbour, Anthony Grant (later Sir Anthony), a solicitor who became the Conservative Member of Parliament for Harrow and was Minister of Tourism in Edward Heath's government. Our neighbour on the other side was Fred Birtles, who was press and information officer for the Ministry of Defence.

Among the press calls I attended for the Journal were visits to Bernard Matthews' turkey farm in Norfolk ('they're bootiful!'), an ice cream factory, Campbell's Soups in King's Lynn, Wall's meat factory, Cherry Valley duck farm, El Al catering unit at Heathrow, Pilkington's glassworks in Liverpool and a preview of the new luxury liner *Windsor Castle* in Southampton. At Tilbury, we had a tour aboard the Holland-American line's new flagship SS *Rotterdam* and later the P & O's *Oriana*. Margaret accompanied me on visits to catering exhibitions, hotels and restaurants in Belgium and Holland.

One of the most unusual (dare I say 'exciting'?) assignments was to the Spielplatz Nudist Village near St Albans, where new catering equipment had been installed in their restaurant. I was not required to remove my clothes for this visit but I was met by the director, completely naked and interviewed several members in the buff. At one house in the village, the occupier, a lady, opened the door wearing just a pair of shorts. She invited me indoors and then said to me, 'Do you mind if I take off my shorts? I feel so uncomfortable in them!' Of course I did not mind!

Another press occasion was the opening of the first restaurant on the M1 motorway, a Charles Forte operation at Watford Gap.

Up to our move to Surrey, our only means of transport was by bicycle, bus and train. I had a seat fitted on the crossbar of my bicycle for Rosalind.

Before leaving Nottingham, I had a moped for a time but as it had no gears, it could not make it up the steep road to our house in Mapperley. When I failed the driving test, I got rid of it.

In September 1960 I had my first driving lesson with the British School of Motoring, Charing Cross branch. Subsequent lessons took me all round the West End and round Trafalgar Square, a nerve-racking experience for anyone, let alone a learner!

At that time, I had neither a car nor a garage, so I ordered a sectional concrete garage and prepared a concrete base for it alongside the house. I had a load of ready-mix concrete delivered which was dumped in the road just outside our front gate. Then it started to pour with rain and it was imperative that the concrete was removed from the road and placed in the foundation of the garage. Fortunately, a neighbour came and helped me as soon as the rain ceased. After the garage sections had been delivered and I had erected the garage, another neighbour opposite came across to lodge an objection. He said a concrete structure was not in keeping with the tone of the road!

On the day of the Cambridge and Oxford Univerisity Boat Race, Margaret and I were invited by the Knorr Swiss Company to view the race on the Thames aboard the pleasure boat *Boadicea II*, followed by lunch. The boats flashed by in a matter of minutes and, unfortunately, Oxford won!

Two weddings of importance took place in 1960. HRH Princess Margaret was wed to Lord Snowdon on 6 May (I was to meet them in Leatherhead some years later) and in June, my secretary, Anne Armitage, left me to marry Geoffrey Greenwood in Bromley, Kent before moving to Yorkshire.

CHAPTER THIRTY

A Different Environment

The beauty of the morning ...
all bright and glittering in the smokeless air.

William Wordsworth, 1770–1850,
Miscellaneous Sonnets, part two

HAVING BEEN THREE YEARS with the Binsted's, it was time to move on. I left the *Caterers' Journal* on 25 November 1960 and on 28th, started work as features editor on the trade magazine *Heating and Air Conditioning* at their offices in Victoria Street, close to Westminster Cathedral. It had taken me twenty-one years to reach a salary over £1,000. I started my new job at £1,200 per annum!

I had no knowledge of heating nor air conditioning but I acquired basic know-how by degrees. A journalist does not necessarily need to know everything about a subject but to know how to find out the relevant information. I investigated and wrote articles about the ventilation, heating and air-conditioning systems in hotels, ships, theatres and other public places and soon discovered full air conditioning was a rarity in most establishments.

In December 1960, I purchased our first car, an Austin A30 (first registered in 1956) at a cost of £315. I eventually passed my driving test in April 1961 at the third attempt! Margaret had driving lessons later and passed at her second attempt. A gallon of petrol at this time was four shillings!

In May, Margaret resumed her Civil Service career as a part-time typist at the Ministry of Labour headquarters in St James's Square. Exactly a year after working with Princes Press on *Heating and Air Conditioning*, I was offered the post of Administrative Secretary for the National Society for Clean Air at their headquarters in Breams Building off Fleet Street, which I accepted. My commencing salary was £1,125 per annum, £75 less than at Princes Press who offered to raise my salary by half-a-crown a week! I started my new job on 1 January 1962 and for the time being reverted to secretaryship instead of full-time journalism. The society did, however, publish a journal entitled *Smokeless Air* and an annual *Clean Air Handbook* which I assisted in editing.

I continued writing as a freelance and was obtaining a few more acceptances. I was also elected a member of the Freelance Section of the Institute of Journalists. The Esher Division of the Liberal Party invited me to produce a small semi-political journal entitled the *Quarterly Chronicle*, even though I was not a member of their party. Besides articles by leading national and local Liberals, I was also able to include articles on holidays and travel, entertainments, feminine topics and book reviews. I considered that people would be more inclined to look at such a publication if it was not mere political propaganda. I received congratulations from the national chairman of the Liberal Party, Jeremy Thorpe. Incidentally, this was a labour of love as I received no remuneration for my efforts.

Another unpaid assignment was the editorship of the *King Pole*, the magazine of the Circus Fans' Association of Great Britain.

My clean air duties took me to several conferences including Harrogate and Belfast. At the beginning of 1963, I had lunch with a Mr Jack Chudley, an Exeter printer, Mr Neville Augur, who was the contractor for staging the Clean Air Exhibitions and his associate Mr Reg Lawson. All three were freemasons and they asked me if I would edit the *Freemason's Magazine* and the *Masonic Record*. I was not a member of that fraternity but my father was a mason and as this came within my freelancing role, I accepted. Travel writing was becoming a specialist subject with me and in April, I joined a party of fellow travel writers on a familiarisation tour of the Pas de Calais region.

January 1963 was the month of the big freeze all over Britain. Wisley Lake in Surrey was frozen and on the 26th of the month, we motored to Windsor and Rosalind walked across the River Thames at Runnymede where the River was completely frozen over.

Later in the year, the exhibitions officer and organiser for the National Society for Clean Air resigned and I was offered the job, which I willingly accepted. A Mr Alan Mister was appointed to take over my secretarial and administrative duties and I was given a very attractive young secretary, Miss Janet Negus to assist me and together we set about organising the 1963 National Clean Air, Fuel Efficiency & Domestic Heating Exhibition which was to be held in Scarborough in association with the society's annual conference. We required 20,000 square feet of exhibition space and I booked The Spa on the seafront, adjoining the Grand Hall where the society's conference would take place concurrently with the exhibition. One big problem was to accommodate several major exhibitors such as the Gas Council, the Solid Smokeless Fuels Association, the National Coal Board, Coalite and the Coal Utilisation Council who needed outside flues for burning appliances. We even had to hire a crane to lift some of the heavy equipment into the exhibition space.

The exhibition was a success and for the next NSCA conference, the Royal Hall and the adjoining Exhibition Hall in Harrogate were booked for October 1964. I managed to sell all fifty-six stands without difficulty and all the advertising space in the conference and exhibition catalogue. But I was not content to rest on my laurels. I wanted to get as much publicity as possible about air pollution so I arranged in conjuction with ABC Television a children's television storyboard competition, open to all children within twenty-five miles of Leeds. They were asked to draw a story board for a television commercial, telling viewers the advantages of clean air, the danger and discomfort of atmospheric pollution caused by such things as smoke from house chimneys and factories, dust, grit and fumes and/or the comfort and benefit to the housewife and her family of modern, smokeless heating methods.

Over fifty entries were selected for display in the Exhibition Hall and members of the public were invited to select in order of merit the best ten. The overall winner was a girl in her early teens and her prize included a visit to London with her parents, staying in a top London hotel, with visits to famous places in the capital, a theatre show and lots of other treats. She had never been to London and I met her and her parents when they arrived and took them to the hotel. She was overwhelmed with such luxury and shed a few tears.

The following year's exhibition and conference was staged with equal success in Eastbourne.

Nineteen sixty-four was a year for travelling – not only on holiday but also on journalists' familiarisation trips and visiting exhibitions and conferences relating to my work with the NSCA. The most interesting was a press visit to Algeria, arranged by the Gas Council, to the natural gas fields and the methane terminal at Arzew in the Sahara Desert. We flew to Oran and over the desert and was surprised to see plantations of trees, the work of an international organisation. It reminded me of the prophesy in the book of Isaiah in the Bible, chapter thirty-five, verse one. 'The desert shall rejoice and blossom as the rose.' This was even more appropriate when we reached our destination, the natural gas plant at Arzew. This was being run by British technicians who were housed in two rows of wooden huts. In the space between the rows, the men had sown a grass lawn and planted rose beds, a real piece of England in the Sahara!

The natural gas from the ground was liquified and transported by pipeline to the coast from where it was shipped to Canvey Island in the Thames and converted back again into natural gas for domestic supplies. On leaving Arzew, we stopped at the Oasis of Guardina, with its tall date palms, vegetable crops and a small lake. The oasis was full of men doing absolutely nothing except talk and drink (presumably mint tea) and during our stay, we did not see a single woman or child. They were probably inside the houses, doing all the work!

A few weeks' later, I went to Canvey Island to witness the arrival of a tanker from Algeria and see the Gas Council's natural gas plant. In November, I attended the Northern Ireland Clean Air and Home Heating Exhibition in Belfast, my first time in the province. Our visit to the Balearic Islands was a press occasion to mark the opening of Fred Pontin's first holiday projects abroad. Fred accompanied us and the first stop was at the Hotel Pontinental at Sargamesa near Santa Eulalia on Ibiza. The road to the hotel was by way of a grand slalom. A tree preservation order on the island prevented trees growing in the path of a road from being removed, even when in the middle of the highway, so vehicles had to zigzag to get round them. A drunken driver would find it very easy!

On Majorca, Fred opened a Pontinental Holiday Village at Cala Mes-quida in the north of the island. Here, he introduced waitresses in the dining room, the first time girls had been employed in this capacity in Majorca. As a result of this Balearic tour, I managed to get three articles with photographs published – 'Go Pontinental in Spain' in the *World's Fair*; 'Now it's Go Pontinsnorkel' in *Watersport* and 'How to run a British Hotel on Foreign Soil' in *Caterer & Hotel-Keeper*. Fred Pontin asked for a supply of reprints of all three articles for publicity purposes.

On the 24 January 1965, the death occurred of the war-time leader and prime minister, Sir Winston Churchill. A state funeral took place six days later along the River Thames and both arms of Tower Bridge were fully raised in an upright position, a very rare occurance.

My work now at the National Society for Clean Air was becoming more complicated. The administrative secretary was interfering with my exhibition role and a crisis arose when, without consulting me, he negotiated with the Board of Trade for the society to exhibit at a trade fair in Germany. Furthermore, my very efficient secretary, Janet, left for a new appointment so later in the month, I had an interview with Mr Colin Troup, a publisher, who offered me the editorship of the monthly publication *Domestic Heating News*. As this was a chance to get back into full-time journalism, I took it. I left the NSCA on 6 July and commenced work on my new job the following day at their offices in Red Lion Square in the City.

For a number of years, my father had been a freemason and he persuaded me to become a Brother. I attended for an interview at my father's lodge, Hitchin 6561, and was initiated at a weird ceremony on 11 October 1965. I was blindfolded, had my jacket and tie removed, one shoe replaced by an old slipper and trouser legs rolled up above my knees. Unknown at the time was a noose placed round my neck and a sword pointed at my bare breast, so that if I tried to pull back, the rope noose would have drawn taut and if I had tried to go forward, the sword would have stopped me. After the ceremony, I was seated at the top table for dinner and had to make a speech. I attended the monthly lodge meetings which were held in Letchworth but was none too happy with the psuedo-religious ritual which had no relationship to the Christian Gospel and my commitment as a 'born again' follower of Jesus Christ. So, in the following year, I dropped out of the lodge on the excuse of having to travel from Oxshott to Letchworth for their monthly meetings. Apparently, once a mason, you are always a mason but I have not had any communication from the Order ever since.

Following the previous year's press visit to the Pontinental resorts in the Balearic Islands, Fred Pontin invited us to visit the Hotel Pontinental at Platamona on the island of Sardinia. We found this to be a very windy island, especially on the Costa S'Emeraldo, where royalty and other celebrities had villas.

The National Society for Clean Air stand at the Scarborough Exhibition, 1963. With Margaret and Roy is Mr Arnold Marsh, the society's director.

CHAPTER THIRTY-ONE

Home and Abroad

One man in his time plays many parts.

William Shakespeare, 1564–1616,
All's Well That Ends Well, Act 4, Scene 3

A PART FROM 1 April 1923, the most significant years in my life have been 1933, 1942, 1943 and 1966. 1933 was the year I became a Christian, 1942 was the year I joined the RAF, met Margaret and became engaged and 1943 was the year of our marriage. Now we come to 1966.

At the end of January, Mr Colin Troop informed me that my services as editor of *Domestic Heating News* would terminate at the end of my six months probationary period. I had not fallen down in my work and I had received no compaints from the company but the previous editor whose departure had led to my appointment now wished to return to the job, so I had to relinquish the editorship.

However, I had for some time been providing freelance articles for a monthly publication called *Homes Overseas*, a magazine advertising holiday villas and overseas properties for purchase and investment. The managing editor, Mr Michael Furnell, invited me to become features editor of this publication, together with another monthly, *Homefinder*, which featured houses for sale and new developments in the United Kingdom. I accepted at a salary of £1,600. I left Colin Troop Ltd on 28 February and joined Michael Furnell the following day. This was a full-time appointment but I was able to work from home, with periodic visits to the London office with my articles and collect new assignments. These included travelling to various parts of the country, calling on estate agents and writing features on current and future house building programmes and the state of the housing market. This was for *Homefinder*. In *Homes Overseas*, I described various countries abroad, their climate, their attractions and amenities and details of villas and apartments on the market which were suitable for British purchasers. Our press familiarisation trips abroad provided additional information for these articles.

We were also able to combine research for the two magazines with the annual conference of the Institute of Journalists which, in 1966, was held in Cork in Southern Ireland. Following this was our second cruise, this time on a new ship which bore two names and had two owners. In the summer months, the ship was run under the flag of the Bergen Line, serving as a car ferry between Newcastle and Bergen, Norway, with the name MV *Jupiter*.

During the winter months, the Norwegian shipping line Fred Olsen, took over the vessel and it became the *Black Watch*, serving as a cruise ship from Tilbury to the Canary Islands. Whilst there, the car deck became the hold for tomatoes, bananas and other products for importation to Britain. The lifebuoys on the ship bore the name *Jupiter* on one side and *Black Watch* on the other.

Our daughter Rosalind, now twelve years of age, was causing us quite a headache. Eventually, we decided that a boarding school would be best for her and we managed to get her into a Christian school, Clarendon, near Abergele in North Wales. She commenced there on 28 April 1966.

Now that Rosalind was away at school, Margaret was able to accompany me on my visits to various towns in England for *Homefinder*. Mr Furnell invited Margaret to furnish two showhouses on new estates being built and these were to be featured in *Homefinder*.The first house was in Seaford, near Brighton, and was being built by Laings. We visited shops and department stores in Brighton, selecting furniture, furnishings and accessories with which to furnish the house which was officially opened on 25 May.

The second showhouse was at Woodhams Ferrers, in Essex, built by Cooper Homes. This was another exciting venture which Margaret enjoyed.

We continued to write our travel articles, not only for *Homes Overseas* but for other publications and to edit the *Masonic Record*, the *Freemason's Magazine* and the Liberal *Quarterly Chronicle*. A travel agency, Embassy Travel Ltd of Great Portland Street and Richmond, Surrey, asked us to prepare a holiday guide for 1966, a thirty-six-page booklet in which we described twenty-three holiday destinations abroad, tying in with Embassy Travel's package holidays. We were also commissioned to prepare the official guide for Seaton and Beer in South Devon.

Madeira is one of our favourite islands, having first visited it on our 1951 cruise aboard the SS *Chusan*. Subsequently, we wrote an article entitled 'Madeira – a Garden in the Atlantic'. The Delegaçao de Turisso da Madeira was so pleased with it that they reproduced it in its entirety as a preface to their hardback book of photographs, simply entitled *Madeira*.

CHAPTER THIRTY-TWO

The 'Courier' is Born

All the news that's fit to print.

Motto of the New York Times from 1896

A N ADVERTISEMENT APPEARED in our local newspaper offering a small monthly magazine, called the *Villager* for sale It was more like a parish magazine but contained articles of local interest. We went to see the owner thinking it could be a nice little extra money earner, and we agreed to purchase it. Shortly afterwards, though, we were gazumped by an advertising agency who made a higher offer, so we lost the purchase. We gave it a little thought and we decided that if a small magazine run by someone who was not a journalist could make a profit, why could not we? After further thought, we decided to launch our own publication. We would call it the *Esher & Leatherhead Courier* to provide a link between the two Surrey towns with Oxshott in the middle. We had no capital and did not want to borrow any money. We said that we would go ahead if we could get sufficient advertisement revenue to pay for it.

The *Villager* was distributed free to households by local newsagents and we planned to use the same method. We would pay them one penny a copy for each one they inserted in newspapers they delivered. Margaret and I canvassed all the shops and businesses in Esher, Hinchley Wood, Oxshott, Cobham, Stoke d'Abernon, Leatherhead, Fetcham, Ashtead and Bookham and obtained

ISSUE NO. 1 – September, 1966

sufficient advertisements to pay for the printing, distribution and other expenses and still make a small profit on the first issue.

We had the blessing of Mr Furnell who agreed to release us from full-time employment with him but we agreed to continue to supply him with articles on a freelance basis.

The first issue of the *Courier* was published on 2 September 1966. We had 20,000 copies printed and it consisted of sixteen pages, and twelve inches by eight inches in size.

It was one of the first free newspapers in the country and, needless to say, it was not looked upon very favourably by the local paid-for newspapers.

From the very beginning, our policy was to make it a readable paper, with no more than fifty per cent advertisements. It would be a monthly publication with emphasis on features and background to local news, not competing with the weeklies. In each issue, in addition to district reports, we had features on entertainments, the arts, food and cookery, wining and dining, gardening, feminine topics, book reviews and two or three pages on holidays and travel. Each subsequent issue made a small profit and after a year, we changed the format to tabloid and brought out two editions – one for Esher and one for Leatherhead.

The whole production, apart from typesetting and printing, which we put out to contract, was undertaken solely by Margaret and myself. We gathered the news, wrote the articles, checked the galleys, pasted up the pages and passed the final proofs at the printers.

Margaret took care of the accounts, sending out the invoices and collecting monies due. When an issue came out, we delivered the bundles of papers to the newsagents and then personally gave a copy to every shop and business in our area. In this way, we got to know the shopkeepers and businessmen and subsequently obtained advertisements from them. We also delivered the invoices by hand and in the majority of cases, the recipients paid us on the spot, often with cash from the till. Because of this method, we had very little bad debts and we always had sufficient money to pay our printing bills and other overheads.

One of the places to which we delivered our first issue was to the Moore Place Hotel in Esher. In the ballroom, a dancing lesson was taking place, run by the Frank Harrison School of Dancing. We talked to Mr Harrison and came to an agreement – he would give Margaret and myself ballroom dancing lessons free of charge in return for a free monthly advertisement. This proved to be a very satisfactory arrangement and some time later, we both obtained bronze and silver medals.

We celebrated the beginning of 1967 with a new car, a Vauxhall Viva SL9O de luxe, having traded in our Wolesey. In the spring, we undertook the editorship of *Leather & Saddlery*, the monthly magazine of the Society of Master Saddlers. Later in the year, Mr Furnell asked us to write a book entitled *A Guide to Continental Holiday Villas* which was published in December as a ninety-six-page paperback and published by Homefinders (1915) Ltd. In it we gave information and facts about villa renting companies and agents specialising in these properties; specifying the main locations of the villas in different countries and indicating their price range.

The publication was a success and we were asked to write another *Continental Holiday Villas and Flats, 1969*. This was a 108-page paperback.

Margaret's younger sister, Renée, her husband Ernest and daughters Sheila, Jill and Alison set sail from Southampton on 17 May as ten-pound emigrants to Australia. Ernest had been a bank manager in Nottinghamshire but thought there would be better prospects 'down under'. Meanwhile, Rosalind was none too happy at boarding school and we finally let her leave Clarendon at the end of the summer term. She was now aged fourteen years. In September, she started as a pupil at St Christopher's School in Leatherhead.

On Saturday, 23 September 1967, the Leatherhead Theatre organised a sponsored walk from the town to Worthing, a distance of around fifty-five miles, to raise funds for a new theatre which was to be built in the town. We publicised the event in the *Courier* and 1,700 people of all ages (plus some dogs) set off on the trek. Not everyone got as far as Worthing but over £6,000 was raised by the walk. Margaret and Rosalind walked part of the way (some thirteen and a half miles) before sore legs brought them to a halt. I was following in the car, taking photographs, and I picked them up and took them on to Worthing.

Two years later, on 17 September 1969, we were invited to the gala opening of the new theatre by Her Royal Highness, Princess Margaret, and her husband, Lord Snowdon. The theatre was named after the famous actress, Dame Sybil Thorndike and the small studio theatre was named the Casson Room, after Dame Sybil's husband, Sir Lewis Casson. The new theatre, built on the site of the defunct Crescent Cinema in Church Street, replaced the old Leatherhead Repertory Theatre in the High Street and was the brainchild of actress/director Hazel Vincent Wallace and co-director Michael Marriott.

Dame Sybil was present at the opening performance of *The Lion in Winter* by James Goldman and she appeared in person in the next production *There was an Old Woman*. Many famous stars later appeared in productions in the Thorndike until, sadly, the theatre suffered financial problems in the 1990s and, in 1997, its doors closed and its future is still in abeyance.

One of the seats in the theatre bore a plaque with the names 'Roy and Margaret Sharp, Esher & Leatherhead Courier'. A few years later, we also had a seat named after us in the Wimbledon Theatre.

Back to 1967, we were approached by the tour operators Clarkson's, offering our readers a day excursion to the bulb fields of Holland. The trip would include the flight from Gatwick to Rotterdam, a tour of the bulb fields, a visit to the bulb park at Keukenof and, finally, a visit to The Hague. We arranged transport from convenient pick-up points in the district to the airport and the total cost per person was just under ten pounds. This also included a Dutch lunch! We easily had a full coach and so successful and popular was the trip that we arranged other continental tours with Clarksons, and later, with other tour operators.

In May 1967, we attended the Institute of Journalists conference in Belgium. This included a visit to the historic city of Bruges. Some 300 journalists were asked to assemble in the market square and when the bells in the clock tower chimed seven o'clock, trumpeters dressed in mediaeval costume came out on the balcony of the Gothic belfry overlooking the square and sounded a fanfare. Then the Belgian equivalent of a town crier came out on the balcony and, in a loud voice echoing around the square, announced in English that members of the British Institute of Journalists were bidden to enter the Banqueting Hall underneath the tower to be entertained by the Mayor and burgesses of the city to a magnificent feast.

In subsequent speeches, it was emphasised that the British people would always be considered the very special friends of Belgium and would always be welcome in their country. I wonder if they still feel that way after our football hooligans have run riot? We have made numerous visits to Belgium in the ensuing years and have experienced their friendship and hospitality.

Our Dutch parties proved to be so successful, we arranged a four day Wine Festival tour of the Rhine Valley with Clarksons, visiting Luxemburg, Rudesheim, Coblenz, Bernkastel and Trier. The cost was twenty-two pounds.

It became our policy that all our tours had to be booked through our local travel agents, who would receive their commission from Clarksons. In return, the agents agreed to take advertisement space in the *Courier*. We took no commission for ourselves and personally escorted all tours.

So popular became our tours that we decided to arrange a New Year party for our readers, again through Clarksons. Over fifty of us left Heathrow on 30 December to welcome in 1968 at the Hotel Pueblo at El Arenal on the island of Majorca.

Having seen the success of the *Courier*, another company launched the *East Surrey Trader* in the autumn, covering Surbiton, Tolworth and parts of our district, namely Claygate and Hinchley Wood. Seeing this as a potential rival to us, we decided to buy them out and incorporate the *Trader* in the *Courier*.

Daughter Rosalind now embarked on a secretarial course at Clark's

College in Surbiton. In June, Margaret and I obtained our bronze medals in ballroom dancing and had to give a demonstration of the rhumba at the Medal Ball.

On 3 July 1968, we celebrated our silver wedding in Malta. We rented a villa for a fortnight at Xemxija, near St Paul's Bay and were accompanied by Rosalind and her girlfriend. The temperature was very hot and Margaret certainly did not want to do a lot of cooking. We found self-catering is no joke. After a day sightseeing, bathing, boating, etc., who wants to return to your apartment or villa and get a meal ready? During the day, you exist mainly on salads and at night, you try to find an inexpensive restaurant for dinner. When we weighed it all up, it cost just as much on a self-catering holiday as it would have done staying full board in an hotel! During the holiday, we also visited the islands of Gozo and Comino and took a boat trip to the Blue Grotto.

Back home, we went to see the film *Doctor Dolittle* starring Rex Harrison. A lot of the picture was filmed in the old world village of Castle Combe in Wiltshire. We went to see the location one Sunday in July and found there were no car parking facilities in the village, so we parked behind a long row of cars on the approach road. When we returned, we found that the traffic warden had been along and given all the cars on this road a penalty ticket. When we got to our vehicle, the warden was standing by it.

'You are lucky,' he said. 'I've run out of parking tickets so I cannot penalise you!' The Lord was certainly with us that day!

After our successful New Year party in Majorca, we organised other *Courier* trips for our readers during 1969. These included a three day visit to Paris in February, a repeat Dutch bulb fields tour in April, Bruges in October and the Costa Brava, Spain in October. These short breaks became a regular pattern in the ensuing years.

Margaret entered the Mount Avernia Hospital, Guildford on 16 April and had a hysterectomy operation. This finally ended all hopes of producing our own child. This was not the end of her troubles. A few months previous, she had an operation to remove varicose veins and in August, she entered the eye hospital in Surbiton for an operation to clear a blocked tear duct. The hospital was a small, old building, due for closure, without a lift and Margaret had to be carried up a long flight of stairs to the operating theatre. No mean weight!

Up to now, our *Courier* was not delivered in East and West Molesey because there was already a successful monthly publication, the *Molesey Review* which had been running for a number of years. In November 1968, the owners approached us with a view to selling it to us. We agreed to the purchase which now gave us three papers. To make publication easier, we changed to newspaper tabloid format, introduced spot colour and brought out three editions – the *Esher & Molesey Courier*, the *Leatherhead & Cobham Courier* and the *Surbiton & Tolworth Courier*. All three editions had common pages but we had to change some pages including the front page for each edition. This meant more work, more running around and still only two of us. However, the *Molesey Review* had been distributed to households by a team of senior schoolchildren, so we continued to use them for East and West Molesey. We also appointed a number of freelance correspondents who supplied us with news reports from their own district.

We were not making a fortune but we remained solvent, had a few bad debts and had a modest income on which to live. We would never make good business people, we are not ruthless enough – more prone to give things away than charge people for them. As it says in the Bible, 'It is better to give than receive'.

By now, the *Courier* was recognised both locally and in the profession as a successful new form of publication. An article in the *Financial Times* (22 August 1969) described the rapid growth of local 'giveaway' news-papers, a development which the major publishing companies were starting to exploit. Mr Rupert Murdoch's *News of the World* group acquired three giveaways and other groups getting on to the bandwagon included the Westminster Press.

In the *Financial Times* article, mention was made of the *Courier*. It stated that,

... the founder and owner, Roy Sharp, and his wife are freelance journalists, so their policy is in favour of editorial content. Their attitude is different from most others in that they offer 'national' type features, mainly on gardening, motoring and travel, the kind of thing that is lacking in the local press. Their papers run forty per cent of editorial to sixty per cent of advertising and they get some well-known contributors among their writers. The enterprise has even led to the formation of a travel and holiday club which does a foreign expedition each year.

Sharp emphasises the need to be cutting corners all the time; to plan to go over to web-offset to save £100 a year on printing bills and so on. His costs, from production and distribution come to sixpence a copy and there is little chance of raising the advertisement rates.

The profession's own paper, the *UK Press Gazette* also published an article on 'The Giveaway' (1 September 1969) in which the front page of the *Courier* was reproduced, as well as detailed description of the *Courier*, its contents, printing and distribution.

CHAPTER THIRTY-THREE

Travel Guide and Party Organiser

To travel hopefully is a better thing than to arrive and the true success is to labour.

Robert Louis Stevenson, 1850–94,
Virginibus Puerisque – El Dorado. An apology for Idlers

FOLLOWING THE INITIAL SUCCESS of our *Courier* day trips for our readers, we proceeded to expand our programme, offering longer tours from three and four days to a week and eventually two weeks abroad.

Our first trips to Holland to the bulb fields in 1967 were followed by a four day Wine Festival Tour of the Rhine Valley, a three day sightseeing in Paris, a tour of Bruges and an eight day Fiesta and Flamenco party in October 1968 on the Costa Brava in Spain. The last named was based in the resort of Calella de la Costa and included excursions to Barcelona, Montserrat, Gerona and Ampurias, as well as a boat cruise along the coast. The cost was twenty-nine pounds and included hotel, full board, coach tours and pick-up and flight. It was arranged for us by Clarkson's. It was an enjoyable tour and we took with us around fifty of our readers. We were disappointed though with the beaches. All the brochures specified sandy beaches but they were not sandy. They consisted of very tiny stones which tended to stick between your toes. The sea, too, was none too clean with unmentionable debris floating on the surface. If we had ordered sand from a builder, we would have sent it back. This was definitely *not* sand.

Our first New Year party consisted of eight days at El Arenal, Majorca and in the following year (January 1969), we took almost 100 participants to the Hotel Playa at Camp de Mar, also on Majorca. On Twelfth Night, 6 January, three of our party donned costumes to represent the three kings and we visited children in a local hospital and gave them toys which we had brought with us from England.

In Spain, the main celebrations are not at Christmas but on the eve of Twelfth Night. Large processions take place in most of the towns consisting of tableaux, bands and children and adults in fancy dress, with the three kings bringing up the rear. They would throw out sweets to the spectators. During the night, the three kings would visit each house and leave presents for the children but if a child had been naughty during the year, he would be left a lump of coal. Candy, shaped and coloured like coal, would be on sale in the shops and parents would buy some to place with their children's toys as a reminder that they had not been little angels during the year!

In April, we took a party to Switzerland, based in Interlaken. We climbed to the top the Jungfrau, 11,333 ft. (by furnicular!) and to the restaurant on top of Kleine Scheidegg (by cable car). This was featured in the James Bond film *On Her Majesty's Secret Service* starring George Lazenby and Diana Rigg.

Planning ahead for our 1970 New Year party, tour operators Lunn Poly arranged for me to visit Torremolinos to see whether their holiday met our requirements. Together with their representative, we hired a car and visited Malaga, Grenada, Nerja and Algeciras. From there, we took the ferry to Gibraltar.

In the Crown colony, it was crisis time. General Franco's campaign for the return of the Rock to Spain came to a head and he unilaterally withdrew all Spanish workers from the colony and closed the frontier on the Spanish side. Not wanting to be isolated on the Rock and unable to return to Torremolinos, we recrossed the bay on the last ferry to Algeciras. (This ferry service still has not been restored in 2002.) We then drove along the coast to the frontier town, La Linea, where we witnessed the last of the Spanish workmen, carrying their tool kits, passing through the frontier gates before they were slammed shut and locked on the Spanish side. Those on the British side, though, remained open.

Many of the Spanish men were in tears and were greatly distressed.

'What am I to do?' one worker asked us. 'I have no work here, I cannot get to my old job in Gibraltar, I have a wife and children to support and we get no financial help from the Spanish government.'

This sorry tale was told to us by other men who were now out-of-work, thanks to General Franco and his government.

Nearly 100 readers joined us for the New Year party to Torremolinos in January 1970, staying at the Hotel Amaragua. One of the excursions we arranged was a day trip to Tangier in Morocco. All went well until we reached Algeciras to catch the ferry across the Straits. When we tried to get our tickets, we were told the boat was completely full and that we would have to wait for the next one in two hours' time. By the time we got aboard, it was lunch time and there was such a scramble aboard that it was nigh impossible to get to the small cafeteria.

Eventually, we arrived in Tangier, two hours later than we had planned. A tour had been arranged for us but this now had to be cut short and we were only able to have a quick tour of the Casbah and visit a souvenir shop before we were taken back to the ferry for the return trip to Algeciras.

This was not one of our most successful outings! Fortunately, the rest of the holiday went smoothly.

A spring party in April followed and we took forty people to the Hotel Miramar in Puerto de la Cruz on Tenerife, one of the Canary Islands. The weather was perfect and everyone had an enjoyable week. At dinner one night, we were served a whole Dover sole. Whether it had seen Dover or not I would not like to say but it was such a large fish that it protruded over the edge of the plate.

In the following month, we took another large party to Keukenhof and the Dutch bulb fields and in September, once more with Clarksons, our readers explored the Black Forest and the vineyards of Alsace.

On the last day of December 1971, Margaret's sister, Renée, and her daughter Alison arrived from Australia. They stayed with us at Oxshott for three days, during which time, Alison saw her first fall of snow, then we picked up sixty of our readers for our *Courier* New Year party and took them to Gatwick airport. Our destination was Palma Arenal in Majorca.

When we reached the airport, the whole area was enshrouded in thick fog and our flight was, therefore, delayed. By one o'clock in the afternoon, it had not lifted and so our party was provided with complimentary refreshments. The minutes ticked by until three o'clock when I, as party leader, was informed that there was no prospect of a flight that day. Accordingly, the tour operator, Clarksons, provided us with a coach to take everyone to Brighton where they booked us into the Old Ship Hotel on Marine Parade with complimentary dinner, bed and breakfast.

The next day, Monday, was sunny and bright in Brighton and I telephoned the tour operator for instructions. We were told that, although the south coast was clear, Gatwick and the rest of the country was still covered with fog. Another call at midday still informed us there was little chance of flying today, so after a complimentary lunch at the hotel, the party dispersed – some to wander round the town and shops, some even went to the cinema.

Shortly afterwards, another telephone call came through to say the fog was lifting and I was to put my party on the train to Gatwick without delay. This meant a frantic round-up by Margaret and myself until everyone had been found and put safely aboard the train. Arriving at Gatwick station, an announcement on the public address system said that the *Courier* party should *not* alight as the airport was now closed and that we were to continue the journey to London.

At Victoria station, we were met by a Clarkson's representative who took us to the Grosvenor Hotel opposite the station where we were allocated rooms for the night. We were then taken to the Chicken Inn Restaurant across the road for dinner. Half way through our meal, I received another telephone call from Clarksons. Although fog still covered the whole country, there was one airport still operating, Ringwood, Manchester. Seats had been booked for us on a train to Manchester and I was to collect our party and their luggage and proceed immediately to Euston Station where they were holding up the train for us.

Another mad scramble as our party left their unfinished meal, returned to the hotel to collect their luggage from their rooms and then grab taxis to take us all to Euston. Once more, we were on the move, but one couple out of the party of sixty decided they had had enough and did not want to proceed any further. The rest of us caught the 11 p.m. train but even this was not plain sailing.

A little way from Crewe, the engine broke down and we had to wait over half an hour for a replacement locomotive!

We finally arrived at Manchester Piccadilly at 4.00 a.m. to find just one coach waiting for the airport. The driver indicated that this was the last one so we all crowded on board and eventually reached the terminal and checked in our flight.

'We are sorry, the flight is delayed,' we were told. More frustration but at last, we made our way to the aircraft, a Dan Air Comet IV. We fastened our seat belts and waited for take-off. Then the captain came on to the intercom and announced he could not take off because the aircraft was frozen and had to be de-iced. But having come so far, we were determined we were not going to be moved again and decided to sit tight and remain on board until the de-icing operation had been completed. At long last, we finally became airborne and touched down in Majorca at 7.30 a.m., Tuesday morning, two days late!

One recently married couple, a Mr and Mrs Smith (that really was their name!) sent postcards to their relatives from Gatwick, Brighton, London, Manchester and Majorca – a touring honeymoon. When they signed the register at the Old Ship Hotel, Brighton, as Mr and Mrs Smith, the management did not believe they were indeed married!

In spite of lack of sleep, most of us managed to watch the Three Kings Procession in Palma later that evening (Twelfth Night, 6 January). The remaining five days made up for all our hassle – sunny weather, full board at the Hotel Flamingo, Arenal, a night at the Tagomayo Night Club and tours of the island, concluding with a gala carnival party on our last night.

But even now, our troubles were not yet over. Our return aircraft was diverted to Luton, where we had to wait for our coach which had gone to Gatwick to meet us. Altogether, a unique holiday experience which we hope will never be repeated.

Margaret's sister, Renée and her daughter Alison, left England at the end of this holiday to return to Australia.

CHAPTER THIRTY-FOUR

Home and Away

'Hence! home you idle creatures, get you home; is this a holiday?'

William Shakespeare, *Julius Caesar*, Act 1, Scene 1

OUR DAUGHTER ROSALIND had always been a bit of a rebel, always siding with the underdog and was never an ideal pupil at school. After boarding school in North Wales and St Christopher's School in Leatherhead, we sent her to Clark's Business College in Guildford to learn typewriting and secretarial subjects. But after a time, we discovered she was absent part of the time. We would drop her off at Guildford but instead of going to college, she would make her way back to Leatherhead where she would pass the time at a youth club called the Blue Set. On her end of term school report, where the headmaster was required to assess a pupil's progress and general behaviour, he wrote 'Refuse to comment!'

Now aged fifteen years, we decided it was time Rosalind started work. She had a succession of jobs including a shop assistant, factory worker, office clerk, waitress and apprentice hairdresser, none of which except the last-named lasted more than a few weeks.

She was at this time mad about boys. Even when she was at Clarendon, the school was next to an army camp and it was not unknown that she would slip out of the school grounds to visit the boys. At weekends, she would often go with friends to Brighton or to Gatwick airport to watch the planes.

The 16 July 1969 is a landmark date in history for on this day, three American astronauts – Neil Armstrong, Michael Collins and Edwin Aldrin – reached the moon in spaceship Apollo 11. Aldrin and Armstrong walked on the moon for two hours four days later (20th) and then they returned safely to earth. Total time on the journey there and back was eight days, three hours eighteen minutes and thirty-five seconds. Neil was the first man to step on the lunar surface with the words: 'One small step for man, one giant leap for mankind.'

Rosalind, now aged seventeen, much against our wishes, went to live with Anthony (Tony) Simpkins, a Leatherhead boy, and as a result, a daughter was born on 3 December 1970 and named Maria Evandra, our first grandchild.

During the year, we attended many local functions and dinners as editors. We also arranged a series of dinner dances for our readers at the Burford Bridge Hotel, Box Hill near Dorking, a Trust House Forte establishment. In conjunction with the management, we arranged the menu, the theme of the evening and the entertainment. The first one took place in May 1969, and over 100 readers attended. The theme for the evening was Caribbean and the menu included West Indian dishes. For entertainment, we had limbo dancing and the Ross Henderson Steel Band. Mr Frank Harrison, who had now opened his own school of dancing at Hampton Wick, acted as Master of Ceremonies and I engaged members of Gilbert's International Circus from Chessington Zoo to provide the cabaret.

Such was the success of this venture that in the following years, we organised a number of similar events. The next one was held at another Trust House Forte hotel, The Greyhound at Hampton Court. We decided on a Norwegian evening and I contacted Fred. Olsen Shipping Line for suggestions for re-creating their famous hot and cold table. They replied by offering to send one of their top chefs to help to provide an authentic Fred Olsen table. The food was prepared on board their ship *Braemar* as she sailed from Christiansand, the gateway to Norway, to Newcastle-upon-Tyne. When she docked, the food was sent direct to Hampton Court by train, accompanied by two pantry cooks, Miss Pal and Miss Knuts, who would be assisting in serving the food. Fred Olsen's chief catering advisor, Mr Martin Johanssen, was also on hand at The Greyhound during the evening to answer questions about the dishes which included a wide variety of fish and cold meats with appropriate salads and vegetables. The cost per person was £2.50.

We provided another themed dinner at The Greyhound in May 1972, This we called 'Dining Around the World' with dishes from Scotland, France, Spain, Alsace, Greece, Majorca, Italy, Russia and England. One of the dishes we wanted to serve was grilled swordfish steaks. In 1972 swordfish was not generally available in the UK so I arranged for a supply to be sent to us from Spain with the co-operation of British European Airways. Unfortunately, my suppliers got the dates wrong and sent them the previous Saturday. The air hostess on arrival did not know what was in the package so instead of contacting me or the hotel, she placed the fish in her locker at the airport and went off for the weekend. When we eventually retrieved it, we were doubtful whether it was fit for human consumption. The hotel manager said he would put it in his freezer and come to a decision on the day of the dinner. He finally decided to risk it and it was served as the second course. Our diners voted the steaks as one of the best dishes and no one reported ill afterwards!

We continued to promote special dinner dances at the Burford Bridge Hotel. One of these was a Thai evening and through the Thai Embassy and Thai International Airline, we had exotic foods, flowers and fruits flown in from Bangkok. We also had two Thai dancers performing traditional dances.

A safari evening was organised with the Kenya Tourist Office and British Airways and a Caribbean carnival night in co-operation with the Trinidad & Tobago Tourist Board. P & O Cruises helped us to stage a cruise night.

On 31 March 1970, we were guests of Ronnie and Kay Smart

Tree-planting at the Burford Bridge Hotel, Box Hill, Surrey

and the Billy Smart's Circus family at the royal opening of their Windsor Safari Park by HRH Princess Margaret.

This year saw an increase in the number of overseas press trips and our *Courier* reader parties. They included Sicily, visiting Taormina, Catania, Syracuse and a climb up Mount Etna where we watched smoke, flames and large chunks of rock being thrown high into the air from the volcano. The Institute of Journalist's conference this year was held in Jersey, after which we went to Copenhagen and another trip to Tunisia.

CHAPTER THIRTY-FIVE

A Life on the Ocean Wave

If one does not know to which port one is sailing,
no wind is favourable.

Seneca the Younger, 4 BC–AD 65, Roman Philosopher & Poet
Epistulae Morales, No. 71 Section 3

WE HAVE ALWAYS CONSIDERED a cruise to be one of the most satisfying holidays. It is an all-inclusive package with accommodation, all meals, entertainments and travel, visiting famous ports throughout the world. At the time of writing, we have been on forty-three cruises with some of the leading cruise lines.

Apart from the two occasions when I was 'guest' of His Majesty's forces in 1943 and 1945, our first cruise (for which we paid £62 each) is described in chapter twenty-four. Our second cruise took place in 1966, courtesy of Fred Olsen aboard the new ship which bore two names, *Jupiter* and *Black Watch*.

Fred Olsen also had another ship, the *Black Prince* and this alternated with the *Black Watch*, one sailing from London every Thursday and the other from Las Palmas every Saturday. Since then, we have had twelve cruises with Fred Olsen.

On 15 November 1996, we journeyed to the new cruise terminal at Dover to join the new *Black Watch* on its inaugural cruise. Formerly owned by the Norwegian Cruise Line, the 28,492 ton vessel had been acquired by Fred Olsen and it had just completed a £4 million refurbishment at the A & P shipyard in Southampton.

What should have been a wonderful send-off turned out to be a nightmare. Work on the refurbishment had not been completed, leaked water pipes had flooded some of the cabins and rendered them unoccupiable, non-delivery of supplies and other problems prevented the ship from sailing. After waiting several hours in the departure lounge in the Dover terminal, an announcement was made to the effect that *Black Watch* would not be sailing that evening. Several hundred would-be passengers were told the cruise was off and were sent home. We were among those whose cabins had not been flooded or upset but because of electricity failure, the ship was unable to provide us with an evening meal. We and the remaining passengers were told to take taxis and find a hotel or a restaurant in or around Dover for dinner and we would be re-imbursed the cost. It was now around seven o'clock in the evening and with so many people seeking an evening meal, we could not find anywhere in Dover where we could be accommodated. Our taxi driver, however, said he knew of a place some miles out of the town and here we were able to be served.

After our meal, we were back on the ship where we spent the night. The next morning, we were served a cold breakfast and cold lunch and after twenty-two hours' delay, we at last weighed anchor and set sail on the inaugural. However, our troubles were far from over. Several times the electricity failed and meals were not always as per the menu. To try and placate us, all drinks in the bars were complimentary but before long, supplies were exhausted as passengers imbibed to their hearts' content!

Our first port of call was Gibraltar, a day late, but to make up some of the time, the captain decided to omit our next stop, which should have been Malta. After Crete, we arrived in the port of Alexandria, Egypt. When a ship is in port, regulations stipulate that the ship's shops on board must remain closed. Egyptian port authorities and police came aboard and immediately demanded that the shop be opened and then they proceeded to help themselves to various articles (for which, of course, they did not pay!).

Most passengers, including ourselves, disembarked in Alexandria and proceeded by coach to Cairo. We were taken to see the Pyramids at Giza and the Sphinx but disappointingly, we could not see the tops of the Pyramids because of low mist. From there, we dined in a four star hotel for lunch and then made a tour of the city and visited the Cairo Museum with its display of exhibits from the tomb of Tutankhamen.

In the meantime, our ship had sailed from Alexandria and we were due to rejoin it at Port Said. For the journey from Cairo to the Port, our coach had a military escort because of the possibility of terrorist activity. We arrived in Port Said in the early evening but there was no ship. Our party waited a while on the quayside and then our escort took us to a hotel nearby where we were served refreshments. At last, just before midnight, the *Black Watch* appeared on the horizon and at long last we were back on board. The captain explained that they had been held up until ships had cleared the Suez Canal where a one-way system operates!

From Egypt, our next port of call was Ashdod in Israel but even here, all was not plain sailing. Because we had called at Egyptian ports before coming to Israel, the authorities showed their spite by insisting every passenger appeared before their immigration officers with their passport to have it examined and stamped. This delayed our disembarkation by several hours and cut short the time we had ashore. This was particularly irritating for us as a representative from the Israeli Tourist Board was meeting us at the quayside to take us on a tour. This included a visit to Neot Kedumim, the Biblical Landscape Reserve near Ben Gurion Airport, which we describe in a later chapter.

On our voyage westwards after leaving Israel, our ship was suddenly diverted. The captain announced over the loudspeaker that he had been ordered to change course and avoid the way ahead because the United States Navy was holding manoeuvres in the area! As a result of this delay, our final port of call, Tangier, was by-passed!

At the end of our three weeks' inaugural cruise, all the passengers were told they could have another cruise free of charge.

'This has not been our usual cruise,' the captain said, 'rather a voyage of adventure!'

Our compensatory cruise was taken the following year when we visited the northen capitals of Stockholm, Copenhagen, Tallin (Estonia), Helsinki (Finland), St Petersburg, Rostock and Amsterdam. We sailed through the Kiel Canal and from Rostock, we made an excursion to the city of Berlin.

On our return from the inaugural, we were invited to appear on Meridian Television News to describe our experiences.

Twice I have been on a cruise aboard the Cunard flagship *QE2*. The first time Margaret was unable to accompany me. It took place in July 1972 and was an historic voyage because it was the first time this ship had visited Copenhagen, Hamburg, Stockholm and Oslo. At each port, we were given a tremendous welcome, especially Hamburg. Crowds of spectators lined the banks of the River Elbe all the way from the sea, aircraft flew overhead and flags were flying everywhere. In Hamburg, I went to the famous Carl Hagenbeck Zoo in the Tierpark and I strolled around the city's famous red light district, the Reeperbahn in the heart of the St Paul entertainment district. I hasten to say I did not avail myself of the services of the ladies of the town!

Prior to my cruise, I had contacted the national tourist offices of Norway, Denmark and Sweden, requesting assistance when I disembarked in their countries. The family who shared my table at dinner on board expressed surprise that at the three northern capitals, an attractive young lady was waiting for me on the quayside to escort me round the city!

In all our articles, we always emphasize to our readers going on holiday to allow themselves plenty of time to get to their point of departure. But in June 1971, we failed to heed our own advice. We had booked our seventh cruise – two weeks on the Shaw Saville Line's SS *Northern Star*. The ship left Southampton on Whitsun Saturday *but the ship went without us*! We left Oxshott early in the morning, giving us, we thought, plenty of time to reach the port. Being a Bank Holiday weekend, we took the country route to Guildford instead of the A3 to avoid holiday traffic. But just after Great Bookham, we became stuck behind a long line of vehicles which were crawling behind a farm tractor all the way to Guildford and as the road was narrow and plenty of on-coming traffic, it was impossible to overtake. From Guildford, we joined the A3 but after the Hog's Back, we came to a halt near Alton because road works were in progress, building a dual carriageway. For over an hour, we did not move and time was ticking away. It soon became apparent that we were not going to reach Southampton before the ship sailed.

Eventually, I turned the car round and drove into Farnham to the nearest travel agency. The first port of call on this cruise was Gibraltar, so we decided to beat the boat and fly to the Rock and there join the *Northern Star*, having first informed Shaw Saville of our intentions. It seemed that we were not the only passengers to miss the boat.

The agency booked us seats on a BEA Vanguard to Gibraltar via Madrid for Monday 31 May and hotel accommodation for the night at the Astoria Lodge Hotel. Our neighbours were astonished to see us returning home. 'We missed the boat!' we told them but by so doing, we were able to attend and report on the opening of the 1971 Molesey Festival on the Sunday. We duly arrived on the Rock on Monday and on the following day, watched the arrival of the *Northern Star*. Earlier that morning, we observed many of the shopkeepers along Main Street changing the price upwards of their goods in anticipation of the arrival of cruise passengers.

We were welcomed on board – 'better late than never!' – and our cruise commenced at 1.00 p.m. We discovered that the Bay of Biscay had been rather rough so this was a blessing in disguise.

A memorable cruise was aboard the Norwegian Caribbean Line's flagship, SS *Norway* in 1985. The ship was originally the SS *France* and vied with Cunard's *QE2* for the Blue Riband of the Atlantic. The ship had a length of over three football pitches (1,035 ft.) and her stacks rose over seventeen storeys above the sea. If stood on end, she would be only 100 feet short of the Empire State Building. In gross tonnage (70,202), she was the fourth largest passenger ship and the longest ever built. She carried 2,400 passengers and had a crew of 850 from thirty different nations. Our cruise commenced in Miami and we visited St Thomas in the US Virgin Islands, Nassau and Stirrup Quay, the company's own private island in the Bahamas.

The Caribbean is our favourite cruising area and we have visited a total of sixteen different islands on various cruises aboard the P & O *Sun Princess*, Carnival Cruise Lines *Mardi Gras*, Royal Caribbean Cruise Lines *Song of America*, Premier Cruise lines star ship *Majestic*, Chandris Line Celebrity Cruises MV *Horizon* and Royal Caribbean Cruise Lines *Majesty of the Seas*.

Other cruises which we have taken in the Mediterranean, the Atlantic and northern waters have been on the *QE2*, *Canberra*, *Melina*, *Meltemi*, *Itthaca*, *Sea Princess*, *Vacationer*, *Orpheus* and Orient Lines *Crown Odyssey*.

The last named cruise took us to the Middle East. We flew from Heathrow to Istanbul, where we joined the *Crown Odyssey*. All was not well, though, for when we arrived at Istanbul, we found that one of our bags had not been put on the aircraft before we left. As we were going straight from the airport to the ship, British Airways undertook to fly the missing bag to Turkey and then on to our first port of call. Needless to say, the bag never reached us and in spite of much searching, it vanished after reaching Turkey. Not only had we lost shoes and items of clothing but our second case, a new one, was damaged and the zip broken. Luckily, this case was repaired for us by the ship's maintenance department.

Our first port of call was Nesebur on Bulgaria's Black Sea coast. Founded by Greek seafarers nearly 3,000 years ago, it is today a UNESCO World Heritage site. There are over forty churches and basilicas from the Byzantine Empire scattered within the remains of the mediaeval fortress walls of the old town. During the reign of the Ottomans, the Turks decreed that no church could be built taller than a man seated on a horse, so in consequence, many churches dating from that time are half underground. Today, there is only one church used for Christian worship.

Our next port of call was Odessa in the Ukraine and then Yalta in the Crimea. We were able to visit the late Czar Nicholas II's summer palace where Winston Churchill, President Roosevelt and Joseph Stalin met in 1945 to plan post-war Europe.

The highlight of the cruise was a visit to Ephesus, a few miles from the port of Kusadesi, where our ship docked. Ephesus was one of the most prosperous Greek cities of ancient times, now a splendidly restored site of antiquity. We were surprised at the extent of the city, over a mile in length and it formerly had a population of around 300,000. After the resurrection of Jesus Christ and His ascension into heaven, His apostles began their mission of spreading the Gospel of salvation and St John the Evangelist, together with the Virgin Mary, went to Ephesus. He gathered around him a great number of monotheistic Jews who became converted to Christianity. Both John and Mary are said to have died in Ephesus and to be buried there. The house of Mary has been restored and is one of the focal points for pilgrims.

St Paul arrived in Ephesus in 53 AD and baptised twelve Christians in the name of the Lord Jesus and the Holy Spirit came upon them. Paul argued persuasively about the Kingdom of God in the synagogue but some of his hearers became obstinate and refused to believe and publicly maligned the Gospel. So Paul left them and took the disciples with him and had daily discussions in the lecture hall of Tyrannus. This went on for two years, so that all the Jews and Greeks who lived in the province of Asia heard the Word of God.

As the number of converts increased, so did the opposition from the worshippers of the goddess Artemis, especially from the craftsmen. One of them, a silversmith named Demetrius who made statuettes of the goddess, was losing business and called upon his fellow tradesmen to protest. A riot ensued and the whole city was in an uproar, proclaiming 'Great is Artemis of the Ephesians'.

Paul's travelling companions from Macedonia, Gaius and Aristarchus, were seized and dragged to the amphitheatre, Paul wanted to address the crowd in the theatre but was persuaded not to do so. The crowds started to beat any Christian upon whom they could lay their hands. Finally, peace was restored by the authorities.

After Paul had departed for Macedonia, the number of converts continued to increase. Paul subsequently wrote his letter to the Ephesians from his prison in Rome and the church continued to flourish for some time but later heeded the warning given in the book of Revelation, chapter two. You can read all about these happenings in Ephesus in the nineteenth chapter of the book of Acts in the Bible.

Up-to-date, only five per cent of Ephesus has been excavated and there is much more to be uncovered. There are three main streets and we made our way along them, passing the ruined basilica, the city hall, the Baths of Various, the Temple of Hadrian, the magnificent library of Celsus, the public baths, 'communal' toilets and the commercial Agora. The lecture hall of Tyrannus has not yet been discovered. We continued along the Marble Road to the amphitheatre which could seat up to 25,000 spectators and this is where Paul's companions were taken and the riots took place.

Cruising has become *the* holiday vacation at the turn of the century with more and more ships entering into service. Although the majority of passengers still seem to be on the 'heavenly side of fifty', the age is gradually coming down with cheaper cruises on offer.

What are the attractions of a cruising holiday? The plus factors include an inclusive fare for accommodation; five meals a day of the highest culinary standard; all kinds of recreational activities from deck quoits, carpet bowls, table tennis, shuffle board and even, on the larger ships, mini-golf; indoor games from whist drives and bridge, Monopoly, Scrabble, etc.; ballroom and line dancing with instructors; arts and craft classes for beginners; heated swimming pools and jacuzzi, 'dolphin' racing, quizzes, lectures and bingo.

There are films shown each day in the ship's cinema or on video in one's cabin, classical concerts, music from the ship's orchestra, cabaret shows and spectacular shows in the theatre. You can relax with a book from the library, take in the sun on a deck chair, enjoy drinks in the various bars or simply put your feet up and do nothing! You only have to pay for drinks and shore excursions. In our opinion, a cruise is the best type of all-inclusive holiday.

If we are spared, we hope to embark on two cruises in 2003 to celebrate our diamond wedding. One is on our familiar friend the *Black Watch*, sailing to Amsterdam, the Shetlands, the Faroe Islands, Iceland and Norway.

The other will be a first for us, the Radissson Seven Seas Cruise Line. Way back in June, 2002, we were entertained aboard their latest luxury liner, the *Seven Seas Mariner* (50,000 tons gross), an all-suite, all-balcony ship with culinary creations by famed Parisian Cordon Bleu chefs.

At the time of writing, we are not sure on which of the company's ships we will be cruising. Hopefully it will be on their new vessel, the most opulent *Seven Seas Voyager* (49,000 tons gross), which also boasts all-suites, all-balconies for each of its 700 passengers.

Other ships in their fleet are the *Seven Seas Navigator, Radisson Diamond, Song of Flower* and the *Paul Gaugin*. The last named is a luxury mobile resort, gliding from island to island in French Polynesia.

The six-star *Voyager* is due to be launched in March 2003 at an estimated cost of £170 million. She will be almost identical to the *Mariner*, accommodating her 700 guests in a cradle of elegance and refinement. She will have four restaurants, each with its own ambience and culinary specialities, and each one offering contemporary Anglo-French Cordon Bleu cuisine.

Standard ocean-view suites will stretch to more than 300 square metres, including living space, full bathrooms with separate shower and bath tub, walk-in wardrobes and private balconies.

Radisson Seven Seas Cruises is part of Carlson Hospitality World-wide, a global leader encompassing more than 1,400 hotels, resorts, restaurants and cruise ships in seventy-nine countries.

We cannot wait to get aboard.

The Fred Olsen cruise ship *Black Watch*.

CHAPTER THIRTY-SIX

From Louisiana to Missouri

*Frenchmen and Spaniards, pirates and generals, European
Royalty and Southern belles have all bowed to the fascination of
the Queen of the Mississippi, New Orleans.*

Sidney J. Barthelemy, Mayor, City of New Orleans

ONE HUNDRED YEARS AGO, more than 11,000 paddle-wheelers plied
the Mississippi and Ohio Rivers, carrying passengers ranging from
Southern belles and diamond-studded gentlemen to trappers and gun-totin'
gamblers. The rivers were the highways of their day, bristling with vessels.
Towns sprang up along their banks and thrived on the passenger trade
from the steamboats as well as deliveries of cotton, sugar cane and other
goods. Competition for passengers was fierce among the steamboat companies, so the boats became floating palaces. They vied with each other
for famous chefs, orchestras and elaborate furnishings, establishing a
tradition of grandeur which is still a part of steamboating today.

You can imagine our excitement when, in October 1989, we received
an invitation from the Delta Queen Steamboat Company of New Orleans
to be their guests on an eight day cruise aboard their flagship, the *Mississippi
Queen* on the River Mississippi from St Louis to St Paul, Minneapolis.

From Margaret's schooldays, she had corresponded with an American
girl, Louise, who lived in Bossier City, Shreveport in Louisiana. They had
never met, so in 1987, we planned to go to New Orleans for the Mardi
Gras Carnival and then go on to visit Louise. We had to cancel this trip,
though, because of two deaths in the family. The first was John Bamford,
husband of Margaret's sister, Winnie. John was a survivor from Dunkirk
in the Second World War and after being rescued and returned to England,
was sent two days later to join the Eighth Army in North Africa, where
he drove a tank.

On 24 December 1986, my father had a heart attack and was admitted
to Lister Hospital, Stevenage. This was his ninetieth birthday but was
allowed home a few days later, only to be readmitted in February the
following year. On 25 February, I telephoned the hospital to see how he
was and was told he had collapsed on the way to the toilet and died that

morning. We had to go to Hitchin to register the death and make arrangements for the funeral which took place at the Stotsley Crematorium on 4 March.

Now with this invitation from the Steamboat Company, we were able to arrange our postponed trip to Louisiana and visit Margaret's friend, Louise.

To get to Louisiana, we first had to fly to New York. Our flight was by Pan American World Airways to J. F. Kennedy airport. Our reception in America was anything but welcoming! Non-US citizens joined a long queue to pass through Immigration and Customs. Two very dominating females – we were reluctant to call them 'ladies' – one white, the other black – stood at the head of the queue and directed the 'aliens' one by one to numbered desks to be interrogated by officials. These two ladies would not have been out of place in Hitler's SS! One of them brandished a stick and shouted at individuals, 'Get back into line. I said desk number fourteen, not thirteen!' and, 'I don't care whether you have a flight connection to catch, you will come when I say so!'

So much for friendly New York and welcome to visitors from overseas! We were glad we were not staying in the Big Apple! We heard our names being called over the loud speakers several times to join our flight to New Orleans but to no avail. We were not allowed to pass the female gauleiters and it took us an hour and a half before we were eventually admitted to the USA.

By now, the once a day flight to New Orleans had departed without us. The thought of being stranded in New York for twenty-four hours did not appeal but we managed to find a Delta Airlines flight which had been delayed and was about to depart for New Orleans and we caught it with minutes to spare.

The tourist bureau had booked us into the New Orleans Hyatt Hotel, situated in the central business district of the city, adjacent to the famous Lousiana Superdrome, the scene of major sporting events and spectacular shows. The hotel had 1,196 luxurious rooms and suites and included an enclosed mall with dozens of boutiques and shops.

New Orleans was not quite what we had expected. We thought it would be more brash, noisy; a carnival atmosphere with an exciting and vibrant waterfront and promenade. No doubt it is all that during Mardi Gras with its street parades and jazz festivals. We liked the modern shopping precincts, the streetcars, the paddleboats on the muddy Mississippi River, the historic French Quarter with its pavement artists, the market, fine Victorian mansions and houses and Jackson Square.

There are many sightseeing tours starting from New Orleans going out into the countryside. We went on the Honey Island Swamp tour. This is by boat through swamps in south east Louisiana, some forty-five minutes' drive from the city. This is a river swamp in the delta of the Lower Pearl River and is one of the wildest, least altered natural swamp left in America. It is semi-wilderness with towering cypress trees and abundant wildlife, small bayous and backwater sloughs. During our two-hour safari, we saw alligators, snakes, turtles, egrets, a racoon, herons, wood duck and many birds which we could not identify.

Shreveport and Bossier City

From New Orleans we flew north-west to Shreveport, known as the Sportsman's Paradise. This plush heartland is a scenic setting for fishermen, hunters, watersports enthusiasts and nature lovers. You can take a scenic boat ride on the Red River or the beautiful Ouachita River in Monroe.

At Shreveport's airport, Margaret's friend, Louise, was waiting to greet us. She had also alerted the local press who were there to interview us. We did not want to impose ourselves on Louise and her husband's hospitality and booked into the Bossier City Sheridan Hotel. Bossier City is virtually a suburb of Shreveport which is where Louise resided. They acted as our guides during our stay in the city and we visited the American Rose Centre, the headquarters of the American Rose Society. Here are over thirty individual gardens located among meandering pathways and the roses encompass all types from the old garden varieties to the newest introductions – hybrid tea, floribunda, grandiflora and miniatures.

In Bossier City is the Eighth Air Force Museum where visitors can see how aviation has developed since World War One to the present day. Bossier City's history is filled with tales of the Civil War but its most significant contribution to the development of the area was transportation. Shed Road, built during the 1870s was the South's original year-round turnpike. It was actually a nine-mile shed with a road running through it which made the transportation of outgoing cotton and incoming supplies a reality. Much of the history of the district can be seen in the various museums and galleries in the two cities.

St Louis, Missouri

Our too-short a stay in Louisiana soon ended and Louise and George took us in their car across the stateline into Texas. Texas, we know, is a large state but we were only able to venture a few miles inside to the small town of Marshall. Our impression of this place was not very favourable, a community whose heart had stopped beating. We made for

Margaret picking cotton in Louisiana

the railway station and here our impressions of bygone days were confirmed. The station buildings were derelict, windows broken and the walls covered with graffiti. If this was Texas, then they were welcome to it!

We crossed a patch of waste ground to a raised platform, overgrown in places with weeds and grass to await the arrival of our train which was to take us overnight to the city of St Louis in the state of Missouri. The Amtrak train, named *The Texas Eagle* arrived on time, whistle blowing and bell clanging and the conductor descended and examined our tickets.

'Oh', he said, 'you have a de luxe bedroom compartment in the last coach', some nine coaches away from where we were standing. As we picked up our luggage, the conductor said, 'There's no need to walk down there, I will move the train for you. Thereupon, he spoke on his portable radio to the engineer and the fourteen coach train slowly moved forward until the last coach reached to where we were standing. Then, to our delight, we heard those immortal words, 'All aboard!'

The train was a double decker and we had to climb the stairs to reach our compartment. This consisted of a large sofa which at night converts into a single bed. The second bed lets down above it and has to be mounted by means of a ladder. There was also a swivel chair, wash hand basin, mirrors, a fold-away table and a toilet. When you closed the lid of the toilet, you sit down upon it and the unit becomes a shower with water issuing forth in short ten second sprays! We had visions of flooding the train.

Regrettably, it became dark soon after leaving Marshall and we were unable to view the scenery from the train's observation lounge. Our ticket included dinner, so we made our way to the dining car where we were served a three-course meal including a very fine New York steak. The meal was excellent but it lost some of its gloss by being served on plastic plates, with the drinks in paper cups.

The train arrived in St Louis (the Americans pronounce it Saint Lewis, not in the French way as we do) at the end of an eleven-hour journey. The time was 6.10 a.m. and was forty-five minutes *early*. We made our way to the Radisson Hotel, formerly the Clayton Inn in the heart of the business district. We found St Louis a beautiful, friendly city, full of interest and exciting leisure facilities.

During the next few days, we toured the seventy-nine-acre Missouri Botanical Gardens, now at its best with its autumn red and gold foliage, and some outstanding sculptures, including two reclining figures by Henry Moore. The most outstanding feature in the city is the Gateway Arch on the river front. Standing 630 feet, it is the nation's tallest and most elegant monument, commemorating the role St Louis played in the United States' epic surge westwards. Built of stainless steel, it is hollow inside and a 'tram' takes visitors right to the apex where you can look through windows across the vast panorama of the city and the great River Mississippi.

St Louis is the third largest railway centre in the States but if you go to the city's Union Station terminal, you will not catch a train. The huge domed building has been redeveloped as a festive market place with speciality shops, restaurants and entertainments and it leads into the Hyatt Regency Hotel.

On our second day in the city, we made our way to Grant's farm, the former home of the USA's eighteenth president, General Ulysses S. Grant. Transport takes you on a tour of the estate through game reserves and a miniature zoo, the Trophy Room and the collection of horse drawn carriages and sleighs and to meet the huge Clydesdale stallions.

Back in the city, we visited the famous St Louis Zoological Park with its $17 million education centre which fuses high technology and living animals with the object of presenting a unified picture of life. Here, you encounter 150 different kinds of animals ranging from jelly-fish, worms and insects to over 2,800 animals living in natural surroundings in the eighty-three-acre park. Visitors view these from an overhead monorail.

There were so many other attractions in St Louis but we just did not have time to see them. One, however, we did find extremely interesting was the beautifully restored 6,000 seat Fox Theatre. But we had to make our way to the riverfront to board the great *Mississippi Queen* steamboat for an historic cruise to Minneapolis.

But should we get another invitation to *Meet me in St Louis,* we will certainly answer the call!

CHAPTER THIRTY-SEVEN

Way Down the Mississippi

There is no better way to see America than from the deck of a paddlewheel steamboat.

Tom Greene, The Delta Queen Steamboat Company

IF YOU SUFFER FROM 'mal-de-mer', or the thought of a rough passage through the Bay of Biscay or an English Channel ferry crossing in a force eight gale turns you green, then you should consider a river cruise as an attractive alternate vacation. Some people like messing about in boats on the rivers of England or on the Norfolk Broads. You can cruise the canals of France or take a cruise along the River Rhine from Holland to Switzerland. This we have done on several occasions and is very commendable.

But in October 1989, we took the ultimate river cruise, aboard the mighty paddlewheel steamboat, the *Mississippi Queen*. Aboard, you can experience all the romance, fun and excitement of bygone days whilst cruising along the world's fourth longest river, the mighty Mississippi. There are still a number of steamboats on pleasure trips along the river, mainly from New Orleans, but only three undertaking cruises from three days to two weeks.

The *Delta Queen* is the last of the truly authentic steamboats and was built in 1926 at the Isherwood Yard, Glasgow, the same yard in which the great Cunarders were built. With decks of Siamese ironwood, cabins furnished in oak and trimmed with mahogany and walnut, stained glass windows and an early air-conditioning system, she set a high standard of opulence. She was taken over by the United States Navy for service during the Second World War and was bought by the Delta Queen Steamboat Company in 1946, an organisation which traces its history back to 1890.

The *Mississippi Queen* was built in 1976 by James Gardner of London, designer of the *QE2* and at that time was the largest ever built, rising seven decks high, 382 feet in length and displacing 3,364 tons. She has twin rear paddlewheels and carries 438 passengers and a crew of 156. Both the *Queens* travel at an average speed of eight miles per hour.

In 1995 a third vessel joined the fleet, the *American Queen*. At 418 feet

The *Mississippi Queen* steam boat

in length and six decks high, she is now the world's largest steamboat, even though she does not carry any more passengers than the *Mississippi Queen*. She blends yesterday and today with the comforts of a de luxe ocean cruise ship and the design of a traditional steamboat floating palace. We received an invitation to cruise on her soon after her maiden voyage but circumstances prevented us from taking up the offer.

We joined the *Mississippi Queen* at St Louis for a seven day cruise through the states of Illinois, Iowa, Wisconsin and Minnesota to the city of St Paul and, on the opposite bank, Minneapolis.

As we set sail, life took on a new meaning as we gently glided past riverside towns, plantations, historic battlefields and miles of virgin forests and woods. We had been greeted on board as we crossed the red carpeted gangplank and the steam operated calliope played Southern tunes. We were escorted to our stateroom containing a king-sized brass-knobbed double bed, large picture window and a veranda, enabling us to watch the ever-changing scenery. As this was a 'Fall Foliage' cruise, the trees were changing to red, bronze and gold.

Dining aboard was sheer delight, starting with a lavish buffet on the first night and then each day, a new and different menu, offering shrimp remoulade, prime ribs of beef, crabmeat Louisiana, Tennessee fried catfish, pecan pie, jambalaya and Creole gumbo. From hearty Southern breakfasts to sumptious evening gourmet fare, each meal was an event. Film shows, dancing, cabarets and lectures, as well as bird watching were all part of our day between meals.

Our first stop was Hannibal, Missouri, the birthplace and boyhood home of Mark Twain and the setting for the adventures of Tom Sawyer and Huckleberry Finn. We visited his home, now a museum, and the Mark Twain Cave, in which Tom Sawyer and Becky Thatcher were lost in *The Adventures of Tom Sawyer.*

The next stop was Dubuque, Iowa, where a coach was waiting to take us across the river into the state of Illinois and the town of Galena. Here, we visited the home of the Civil War General Ulysses S. Grant, who later became the eighteenth president of the United States. Where the Black River and La Crosse River meet the Mississippi lies the town of La Crosse (Wisconsin). Founded in 1842 as an Indian trading post, the town specialised in lumber and sawmill products until the surrounding forests were completely ravaged. A famous landmark there is the brewery built in the shape of a six-can pack of beer.

One of our last stops was Wabasha, Minnesota which was settled by the 'Laurel' people in about 900 AD. They buried their dead in sitting positions near the river's edge, believing their spirits would flow down river to the great sea with the next rainfall. Today, the town features one of the largest early Indian artefact exhibitions in the States.

Minnesota's oldest hotel, the Anderson House, is a country inn and all its rooms are furnished with antiques dating back to its opening in 1856. Besides its famous cuisine based on Grandma Anderson's original recipes, the hotel has another unique feature. On request, it will provide you with a cat for the night to act as a bedwarmer! Alternatively, you can opt for a mustard bath and a hot brick in a quilted envelope to keep you warm on chilly nights. There is a cookie jar in the lobby and if guests wish, they can go out fishing in the nearby waters and the hotel will cook their catch for them. Having chosen your cat for the night, the hotel provides you with a cat basket and cat food! No wonder Anderson House is included in the National Registry of Historic Places!

During our seven day cruise, we travelled a total of 669 miles and climbed 420 feet by means of twenty-seven giant locks. Arriving at each lock is a special occasion, with blasts on the boat's horn and music from the calliope. Townsfolk line the river banks and passengers throw silver-wrapped chocolate dollars to the children on the shore. Only twice a year do they see the *Mississippi Queen* so far up river, once going up and again on its return voyage.

As Tom Greene said, 'There is no better way to see America!'

Our cruise terminated at the twin cities of St Paul and Minneapolis. The Mississippi River was central to St Paul's history and was the reason for its settlement. During its earliest years in the 1840s, the city was a French village settled by French-Canadian voyageurs. In 1849, Minnesota became a territory and St Paul the territorial capital and remained so when Minnesota became a state in 1858. The twin cities are lovely urban centres with a wide range of attractions. They share the common heritage of their German, Irish and Scandinavian settlers.

The cathedral of St Paul was modelled after St Peter's in Rome and many of the mansions date from the Victorian era. Minneapolis has achieved international recognition for its focus on the arts with the Guthrie Theatre one of the leading repertory playhouses in the States. Modern art is displayed in the Walker Art Centre and over forty works are set among tree-lined courtyards in the adjacent Sculpture Garden.

But all good things must come to an end, so we reluctantly had to make our way to the international airport for our flight home via Washington.

The city of St Louis, Missouri with the Gateway Arch on the river front.

CHAPTER THIRTY-EIGHT

Food, Cookery and Travel

There is no love sincerer than the love of food.

George Bernard Shaw, 1856–1950,
Man and Superman, Act 1

PROBABLY the three most interesting and enjoyable subjects in which a journalist can specialise are food, travel and the leisure industry. I was fortunate to choose all three and it has provided me with much pleasure and, although it is more than a full-time occupation, I have never looked upon it as 'work'.

Life returned semi-normal at the beginning of 1971 (if you can call a journalist's life normal) and, apart from a tour of Devon and Cornwall, we were based at home until 1 August when Margaret and I flew behind the Iron Curtain for a two-week break in Communist Romania. We stayed in the modern purpose-built resort of Mamaia on the Black Sea coast.

All along this coast, holiday complexes have been built, almost all identical, and given the names Venus, Jupiter and Neptune. During our stay, we visited Constanza and took a boat trip on the River Danube and the Danube delta where we saw Europe's only wild pelicans. Other diversions included a visit to a sanitorium, mud baths, a nudist beach (a separate one for men and women), vineyards, an oil field; and we even attended a Romanian folk dance and a wedding feast.

Our hotel was comfortable, the food adequate and enjoyable and we found the Romanian people very friendly. However, we were not allowed to check out of our hotel at the end of our holiday until the management had checked our room inventory to ensure that we had not purloined any towels, soap, ashtray or other furnishings and fittings from the room! They obviously did not trust the British tourists!

One of our problems in producing the *Courier* was printing. Prices kept rising and we had to shop around and find alternative printers. One of these was in Aylesbury and on 24 September, having been at the printers all day checking and passing pages, we were driving home through Amersham in pouring rain when we were involved in a head-on collison with another car. The road was for two-way traffic with a middle lane for overtaking. I moved into this lane to overtake a vehicle when another car coming in the opposite direction decided to do likewise. I braked hard but did not realise what would happen if the wheels locked on a wet and slippery road. In consequence, our car slid sideways across the road and crashed headlong into another vehicle in the opposite lane.

We were certainly under Divine protection for although our car was only a few weeks' old, it was a complete write-off and we only sustained bruises. We were saved by wearing our seat belts. The driver of the other vehicle was only slightly injured.

Three consequences followed the accident. I was prosecuted at the Amersham Magistrates Court on 16 December for driving without due care and attention and was fined £20, plus £1.85 witness expenses and my licence was endorsed. As my new car was a write-off, my insurance company paid me in full and I bought a new Austin Maxi.

The third consequence of our accident was that Margaret developed a lump on her left breast. We were very worried, fearing this might be cancerous. She had an operation in October in the Epsom District Hospital and had the lump removed. Thanks be to God, it was not malignant and the incision healed nicely.

Back home, Margaret was invited to be a judge in a Better Sandwich contest which was held in the Bull Hotel, Leatherhead.

At the end of the year, we were invited to meet the management committee of the Cookery and Food Association, who offered us the editorship of their journal, *Food & Cookery Review*, which was first published in 1897. We accepted the appointment and took it over from January 1972.

The association, originally known as the Culinary Society, came about through a cookery exhibition held in London on 5 May 1885 under the chairmanship of Eugene E. Pouard, chef to the Officers' Mess of Her Majesty Queen Victoria's bodyguard at St James's Palace. Following the promotion of a second exhibition in December 1886, Monsieur Pouard was encouraged by colleagues to examine the formation of a properly constituted organisation and in the following year, the Culinary Society was renamed the Universal Cookery and Food Association. The present title – the Cookery and Food Association – was adopted in 1958 and in 1965, it formed a separate division known as the Craft Guild of Chefs, incorporating the Worshipful Company of Cooks.

Since 1898, the association has been privileged to enjoy royal patronage, including that of Her Majesty Queen Alexandra, Her Majesty Queen Mary and Her Majesty Queen Elizabeth the Queen Mother. Traditionally, the presidency of the association is held by the Master of the Royal Household.

The aim of the association is to promote and develop the art and technology of cookery and allied professions. Principal objectives include the establishment of codes of practice and conduct for people within the industry; the organisation and support of culinary competitions and exhibitions; the furtherance of education and training, especially for young persons, in the catering industry. Education in the art of science of food and cookery in all its facets has played a major role throughout the years. The outcome of the setting up of the association's school in Vauxhall Bridge Road, London, at the turn of the century to teach boys professional cookery led to the establishment of the first Hotel School, Westminster Technical Institute in 1910 (now Westminster College), the forerunner of over 300 colleges, polytechnics and universities offering courses in catering and allied subjects today.

Members are elected to the association from suitably qualified persons directly concerned with or engaged in catering management, cookery or allied subjects or in the teaching of any of those subjects. Members belong to one of the regional divisions, including the Craft Guild of Chefs and the Restaurant Services Guild. The Association's motto is *Docendo Discimus*, which roughly translated means 'Through teaching we ourselves learn'. Among its activities is the promotion of culinary exhibitions and salons culinaire and every two years, the Craft Guild of Chefs organises the Craft Guild Chef of the Year competition.

As a result of becoming its editors, we attended many culinary functions and dinners throughout the country; food presentations, trade exhibitions and press facility visits to farms, food factories and demonstrations.

In May the following year, we were invited to join the team of judges at the Jersey Food Festival in the Channel Isles. This meant dining at a different restaurant for lunch and dinner each day for three days and awarding marks on the culinary merits of the menu and the service and presentation of the meals. No wonder we put on weight! But indulgence did not stop there for two days' later, we were off again to the Austrian Tyrol and Innsbruck, with a short trip across the border to Merano in Italy.

This was followed by two cruises – the first on the Greek ship *Meltemi* around the Greek Islands and then on the *QE2* around Scandinavia.

In order to improve our cookery skills, we both attended courses at the Tante Marie School of Cookery in Woking. We spent the mornings preparing foods for lunch which we all partook and then in the afternoons, we had lectures and demonstrations.

The Cookery and Food Association's annual banquet and ball in 1976 was held at London's Dorchester Hotel at which their Royal Highnesses, the Duke and Duchess of Gloucester were guests of honour. After the meal, we had the honour of being presented to their Royal Highnesses, who were very interested to hear about our journal, the *Food & Cookery Review*.

In the same year, we organised our own banquet and ball at the Leatherhead Leisure Centre to celebrate the tenth anniversary of the *Courier*. Frank Harrison of the Park View Dancing School acted as Master of Ceremonies and he and his partner gave a demonstration of Latin American dances. Liz Field provided her Roaring Twenties cabaret show and music was provided by Russ Henderson and his West Indian Dance and Steel Band. We devised an international menu comprising six courses and T. Wall & Sons provided us with a huge anniversary ice-cream gâteau.

Ten years later, we held our twentieth anniversary dinner and dance, again at the Leatherhead Leisure Centre.

Members of the Cookery and Food Association were invited to have tea with Queen Elizabeth the Queen Mother in St James's Palace in 1978. We were among the guests and we had to wait in a line until Her Majesty entered the room and was introduced to us all. We had the honour of being presented to her and altogether she spent nearly two hours in our presence. When it was time for her to leave, her two corgis entered the room and that was the signal for her departure.

Her Majesty the Queen Mother considers whether to walk under the ladder or to go along the corridor (exclusive photograph by Roy Sharp)

We met the Queen Mother on another occasion in Leatherhead in July 1984 when she visited the Queen Elizabeth Foundation for the Disabled, of which she was the Royal Patron. Previous to that, in 1980, she opened some new nurses' quarters in Oaklawn Road, Leatherhead. As she toured the premises, she came to a narrow corridor. Half way along it, a workman had left a ladder leaning against the wall. There was no way round it. I waited with my camera to see what the Queen Mother would do. As she approached the offending obstacle, she looked up at me and said, 'I suppose you are hoping I will walk underneath?' I replied, 'Yes, Ma'am'. Without further ado, she smiled and walked under it and I took my picture.

Other royal occasions at which we were invited ranged from the visit of the Duke of Edinburgh to the Electrical Research Association in Leatherhead; the opening of Chessington World Of Adventures by His Royal Highness Prince Edward; the opening of the Thorndike Theatre in Leatherhead by Princess Margaret and Lord Snowdon, and a visit to the ERA establishment by the Duke and Duchess of York in 1987. The last-named were asked to try and locate objects buried in the ground with a metal detector. When Fergie had a go, she said, 'It's like using a Hoover!'

Also during our 'reign' as editors of the *Courier*, we had tea with His Majesty Constantine II, ex-king of Greece, and his Queen at the QEFD in Leatherhead.

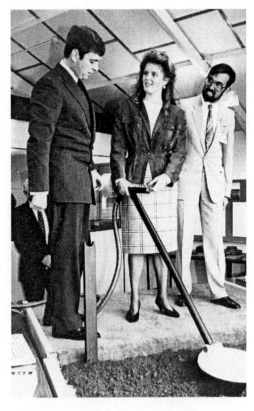

HRH the Duke of York looks on as the Duchess uses a metal detector at the ERA establishment in Leatherhead in 1987
(Photograph by Roy Sharp)

This beautiful model of a Mississippi steamboat in pastilage and icing sugar was an exhibit in the Hotel and Catering Exhibition.

CHAPTER THIRTY-NINE

So Near and So Far

East or West, home is best!

Bohn, 1855

B Y NOW, readers will have gathered that we like travelling but it is always nice to come home. By the end of a second or third week away, home comforts and home-cooked meals seem far more inviting than exotic surroundings abroad.

In 1972, after my *QE2* cruise to the northern capitals, we were invited to spend two weeks in Elba, Italy. For sometime, we had been contemplating installing central heating into our Oxshott home. As we were preparing for our Elba trip, the heating contractors telephoned us and offered us a reduced price for the system if we could have it installed in August. This was just the week we would be away, so we asked my father and mother whether they would like to take over our house whilst we were on holiday and supervise the central heating. When we returned after our holiday, everything was completed.

'Trust you to avoid all the mess and upheaval' commented my father.

Returning from a quick four day trip to the Algarve in September, we received an invitation from the Royal Air Force to inspect the catering facilities at the Royal Air Force Cyprus base at Akrotiri, with a view to writing an article in the CFA magazine *Food & Cookery Review*. We drove to the RAF transit camp at Brize Norton in Oxfordshire and spent the night in the VIP suite in the RAF hotel, Gateway House. In order to faciliate our visit and ensure we obtained co-operation and VIP treatment in Cyprus, I was accorded temporary rank of a wing-commander (rapid promotion from my wartime rank of sergeant!).

We were up very early the next morning and we took off in an RAF Air Support Command Britannia turbo-prop aircraft at 3.15 a.m. We touched down at RAF Luqa on the island of Malta for refuelling. No one disembarked from the aircraft except ourselves and we were whisked away in a staff car to the Officers' Mess where we were served breakfast. After our short break, we returned to the aircraft and continued our flight to

Celebrating the Golden Wedding of Roy's parents in 1972
Back row: Roy, brother-in-law Eric, niece Hazel
Middle row: sister Eileen, Margaret, Roy's father, Aunt Esther
Front: Roy's mother with Hazel's son, Andrew

Cyprus where we had been booked into the new Apollonia Beach Hotel, Limassol for the next four nights.

During the day, we were able to see something of the island. Although not divided into two entities – Greek and Turkish as it was later – there was still a lot of tension and the RAF was constantly on the alert for trouble.

Akrotiri was, at that time, the biggest and busiest station of the Royal Air Force. It was the home of five operational squadrons and was used by some seventy transport aircraft every week from as far afield as the UK and Hong Kong. Here, there was no beginning or end to the day's work with well-ordered activity every twenty-four hours throughout the year. This meant that thousands of men and women, both establishment and those in transit, had to be fed – some 670,000 meals in one year, almost half of which were packed and stowed aboard aircraft for consumption during flight. This accounted for three tons of meat and poultry, one and a half miles of sausages, 9,000 pounds of bread, cake and biscuits and well over a ton of butter and fats every month! All the catering on the station was run by forty RAF personnel and a similar number of Cypriots.

When visiting the station, we dined in the Officers' Mess but we visited both the airmen's dining room and the Sergeants' Mess. The last-named was a real eye-opener. You could not have fared better in London's Savoy Hotel! In charge of the Mess were head chef Flight Sergeant R. Holwarth and assistant head chef Sergeant J. Heneghan, both of whom happened to be members of our Cookery & Food Association. Mess members had a choice from a most comprehensive à la carte menu. There were so many choices that sergeants, if they wished, could have something different every day throughout the year!

Among the items on the menu were thirty-six different omelettes, eighteen chicken dishes, twenty-seven fish dishes and wide selection of entrées, grills, vegetables, salads and desserts. It made us wish we had eaten with the sergeants rather than with the officers!

The year 1973 saw us travelling extensively on press familiarisation trips and with *Courier* parties. These included Benidorm, Rome, Lanzarote, Gran Canaria, Majorca, the Austrian Tyrol, Vienna, Bavaria, Hitler's retreat at Berschegarten and the Eagle's Nest, Brindisi, Tangier, Madeira, Thailand, Malaysia and France. We also embarked on our tenth cruise, this time on the Shaw Saville Lines SS *Northern Star* to Spain, the Canary Islands, Madeira and Morocco.

In February we were invited to plant a tree outside the entrance to the Forte Trusthouse Burford Bridge Hotel at Boxhill, Surrey.

Influenced by our association with Michael Furnell and the *Homes Overseas* magazine, we decided to buy a new apartment at Calpe on the Costa Blanca. We had visions of making money through lettings and to spend a few weeks there in the winter. But our dreams turned into nightmares. We had an agent in Calpe who was supposed to look after the apartment when we were not there and to supervise lettings. These were comparatively few and, each time, the agent said certain repairs needed doing or he needed money to replace various items in the flat.

A few months after our purchase, we were informed that the local authority was imposing a levy on all property owners to pay for a new promenade which was being constructed. The apartment was situated at the end of the main street and we discovered that, in the winter months, the wind blew straight down from the sea and the place was cold – not the warm weather we had expected at that time of year. The final straw came when we were informed that the lift was not functioning properly and had to be replaced. We decided thereupon to sell before any more expenses occurred. In fact, we never once spent a night in our apartment!

We were able to find a cash buyer and the sale was completed. Fortunately for us but regrettably for the purchaser of our flat, he died a few weeks after moving in.

We ourselves suffered a bereavement in 1973. My mother, Gladys Valentine Sharp, had not been well for some time and had for a while been a patient in the Masonic Hospital, London. She died on 27 December, following a stroke, aged seventy-eight years.

On 6 July Rosalind married Anthony Simpkins, shortly after the birth of her second child, Michael, on 3 June 1973. Her husband, Tony, helped his brother and father run a workshop repairing and servicing lawn mowers in Fetcham. One day, Tony had an accident in the works whilst working on a mower and chopped off the end of his finger. His brother's dog, who was lazily resting close by immediately sprang up, picked up the end of Tony's finger and ate it!

On 5 September Margaret had an eye operation for a blocked tear duct at the Surbiton Eye Hospital. This was a very old building with no lifts and patients had to be carried on stretchers up and down several flights of stairs to the operating theatre.

We attended the Institute of Journalists' conference shortly afterwards which was held in Le Touquet, France. We crossed the Channel aboard the Townsend-Thoresen car ferry *Free Enterprise* and then by coach to the resort. Highlight of the conference should have been the Institute banquet at the Palais de l'Europe. Our table was the last to be served and when it came to the fish course, there was none left for three of us. The waiter, thereupon took pieces of fish off the plates of nearby guests to make up the remaining plates! So much for French haute cuisine!

To complete the year, we paid our accustomed visits to the pantomimes and other festive shows. One of these was at the Round House, Chalk Farm, which used to be a railway workshop and had been converted into a theatre. We were watching an historic drama *Feast of Fools* but no sooner had the performance started than there was an IRA bomb alert and the entire theatre had to be evacuated. It turned out to be a false alarm but we did not go back to see the rest of the performance.

The year 1974 began with my mother's funeral on 3 January at Luton Crematorium, followed by our *Courier* New Year party at the Hotel Dom Joao II at Alvor on the Portuguese Algarve. Subsequent tours included Geneva, Chamonix and Mont Blanc in France. The latter was in March and was the coldest place we had ever experienced. It took our breath away. We regained our warmth in Benidorm on the Costa Blanca!

CHAPTER FORTY

Crocodiles, Elephants and Snakes

A herd of elephants pacing along ...

Isak Dinesen (Karen Blixen), 1885-1962,
Out of Africa

Thailand

OUR FIRST TRIP to the Far East took place in August, 1973 at the invitation of the Thai Tourist Board. We flew to Copenhagen aboard an SAS Caravelle jet and stayed a night in the Danish capital. The next morning, we took off aboard a Thai International DC8 for Bangkok, capital of Thailand, with a refuelling stop in Tehran, Iran. It was an excellent flight, travelling first class by courtesy of the airline.

We were told at the Thai embassy in London not to allow the immigration officers at Bangkok airport to cancel our entry visa as our plans were to go to Malaysia a week later and then return to Thailand. But to no avail; the official who could not speak English, duly cancelled our re-entry visa and it took me nearly two days to get another one – two frustrating days which took up most of our precious time when we should have been sightseeing.

We were booked into the Erewan Hotel in Bangkok and between long waits at the visa office, managed to tour the capital, saw the Reclining Buddha and cruised along the city's river. August is in the middle of the rainy season but this proved not to be as bad as it sounds. For most of the day it is sunny and hot and then it clouds over, followed by thunder and lightning and for between twenty minutes to two hours, the heavens open and a tropical deluge occurs. Then the clouds disperse, the sun comes out again, the floods in the street drain away, the water start to steam and everything is back to normal. It rains most days like this, mostly towards evening, but it is not unwelcome and helps to cool the air.

A 'must' for every visitor to Bangkok is a visit to the floating market. For hundreds of years, Thai life has been closely associated with its rivers and canals. Until the twentieth century, there were few roads and most houses and businesses were of necessity located on the natural rivers and man-made waterways, which the inhabitants call *klongs*. The first European visitors to the capital dubbed it 'the Venice of the East'.

The most important river in central Thailand is Chao Phraya, formed by four smaller rivers, the Ping, Wang, Yom and Nan, and this flows through Bangkok to the Gulf of Thailand, thirty kilometres away. The river plays a major role in the life of the people. Its waters irrigate the vital rice fields and along its banks and the canals which branch from it, a complex river life has been established.

We embarked on our river trip on a 'taxi boat' from the landing stage of the Oriental Hotel at seven o'clock in the morning in order to visit the floating market. Like traffic on Bangkok streets, everything on the rivers and canals moves fast. The roaring 'long-tail' boats whose powerful engines sound like a jet-plane taking off, leave huge wakes behind them as they race along like speed boats, causing smaller craft to rock and roll frantically. On both sides of the river are old Thai houses, built on stilts amidst tropical vegetation, bananas and coconut palms, interspersed every so often with a gaudy Buddhist temple. Passing under the Bangkok Bridge, we turned right along the Dao Kanong Canal to the famous floating market at Wat Sai, one of the strangest commercial centres in the world. This is the largest and best-known of hundreds of similar markets throughout Thailand, where people who live on or near the water can bring their produce to barter.

Hundreds of big and small boats laden with all kinds of produce converge here every morning with fruit, vegetables, flowers, kitchen utensils and cooked foods in abundance. The vendors for most part are pretty Thai girls, wearing the traditional straw hat which sits high on the head and permits the air to circulate freely underneath. Whether or not you buy from the girls, you will certainly be busy with your camera.

A forty minute taxi ride from Bangkok brought us to Jak Nam, where the world's largest crocodile farm is located. Here, over 10,000 crocodiles are bred like battery hens and we saw babies from a few inches long to twelve foot monsters. They are reared for their skins which are shipped all over the world to make handbags, shoes and accessories.

Crossing the road in Bangkok is a dance with death. Although vehicles drive on the left, they overtake on the left, right and down the centre. Traffic jams are continuous and a journey from one place of interest to another can be most frustrating. Fortunately, most of the taxis are air conditioned but when I alighted from one, my glasses immediately steamed up, because of the humidity and heat outside. In contrast, the hotels' public rooms are close on freezing. When one guest asked for a bottle of red wine, the waiter asked him if he wanted it at room temperature. 'No fear', the guest replied, 'I want it warm!'

We found many of the pavements very uneven and full of pot-holes, a strange contrast to the fine modern buildings and general high standards elsewhere.

Life in Thailand has not been influenced by Western culture as much as some other south-east Asian countries. The people are fun-loving and predominantly Buddhist, with a small minority of Muslims, Confusians and Christians of various denominations. Feasts and festivals usually have a religious basis and are connected with the changing seasons. There are approximately 20,000 monasteries throughout the kingdom and Bangkok alone has more than 300 of these Buddhist constructions. The Thai word for a temple is *wat* and there are seven major ones in the city. Ladies are not allowed in them if they are wearing trousers or shorts and everyone must remove their shoes before entering.

The first temple we visited was the Wat Phra Keo in the grounds of the Grand Palace. Within its walls is the private chapel of the King and Queen of Thailand where the sacred image of the Emerald Buddha is kept. The most extensive monastery in the city is Wat Po with a colossal Reclining Buddha, four large and ninety-one small chedis (pagodas) and the largest collection of Buddha images in the country. The other major temples are Wat Trimitr, the Monastery of the Golden Buddha; Wat Sutat with its giant swing; Wat Sraket, the Golden Mount; and Wat Arun, the Temple of Dawn.

At last we got a new re-entry visa so were able to fly from Bangkok to Kuala Lumpur, capital of Malaysia. On our return to Thailand, we had no visa trouble. Awaiting us was an invitation to dine at the Aswan Hotel in Bangkok.

We were now ready for our dinner at the Aswan, a fine five-star hotel. On entering the large foyer, we came face to face with a huge floral display, in the centre of which was a large placard bearing the words in English:

The Thai Hotels Association welcome Roy and Margaret Sharp as their honoured guests for dinner.

We were taken completely by surprise but the welcome was very warm and an excellent meal ensued. On the following day, we were taken aboard a pleasure boat, *The Oriental Queen*, for a river cruise to the ancient capital Ayuttaya and to the Bang Pa-In Royal Palace.

Day eleven, we joined a small group of international journalists from Japan, Switzerland, Germany, Denmark, Belgium, Italy, the USA, Sweden and France for a flight to Chiangmai in the north of the country for a four day tour, led by representatives of the Tourist Organisation of Thailand. The flight took ninety minutes whereas if we had gone by road, it would have taken us eight hours through the jungle. The first thing we noticed on leaving the airport at our destination was the slower pace of life compared with the capital. The traffic was considerably less and crossing the road was not quite as hazardous! Everywhere were bicycles – British Raleigh Sports, made in Margaret's home town, Nottingham – and tricycle 'taxis' called 'trishaws'. Men and women were busy in the paddy fields, knee-deep in water, planting rice, whilst grey water buffalos wallowed in the mud.

One of the big attractions in the north of the country is the wild orchids, which grow in great quantities in a large variety of colours and sizes. There are over 1,000 species of orchids and growers have cultivated many hybrids. One of the best wild varieties is *Vanda Coerulea*, a native to northern Thailand, Burma and India. These large blue flowers on upright stems vary almost white to a rich purple/blue. There are also some pink varieties to be found.

Chiang Mai is both a city and a province. It is the second largest city in the country with a population exceeding one million. It is the centre for arts and crafts and abounds in legend and folklore. It is 1,000 feet above sea level and around it are mountains rising 3,000 to 4,000 feet.

The elephant figures abundantly throughout Hindu mythology and is not an unfamiliar sight in Thailand. Even in Bangkok, we saw a baby elephant tied to a parking meter near a petrol station, obviously being refilled! But the place to see elephants is the teak forests of northern Thailand.

We set out from Chiang Mai and drove through the jungle to Lampang. In a clearing just behind the village is the Young Elephant Training Centre where they are taught forestry and lumbering, to lift logs and other skills. Run by the Forestry Industry Organisation, which owns over 120 elephants, there were at the time of our visit seven pachyderm 'students' from three to five years of age, and six baby elephants, no taller than four feet, with their mothers.

The life-span of an elephant is about seventy years and working elephants are retired at the age of sixty. They are not fully grown until they reach twenty-five and they work nine months of the year and have three months of freedom in the jungle. The training course lasts five to six years and the daily lessons last six hours. They have a holiday on religious days and when it is a half moon and a full moon.

First of all, the student has to get to know its future master, the mahout, and obey his commands to get up, crouch down, pick-up, move around and stop. Then he gets to feel the weight of the training harness and the drag chains used for pulling the teak logs. When the course is finished, the 'graduate' will have learnt to haul sawn logs from timber sites through

'Kicked by an elephant'

the jungle to the log-yard, where it is transported by trucks, train or water to the market.

As we watched the training session, suddenly a one and a half ton 'baby' elephant broke away from the other animals and made a beeline for us. For some reason, the animal took a dislike to Margaret's colourful floral dress and as it came up to us, it turned and kicked Margaret on the knee with its hind leg. Fortunately, it sounded worse than it looked and no bones were broken but the bruise lasted for days.

By this time, the call of nature overcame us but the only toilet in the jungle was a 'unisex' primitive bamboo and grass hut with a hole in the ground.

We gentlemen allowed the ladies to go first and Margaret went in as number one, followed by the German girl and then the American. Seconds later, the American ran out screaming, 'There's a snake in there!' Two of the Thai men came up with long sticks and cautiously investigated. Sure enough, there was a three foot green and yellow striped snake coiled up under the straw roof of the hut. They knocked it down with a stick and it quickly slithered out of the hut and disappeared in the undergrowth. This was certainly a memorable day for Margaret – being kicked by an elephant and sharing a toilet with a snake! Surely this warrants an entry in *The Guinness Book of Records*?

Snakes are common in Thailand, ranging from harmless grass-snakes to King Cobras and pythons. Thankfully, we did not see any more in the wild but we did visit the snake farm at the Pasteur Institute, the world's second largest, where the reptiles are fed and the venom extracted for medical purposes.

An interesting evening was spent at the old Chiang Mai Cultural Centre where we partook of *Kan Toke*, a northern Thai-style dinner. We had to remove our shoes before entering the banqueting hall and sit on the floor to partake from the wide variety of Thai dishes. During the meal, traditional native folk music and dancing were performed including the 'finger' dance and the candle dance. Other dances were given by people from the hill tribes.

Before returning to Bangkok, we boarded a coach to the seaside resort of Pattaya, where we spent a further four days cruising round the islands, viewing the coral reef from a glass-bottomed boat and relaxing on the sandy beach.

A final dinner in the five-star Dursit Thani Hotel in Bangkok brought our exciting Far Eastern tour to a close and reluctantly, we had to fly back to the UK and prepare the next issue of the *Courier*!

The floating market of Bangkok, Thailand

CHAPTER FORTY-ONE

The Pearl of the Orients

It's very nice to go travelling ...

Lee Yan Lian, managing director,
Malaysia Hotel, Kuala Lumpur

Malaysia

WHEN WE DECIDED to visit Thailand, it seemed a pity not to extend our air ticket and pay a visit to the former British territory of Malaysia, 753 miles south of Bangkok.

Malaysia from the air appears to be mainly jungle – vast stretches of green, interlaced by twisting, winding rivers. In fact, three-quarters of the territory is jungle, untouched by nature or man for an estimated one million years, older than the jungles of the Congo or the Amazon.

Our arrival in the capital, Kuala Lumpur, was pleasant in every respect. No visa was required although a careful check was made to see that we had a valid vaccination certificate against smallpox and cholera. Customs inspection was a mere formality. We were the guests of the Malaysian Tourist Development Corporation and we were greeted in the arrival hall of the airport by their representative and conveyed to the Malaysia Hotel on the outskirts of the city.

The weather was certainly warm, being just three degrees north of the equator, but it was not unbearable. The biggest contrast was stepping into an hotel or a restaurant to be met by freezing air conditioning. Fortunately, this can be adjusted in the bedroom.

Malaysia presented a kaleidoscopic picture of the exotic Orient, with the colourful sarong and kebaya of the Malay women and the slender sheath of the Chinese cheongsam; the graceful Indian sari and the brief mini-skirts of the young girls influenced by the West. The gay dress of the Ibans, Muruts and Kadazans added yet another splash of colour to the Malaysian scene. Malay velvet caps were to be seen in the same street as the Sikh turban and the yard-wide Chinese labourer's straw hat.

A monkey greets Margaret in Malaysia.

There is so much to see in this country and it was our great regret that our stay was so short. Everyone was so welcoming and friendly. We first made a tour of the countryside around the capital, stopping at a rubber plantation to watch a lady gathering the liquid latex in a cup, before we proceeded to the rubber factory. Next, we watched the printing of batek, Malaysia's colourful fabric which is used for the ladies' sarongs and kebayas. Batek means wax printing in an intricate design, a hand process, and the finished result is very attractive.

Coconut palms grow everywhere and there are masses of fruit, ranging from bananas and pineapples to papaya, starfruit, jackfruit (mangka), mangosteens, durian and rambutans.

Our tour of the capital took us to the National Museum with its hall devoted to the wildlife of the country and to the University where, in the Agricultural Department, we saw coffee bushes with the cherries just turning red, pineapples and other produce being grown.

The following day, we were taken by car thirty-two miles to Malaysia's hill resort of Genting Highlands, nestling 5,614 feet above sea level and a breathtaking view over miles of jungle from the Genting Highlands Hotel; our abode for the next two days. The hotel has over 200 rooms, two restaurants (one European and one Chinese), an American-style coffee house and a large casino, crammed full of gaming machines and tables. The Chinese are gambling crazy and spend all night playing Russian roulette, blackjack, baccaret, keno and other games.

We took a walk along a newly-cut jungle track but although we heard the sounds of wildlife all around us, we only spotted a few birds and butterflies.

From the Highlands, we were taken to the island of Penang, separated by two miles of sea from the north west coast of West Malaya. The guide book describes it as the 'Pearl of the Orient' and this is no exageration. It is indeed a lush island as far as vegetation goes with tall waving coconut palms growing everywhere. In the Botanical Gardens, we were besieged by dozens of monkeys emerging from the trees and undergrowth, begging for titbits.

Away from Georgetown, the island capital and seaport, there are many fine sandy beaches. We saw the famous Snake Temple, inside of which poisonous snakes glide everywhere and rest in every nook and cranny. They are said to be under the narcotic spell of incense but nevertheless, we declined the invitation to go inside. One snake in Thailand was enough for Margaret and I was not keen either! Another 'must' is a trip up Penang Hill aboard the mountain jungle railway.

All too soon, our brief visit to this fascinating country came to an end and we had to return to Thailand to continue our tour.

Bali

Bali, it is said, is a gift from the gods. It certainly is an island of gods, Hindu and mythological, and their statues and images are everywhere – by the roadside, in towns and villages, at crossroads, in hotels and gardens; you cannot escape their fearsome glare and menacing teeth, the competing forces of good and evil.

Bali is in the Republic of Indonesia, formerly part of the Dutch East Indies. Indonesia today consists of a chain of islands, more than 13,000 of them, ranging from Sumatra in the east to Java, Bali, and Lombok.

But whereas great changes are taking place in East Java, where the capital, Jakarta, is located, Bali remains very much as it has been for centuries. In the hill villages, there are no sanitation facilities in the houses, ploughing is carried out by buffalo-hauled hand ploughs and villagers draw water from wells and springs.

At the end of the day, you will see men, women and children washing themselves and their clothes in communal baths, or in rivers and streams.

Bali has been described as paradise, but on our first visit into Denpasar, the island capital, on Saturday afternoon, it was the opposite. It seemed that most of Bali's 2.8 million population was out on the roads, walking, cycling, on motor bikes and scooters, trucks, minibuses and cars. Why there were no accidents must have been through the protection of the gods.

Fortunately, this was not a true picture of Bali as we were to discover on our subsequent tours of the island.

Bali is slowly changing as modern civilization takes hold. Tourism is becoming the major money earner and is providing employment for thousands of its people.

An organised tour includes a visit to a Barong open air dance theatre where a comic ballet pantomime is performed; a visit to MAS,

A procession to the temple on Bali.

the wood carving village, Ubud, the village of artists, to Tampaksiring, the holy springs where you can see Balinese men, women and children unashameably having a communal bath, and view Mount Batur, the active volcano.

After lunch, the return journey takes in the Elephant Cave at Bedula, visits to a number of Hindu temples and the silversmiths' village of Celuk.

An afternoon tour takes you to the monkey forest at Sangeh, the home of thousands of monkeys who follow you as you walk along begging for peanuts and other titbits. Also high in the trees, you can see hundreds of giant fruit bats or 'flying foxes' with their immense wingspan.

This tour also takes in the former Royal Temple at Mengwi and concludes with a walk along the west coast to the Temple of Tanah Lot, built on a rocky shelf and surrounded by water at high tide. Here, you watch the sun setting over the Indonesian Ocean.

Everywhere you go in Bali you pass temples. It is said there are over 30,000 of them but no precise figure is known. These range from the great holy temple at Besakih to small village places of worship and family shrines. A common sight is the processions of Balinese on their way to a temple, bearing their offerings of fruit and flowers on their heads.

Whereas the religion on neighbouring Java is principally Muslim, the majority of Balinese practice the Hindu religion but their own variation.

Unlike strict Hinduism as practiced in India, the Balinese have their own customs and even eat the flesh of the sacred cow.

The principal agriculture is the production of rice and everywhere you see the paddy fields, many of them in raised terraces up the hillsides.

For complete relaxation and pleasure, we have no hesitation in recommending the island of Bali. As the brochures declare, 'It's Paradise in Paradise', a land where everyone smiles and greets you and wants to be of service.

Note: *Since writing this article on Bali, a terrorist bomb attack on the Kuta Beach Sari Club took place on 12 October 2002, resulting in over 200 deaths, mainly Australian.*

We hope this will not permanently damage the island's tourist industry and not deter holidaymakers to this paradise location.

CHAPTER FORTY-TWO

Caribbean Carousel

Westward, look, the land is bright.

Arthur Hugh Clough, 1819–61,
Say not the struggle naught availeth

IN 1974 WE MADE OUR first flight across the Atlantic and our first visit to the West Indies. In April, we had arranged to take a *Courier* party to Denmark but Margaret was feeling unwell and decided she was not fit enough to travel. As tour leader, it was essential that I made the trip and, with Margaret's consent, took a mutual friend, Mrs Betty Bore to take her place to assist me with the party. With her husband, Cliff's agreement, Betty said 'yes' and we embarked on the DFDS ferry *Winston Churchill* from Harwich to Esjberg, from where we took the train to Odense.

On our return home, we found Margaret's condition had deteriorated and the next day, she was admitted to Epsom Hospital for observation. It was decided she had to have her gall bladder and appendix removed and the operation was carried out on 2 May. Margaret still has the stones which were removed from her in a jar! She had to spend another two weeks in hospital which meant missing another *Courier* tour this time to Norway, and my father accompanied me in her place.

At the end of May, we organised a *Courier* party to St Lucia, in the West Indian Windward Islands. This was a first for Clarksons, who arranged the tour, using their own airline, Court Line. The party was booked into the Halcyon Days Hotel complex for fourteen days' full board. The total cost including flights was £128. No wonder Clarksons and Court Line collapsed soon afterwards! Because of Margaret's recent operation, it was considered unwise for her to make the flight, so we decided neither of us should go and once more delegated my father to look after our group. The holiday proved to be such a success that we decided to arrange another party to St Lucia on another date.

Our dancing lessons had been progressing over the months and having fully recovered from her operation, Margaret and I attended the dance studio's medal ball in June and we were both awarded our intermediate silver medals after giving a demonstration rhumba.

Rosalind now had two children – Maria, aged three-and-a-half years and Michael one year. Both were christened in St Andrew's Church, Oxshott on 2 June, followed by a party in the village hall.

Margaret was now pronounced fit to fly so we were able to make our trip to the West Indies. Flying from Heathrow on a BWIA Boeing 707, we landed in Barbados and booked into the Barbados Beach Village Hotel on the Caribbean St James's coast. Whilst there, we took advantage of a day trip to St Lucia.

After a week in Barbados, we flew to Port of Spain, Trinidad with the intention of flying on to the island of Tobago. But the aircraft was forty-five minutes late in arriving in Trinidad and we found the last flight to Tobago had already left. The airline gave us a room for the night at the Bell Air Hotel next to the airport, a mediocre room swarming with mosquitoes! We were glad to have an early call at 6.00 a.m. to catch the 7.30 flight to Tobago and our hotel, the four-star Mount Irvine Bay.

For the next two days, we explored this beautiful Robinson Crusoe island, visiting the Buccuo Reef, the Grafton Bird Sanctuary and Turtle Bay. On the third day, the island received a hurricane warning. Guests in the hotel were told to remain in their rooms, to fill the bath with water and, if necessary, to stay in the bathroom. As Hurricane Alma drew near, we could see the palm trees bending over ninety degrees and debris being hauled everywhere. At the same time, the rain came down in torrents. Fortunately, the eye of the storm passed between Tobago and Trinidad, so we did not suffer the full force but the place was littered with debris and fallen trees. There was no electricity in the hotel, so that evening, we were served a cold buffet. Our second visit to the West Indies took place in July 1975. Earlier in the year, we had taken our *Courier* party to C'an Pastilla, Majorca; a tour of Switzerland and a mini-cruise to Gothenburg, Sweden. Back home, having sold our apartment in Calpe, Spain (we never spent a single night in it!), we purchased a bungalow in Ferndown, Dorset and spent most weekends there.

On 29 May, Margaret received a call to go to Nottingham where her mother had been taken ill. Margaret stayed with her until she passed peacefully away the following day.

Our flight to Jamaica in July by Air Jamaica from Heathrow was enlivened by a fashion show, put on by the air hostesses displaying the latest Caribbean dresses. This was one of our most interesting and enjoyable foreign trips. It was arranged for us by the Jamaican Tourist Board and the original plan was to spend two days in the capital, Kingston, four days in Montego Bay and nine in Ocho Rios. But when we were met at the airport, the tourist board representative told us that there was a certain amount of unrest in Kingston and, therefore, we would have an extended stay in Montego Bay at the Bay Roc Hotel.

Montego Bay is the island's second largest town and one of the biggest tourist resorts in the whole of the Caribbean. Set between the blue waters of the Caribbean and the green hills behind, it offers shady, white sandy beaches, a buzzing nightlife and rich historical heritage. There are four excellent beaches, an historic Fort Montego which once guarded the town against unwanted intruders and one of the finest churches in Jamaica, St James's Parish Church, built between 1775 and 1782. On Sundays, the parishioners, dressed up to the nines in their straw hats, brightly coloured dresses with bows and frills and men in jackets, collars and ties all making their way to morning service.

Like every Jamaican town, there is a extensive straw and craft market, with its array of colourful bags, hats, jewellery, clothes as well as fruit and vegetables. When my father was in St Lucia, he espied a huge banana on a stall and promptly bought it. But he was bitterly disappointed for what he thought was a sweet banana was a distant relative, a plantain, which the inhabitants use as a vegetable.

One thing you must do in the market is haggle like mad. You will be considered very odd if you accept the first price asked. It is simply not done! The tourist board advises you to think of a number, halve it and start from there. When the vendor says American dollars, say, 'no, Jamaican dollars'. This will mean an instant reduction of nearly 100 per cent!

During our stay in Montego Bay, we visited Rose Hall Great House where in the past three murders by the mistress of the house took place. She was Annie Parker and she became known as the White Witch of Rose Hall. She herself was finally murdered by one of her vengeful slaves and her ghost still haunts the building. Another interesting building is the Greenwood Great House, built by the Barretts of Wimpole Street.

An exciting experience is rafting on the Martha Brae River. You sit in a wicker chair attached to a raft of bamboo branches and your craftsman stands on the rear end and propels the raft along the river and through the rapids.

Another thrilling experience is an evening on the Great River. This gently flows into the Caribbean ten miles west of Montego Bay. We travelled up the river at dusk in a fishing boat, gliding through a valley with towering mountains on both sides. Dozens of other boats were making the same journey and each craft lights up the river with bamboo torches. Arriving at the disembarkation site, we then walked along the river bank on a torchlit path cut out of the side of the mountain to a recreated Arawak Indian village. Here, drinks flowed freely to Caribbean music and then we were served with a Jamaican-style dinner consisting of rice and peas, chicken, barbecued meat and vegetables. After dinner came the floorshow and dancing. Certainly, a very exciting night out beneath the stars with fireflies flitting and glowing in the undergrowth.

No visit to Jamaica is complete without a tour of the beautiful plantation on the Brimmer Hall Estate. We were conveyed on a tractor-drawn *jitney*, an open-sided carriage, and along the way, we stopped whilst our guide described the exotic tropical fruits and produce such as bananas, pineapples, coconuts, pimento, cocoa, coffee, bread-fruit, papaya, and mango.

A train journey to the Blue Mountains where the famous Blue Mountain coffee is produced is another exciting experience. You board the Governor's Coach and the train travels through Cockpit Country, visiting villages, the Appleton Rum and Sugar Distillery and making a stop at the Catadupa Cloth Market. Here, you can choose a piece of material and on the return journey, you can pick up a dress, shirt or suit made from the material you had chosen.

After our stay in Montego Bay, we transferred to the four-star Shaw Park Hotel in Ocho Rios. Adjoining the hotel is Shaw Park and every Tuesday afternoon, the Governor's Tea Party is held. The Jamaican Police Band, in their splendid red uniforms provided musical entertainment whilst guests sat around under sun umbrellas enjoying afternoon tea and cucumber sandwiches. But like all English garden parties, just when everything was going swimmingly, the sun disappeared and down came the rain. Guests, bandsmen, everybody ran to the marquees for shelter. The rain only lasted a short time but that was the end of the party!

Dunns River Falls, Fern Cally, Swamp Safari, rafting on the Rio Grande, crab racing, a glass-bottomed boat trip to a coral reef and a visit to Lisa Salmon's bird sanctuary were all included in our Jamaican experience, one which we will never forget.

Back home, Rosalind gave birth to a third child, Suzy, on 10 September, so we now had three grandchildren. We stayed in our bungalow in Ferndown whenever possible but although it was an excellent property, we and our friends who stayed there inevitably wanted to go to Bournemouth but the problem here, especially during the summer months, was finding somewhere to park the car.

Then we saw a new apartment block 'Hinton Wood' on the East Cliff of Bournemouth overlooking the sea with a vacancy on the sixth floor. It had two bedrooms, a large lounge with a dining area, kitchen, two luxury bathrooms and two balconies – one overlooking the sea and the other to the rear. It had an underground car park and a large front communal garden. It seemed ideal, so we decided to sell the Ferndown bungalow and buy the Hinton Wood apartment.

CHAPTER FORTY-THREE

Behind the Iron Curtain

So when the sun in bed,
Curtained with cloudy red,
Pillows his chin upon an orient wave.

John Milton, 1608–74,
On the morning of Christ's Nativity

B Y 1976, OUR NEWSPAPER, the *Courier*, was well established. Our holiday and travel features were widely read and even the local travel agents would ring us up and ask our opinion about a specific country or resort. Our escorted holiday parties abroad were very popular. We also organised one day trips to places of interest in the UK with the local coach company, Epsom Coaches, and passengers would be picked up in their own village or locality.

We arranged a Russian tour in April and flew from Gatwick on a Russian airline, Aeroflot, with a woman pilot. All was well until we reached Moscow airport. Then it was discovered that all our party's baggage had been put on the wrong aircraft. The Russian authorities insisted that no one was to leave the airport without their luggage and we were confined to the lounge. We were eventually told our baggage would be arriving in the early evening aboard another flight. After much arguing, the Russian customs and police agreed to allow our party to leave the airport and proceed under escort to the Hotel Intourist in the city with the stipulation that one person from each family remained behind to collect the luggage when it arrived!

Although still under strict Communist rule, we found our movements in and around the city unrestricted. The hotel was very much a pre-war building with ancient lifts and ironwork gates, and a Palm Court orchestra playing in the restaurant. Dinner was booked for 6.30 p.m. and dead on the dot, the first course, usually soup, was set down in each place, whether the person was there or not. Needless to say, after the first night, and for some a cold soup, no one was late for their meals.

On our tours of the city, we had an official Intourist guide, who told us not to be afraid to ask her any questions. In the hotel, we were provided with an English newspaper free of charge, the only one allowed in the country – the *Daily Worker*.

The highlight of our Moscow stay was undoubtedly a visit to the Kremlin and the Armoury and our party was invited to attend a concert by the Red Army Orchestra, singers and dancers. This was held inside the Kremlin in the hall used by the government for its meetings. Our guide told us that, when the interval arrived, to get up and follow the rest of the audience. As soon as the first half of the concert finished, everybody jumped up from the seats and rapidly left the hall. We followed as they made their way to the escalators which took us to a large upper room. Like sheep we all followed, though it was more like a stampede of cattle. On reaching the upper hall, we discovered why everyone was so eager to get there. Refreshments in the form of snacks and drinks were laid out on long tables with the compliments of the Kremlin. After the refreshments, we joined the queues for the toilets and on entering these, we were met by a thick cloud of tobacco smoke. Smoking in the halls is not permitted, so the populace make for the toilets to have their cigarettes!

Other notable experiences in the Russian capital was a visit to the famous Moscow State Circus, the Bolshoi Ballet and a tour of the metro. On the latter, we alighted at each stop on the circuit to admire the fine architecture, mosaics, sculptures and paintings, the pride of each station. Some of the platforms were even lit with huge crystal chandeliers and not a scrap of litter or graffiti could be found anywhere! The same applied to the streets of Moscow. Even before breakfast, we could see Russian women sweeping the streets and no one dared drop any litter.

Moscow's largest department store is called Gum. Here, we witnessed long queues for the smallest article. One such queue was for one banana. The selection and quantity of goods was very scarce and below the quality we would expect in England but in contrast, there was an abundance in the tourist shops where only American dollars and other foreign currency were accepted.

Copies of Russia's newspapers – *Pravda* and *Isvestia* – were displayed page by page on public notice boards for the public to read.

After three days in Moscow, our party boarded a train to Leningrad. This was a day's journey and we thought it would be scenically interesting. But we soon discovered most of the land, the Steppes, was barren, with little to attract your attention. We arrived in Leningrad in the evening and checked in to the Leningrad Hotel. We were pleasantly surprised at the high standard here and for our final dinner, we were served fresh salmon, caviar and chicken.

Although it was April, large ice floes were coming down the river. We visited the Hermitage, the Winter Palace, Puskin and the Leningrad Circus on Ice. All our party agreed that this Russian tour was a great experience.

Some twenty years later, we returned to Leningrad. The Iron Curtain had gone and the city had reverted to its former name of St Petersburg. But these were not the only changes we discovered. Whereas the public buildings such as the Hermitage, the Admiralty and the blue and white swirled 'onion towers' of the Church of the Resurrection of Christ had been maintained in excellent condition, other buildings such as offices, shops and apartment blocks were in a very poor state. A painter could make a fortune here except he would never be paid for his work.

Twenty miles south of St Petersburg lies the town of Pushkin. Here are several royal parks and palaces which have been restored and are in pristine condition. Rastrelli's Catherine Palace, with its ornate blue and white façade nearly 1,000 feet in length is a fine example, as is Emperor Paul's Palace.

Nineteen miles west of St Petersburg is Petrodvorets or Peterhof, on the coast of the Gulf of Finland. Here is the magnificent summer residence of all the Tsars. Founded by Peter the Great, the estate encompasses seven parks and more than twenty palaces and pavilions.

We also noticed on our latest tour of the former Soviet Union people trying to sell you trinkets or playing instruments in the streets and begging for coins. When our coach stopped in the Palace Square opposite the Hermitage, we were immediately accosted by gypsy women carrying their babies and by their children, asking for money.

Our latest visit to Russia (in 2000) was to Odessa and the Crimea. Here, much had been done to restore buildings and the State Opera House in Odessa was nearly complete. The city is known as the Pearl of the Black Sea and was once the playground of the Russian elite. The night before we arrived, there had been a great music festival in the city with many stalls, food vendors and entertainments which meant the streets were strewn with litter. It was only 9 a.m. when we started our tour of the city but already, hordes of cleaners were busy gathering the litter and cleaning up the streets.

Our guide was at great pains to point out to us a canon from a British warship which had sunk during the Crimean War.

Yalta is the capital of the Crimea and we had the privilege of touring the Livadia Palace where the three wartime leaders – Churchill, Roosevelt and Stalin – met in 1945 to demand the unconditional surrender of Germany. Another beautiful palace is the Alupka, designed by a British architect, Edward Blore, for Count Vorontsov in the nineteenth century.

But even here, there were people busking and trying to sell us souvenirs. Russia still has a long way to go to catch up with today's democracies in the West!

CHAPTER FORTY-FOUR

A Royal Jubilee

I think everyone will concede that, today of all days, I should begin by saying "My husband and I".

Her Majesty Queen Elizabeth II on her
silver wedding speech in the Guildhall, 1972

T HE YEAR 1977 WAS extremely important, the year of the Queen's Silver Jubilee, celebrating twenty-five years on the throne. We hoped to cash in on the Jubilee by publishing a souvenir brochure detailing events which were to take place in Surrey. Mole Valley District Council was very keen on the idea and agreed that our brochure should be the town's official publication. We also approached the Elmbridge Borough Council and made a similar offer to them but they replied that they were planning their own but at the last minute, they decided not to publish a rival brochure to ours. We were able to combine the two districts in one publication but reversing the order for each district, hence the Mole Valley edition would start with an introduction to Leatherhead and surrounding villages, a message from the chairman of the Council and then listing all the celebration events in date order, district by district.

The Elmbridge edition followed a similar pattern but the second half of each edition contained the events from the neighbouring authority. A portrait of the Queen appeared on the front cover and inside were the messages from HRH the Prince of Wales, the Mayor of Elmbridge and the Mole Valley Chairman. The brochures were on sale at 25p and were sold through the newsagents. Margaret and I also sold copies to the crowds at the various public events. Although sales were good, we made no money from the venture because of the high cost of printing.

The week of the Jubilee was an hectic one for us as we wanted to cover as many local events as possible. These included a fête and cavalcade of motoring in Cobham; carnival processions in Weybridge, Leatherhead, Claygate, Walton-on-Thames and Effingham; a regatta on the Thames; fêtes and fairs in Thames Ditton, West End, Weston Green, Esher, Great Bookham, Oxshott and Claygate and street parties in Stoke D'Abernon, Weston Green, Hinchley Wood, East and West Molesey, Esher and the Dittons.

Other celebrations included special church services, barbecues, sporting events, dances, bonfires and fireworks. We also attended a huge firework display on the River Thames at Kingston; an open-air historical pageant in Guildford and the Silver Jubilee Exhibition in London's Hyde Park.

On 1 June, the Queen and the Duke of Edinburgh came to Epsom. They had attended the Derby on Epsom Downs and then came to Epsom High Street to receive the congratulations of the townsfolk and civic heads. I had a royal pass to report the occasion, together with my photographer, John Eagle, and occupied a place adjoining the royal dais. I was also able to get my granddaughter, Maria, now aged six, a seat in the special enclosure for children opposite the dais. Grandson Michael, who was only four years of age, only got a glimpse of the royal couple as he and Margaret were well back behind the crowds. He had wanted to give the Queen some flowers!

In chapter thirty-eight, we have described a number of other royal events which we have attended. One such notable occasion was on 27 June 1985 when we were guests at the Centenary Banquet and Ball of the Cookery and Food Association at the Grosvenor House Hotel, Park Lane, London. Over 500 people attended including the President, Vice-Admiral Sir Peter Ashmore, Master of the Royal Household, and vice-presidents Lord Forte of Ripley, Sir Hugh Wontner and Sir Charles Taylor. Guest of Honour was Her Royal Highness Princess Anne, the Princess Royal, and we had the honour of being presented to her.

Back to 1977, we started the year with our New Year *Courier* party. The destination was Torremolinos on the Costa del Sol, the highlight of which was our St Trinian's and Greyfriars Fancy Dress Gala night.

In May, we took a party of readers to St Lucia in the Caribbean. We again chose the Halcyon Days Hotel at Vieux Fort but to our dismay, we found that the hotel had been double booked by an American party. Four years previous, our first party to the island was with Clarksons but when the company went into liquidation, Pegasus Holidays took over and it was they who arranged this year's tour for us.

Pegasus was not responsible for the overbooking but to save an awkward situation, they asked for twenty-five couples to volunteer to move to the Holiday Inn at Reduit Beach to the north of the capital, Castries. They were offered superior accommodation and full board, so we were among the volunteers.

Our transfer from the south to the north of the island was by taxi; a nightmare journey in torrential rain. The road was full of potholes which rapidly filled with water. It then transpired that the cab's windscreen wipers did not work, so the driver kept his window down and, holding the steering wheel in one hand, extended his other hand out of the window and continuously wiped off the rain. This he did for most of the journey with no reduction in speed! Were we thankful to arrive at our destination in one piece! The Holiday Inn was situated on a superb beach of soft, white sand, fringed with coconut palms and the sea was crystal clear. We spotted a humming bird's nest in some overhanging bourgainvillea, exquisitely made and no bigger than an old English penny.

St Trinian's night in Torremolinos. Margaret, Roy and grandaughter Maria

In the shadow of The Pitons, twin pyramids of rock rising over 2,500 feet, near Soufrière on the east coast is Anse Chastanet with a beautiful beach, where you can escape from the modern world. In Soufrière is a restaurant known as The Ruins, formerly a 150-year old French villa and still retaining some unusual architectural features. The roof is supported by the corner posts of the four-poster beds. We expect that ownership of the restaurant has changed since 1977 – perhaps the restaurant no longer exists. But when we were there, it had been purchased by a young lady, Clare Leates from Sheffield. She had previously spent seven years as catering officer for Islington Borough Council. In October 1976, she came to St Lucia on holiday and ended up buying The Ruins and staying on the island. She soon learnt to adapt local cuisine for Western tastes and to haggle with the old ladies in the market and local fishermen for her fresh fruit and vegetables and the kind of fish she required. One of her speciality dishes which we immensely enjoyed was West Indian Pepper Pot consisting of tuna fish cooked in a creole sauce of onions, thyme, celery, tomato, Worcester sauce and anything else she could lay her hands on. Another tasty dish was her Chicken Soufrière with mashed green papaya, kidney beans, macaroni, yams, darkeen, tarmina, sweet potatoes and green salad.

One of the most beautiful bays in the Caribbean is Marigot Bay, which was chosen as one of the locations for the filming of *Doctor Dolittle* starring Rex Harrison.

Whilst in St Lucia, we were recommended to take a trip to the neighbouring island of St Vincent. Our hotel was providing a day trip for £44 but we thought we could do better than that. After making enquiries, we found a local air transport company, Norship Air Ltd., who offered to charter a 12-seater De Havilland Dove aircraft for £216. We had no difficulty in finding ten other people from our party to accompany us, thus reducing the price to £18 each! The flight took twenty-five minutes and the St Vincent Tourist Board provided us with a minibus, guide, a tour of the island and lunch. We visited the Botanical Gardens, one of the most beautiful we have seen. Founded in 1765, it contains a tree grown from a sucker from one of the original bread-fruit plants introduced from Tahiti by Captain Bligh. The gardens cover twenty acres and feature many exotic plants, trees and flowers such as the pagoda flower, bottlebrush tree, the brush and comb flower, orchids, strelitza, jacaranda, flamboyants, red ginger and much more.

Our tour of the island included the historic Fort Charlotte (636 feet), built in the late 1700s and named after King George III's Queen. Inland, we passed through a heavily cultivated region called Mesopotamia. The scenery is dramatic with vistas of the sea to the south and the meeting of the Atlantic Ocean and the Caribbean.

Fresh water streams with names like Yambou, Zenga and Teviot flow through the valley and at many places, the ladies of the island can be seen doing their laundry and then spreading the clothes out on the rocks and bushes to dry in the sun. By the roadside, workers from the plantations, boys on donkeys and hordes of schoolchildren, smartly dressed in gymslips and blouses or crisp white shirts and shorts and carrying their school books, could be observed making their way home.

Our day on St Vincent went by far too quickly. At the airport, we awaited the return of our charter plane. When it arrived, we found that the seats had been removed and the interior filled with goods for the island. We had to wait until these were unloaded and the seats replaced for our return flight to St Lucia.

We went to St Lucia and fell in love with St Vincent.

After the Silver Jubilee celebrations, we led a party on an air and coach tour of Yugoslavia, the Austrian Lakes, Slovenia and Carinthia. This included a visit to the stud farm of the famous Lipizzaner horses as supplied to the Spanish Riding School in Vienna. The stud was founded by Archduke Charles at Lipizza near Trieste in 1580. These horses have a short back, strong hindquarters, a powerful neck and a small head. When they are born, they are black in colour but when they mature, they turn a fawn colour or white. Their height averages fourteen and a half to fifteen hands.

In 1978 we recruited John Douglas, a former representative for a print firm, as full-time advertisement manager for the *Courier*. He proved to be extremely proficient in his job and designed some excellent advertisement copy. He never seemed to bother with lunch, preferring two Mars bars and a pint of beer.

In March we took a *Courier* party on a winter sports holiday to Aprica in Italy. We do not ski ourselves but we like to watch other people. Aprica (7,560 feet), in the province of Sondrio, is a long spread out village on the road between Lake Como and the Brenta Dolomites. Our hotel was the Larice Bianca, right on the ski slopes and we were told we could ski from the front door down to the village. There appeared to be just one drawback to this for whilst we were there, there was no snow! A very mild winter had transformed snow-covered slopes to green grass ones.

To compensate for this, our Inghams' representative arranged transport for our party to another resort in the province, Bormin, as this was higher (9,840 feet) and had some snow. During our holiday, we decided to take the train across the border to St Moritz in Switzerland. The Swiss Tourist Board had booked us overnight accommodation in the Hotel Bellevue overlooking a frozen and snow-covered lake.

During the night, it snowed very heavily and when we awoke the next morning, about a foot had fallen. We were very apprehensive as we were due to catch the morning train back to Tirano and, with so much snow, we doubted whether there would be any trains running, certainly not in England after a similar snowfall.

After breakfast, we poked our noses outside the hotel door and were amazed to see the snow-ploughs had already been out and cleared the road and footpath to the station. By the time our train was due to depart, the sun was shining from a cloudless blue sky and thus began the most exhilarating train journey of our life. The heavy overnight snowfall had transformed the countryside into a sparkling white fairyland. Our train took us on ever-increasing circles as it climbed to reach the mountain passes, giving us repeated views of the spectacular scenery. We finally crossed the Italian border through a tunnel and entered Tirano where there was no trace of snow – two different worlds only a few miles apart!

On our return to England, Margaret was despatched to Scotland to explore Victorian memorabilia in Glasgow and also to visit Rothesay, the Isle of Bute, Stirling and the Trossachs.

May took us across the Atlantic once more to Trinidad where we witnessed hundreds of scarlet ibis and white herons flying in to roost for the night in the trees around a large swamp. We then boarded the P & O cruise ship *Sun Princess*, known as 'The Love Boat' and featured in a film and television series, for an eight day Caribbean cruise, calling at Martinique, St Thomas, San Juan (Puerto Rico), Curaçao, Venezuela and back to Trinidad.

On our arraival at Port of Spain, we made our way to the airport to fly the short distance to the island of Tobago and spent the next five days once more at the Mount Irvin Bay Hotel, where we had encountered Hurricane Alma in 1974.

Five months later, we again crossed to the New World and spent a few days in the famous Hotel Eden Roc on Miami Beach, during which time we went to Fort Lauderdale, the Everglades and the Miami Seaquarium. From Miami, we flew to the United States Virgin Islands with stays in St Thomas, St Croix and St John, and a visit to Buck Island.

To complete our overseas tours in 1978, we spent a week in Gibraltar reviewing hotels and restaurants on the Rock.

Back in the UK, Margaret went up to London to the Palladium to interview the American showbiz star, Liberace, who showed her all the rings on his fingers, including one in the shape of a grand piano.

Roy with his dance partner/instructor Lorna Tribe after gaining his silver medal for ballroom dancing.

CHAPTER FORTY FIVE

The Call of the Virgins

St Thomas is the Caribbean's answer to Fantasyland, a magic kingdom for all to enjoy … it's got to be experienced to be believed.

Virgin Islands Playground, 1978 Edition

WITH SO MANY PLACES throughout the world which we should like to visit before old age finally sets in, we do not often return to the same region or country. But the Caribbean is an exception. In the previous chapter, we mentioned a visit to St Thomas when on the *Sun Princess* cruise. We were so captivated by it that we were determined to pay it a return, longer visit. This we did six months later.

After a two and a half hour flight from Miami, we landed in St Thomas, the largest of the Virgin Islands. We booked into the Secret Harbour Beach Hotel, a secluded spot with a fine sandy beach and set amid lush tropical gardens, a twenty-minute taxi ride from the capital, Charlotte Amalie.

The capital is a shoppers' paradise, especially for jewellery, watches and gold work. Off the main street are dozens of little side streets and shopping malls to be explored, all with intimate shops offering you merchandise from all over the world. In great demand were tee-shirts bearing the words in large capital letters, 'I'm a Virgin' and underneath in tiny letters the word 'Islander'.

Behind Charlotte Amalie lies thirty-two square miles of green-clad volcanic uplands, laced by winding roads which seem to cling to the side of the cliffs and offering superb views across the blue waters of the island-studded bay. Throughout the island you see a white, fragile flower known as the 'poor man's orchid' (*Bauhinia candida*), the bright yellow 'Ginger Thomas', the island's national flower which is really the yellow elder tree blossom, the brilliant scarlet flamboyant trees, masses of bougainvilla and red, orange, pink and white hibiscus.

From the 1,400 ft mountain top, you get a most spectacular panorama of the islands Little Hans, Lollick, Big Hans Lollick and, on a clear day, the British Virgin Islands of Tortola, Virgin Gorda and Ane Gada. But the most tempting sight below is the magnificent Magens Bay, fringed by tall coconut palms and a mile and a half of superb, soft white sand, surely one of the most beautiful beaches in the world!

On the way down from the mountain, we stopped at Drake's Seat, where Sir Francis stood and looked out over nearly 100 islands, the peaks of a submerged mountain chain. We also came across a 200-year old sugar plantation, country churches and little villages. But the biggest and most exciting attraction on St Thomas must be Coral World underwater observation tower and marine park. After looking at the twenty-one aquarium tanks in the Marine Gardens, we walked across a 100 ft long causeway to the observation tower, built on a coral reef in the sea. We entered the domed tower lounge with its bar and spectacular view of the neighbouring island of St John and the British Virgins. Descending a spiral staircase, we came to the second level which is a room surrounded by a circular aquarium in which we saw sharks, stingrays, barracudas and huge sea turtles. But the best was yet to come. We continued down the next staircase which took us below sea level down to the sea bed itself. Wide picture windows run all round the room and these look out into the open sea where we saw the marvels of marine life around the coral reef. Hundreds of brilliantly coloured tropical fish were swimming around in their natural habitat. A long trumpet fish swam up to the glass window and looked at us, puzzled at the weird creatures (us) trapped inside! Here were beautiful coral formations and sea anenomes, angel fish, rainbow fish, parrot fish, pork fish and trunkfish. We were intrigued by the four-eyed butterfly fish, the white-banded butterfly fish with black stripes, the beautiful blue parrot fish and the yellowtail snapper. We could spend hours here under the sea without getting wet or feeling claustrophobic. This is an attraction which every visitor to St Thomas must see.

We found the hotels and restaurants very good on St Thomas, in particular, Bluebeard's Castle, a seventeenth-century tower built by the infamous Bluebeard the Pirate.

St John

All too soon, it was time to leave St Thomas and take the ferry for the half-hour crossing to the island of St John. This lovely island, smaller than St Thomas, is a United States National Park, unspoilt, few buildings and no crowds. You can sun yourself on deserted beaches, follow a friendly mongoose along a woodland trail or do as we did, explore the island by jeep. We were shown mahogany trees, an abandoned eighteenth-century sugar plantation, majestic kapoks and a leaf which, when squeezed, emits aftershave lotion.

If you want to be different and not stay in an hotel, you can camp in a tree in the jungle! The terrain around Mabo Bay consists of a thick wooded slope rising up from the beach within the boundary of the national park. Here, a private company has created a new concept in camping. There are no bulldozed roads, practically no clearing of trees or undergrowth. But by skilful planning, the company has built a zig-zag of wooden pathways among the treetops and at suitably spaced spurs have been erected three-roomed canvas cottages, measuring sixteen feet square and set on plank decks that cantilever over the hillside. Each unit offers spectacular panoramas of the sea, sky, crescents of white sand and peaceful islands. There is a primary sleeping area, a living room that converts into a second bedroom, a screened cooking and dining space and an open porch for sun-bathing. Centrally heated bath-houses are equipped with modern toilets, sinks and showers and each 'cottage' is furnished with electricity, an ice box and a multi-burner propane stove.

St Croix

This is the third and largest of the US Virgin Islands with two main towns, Christiansted and Frederiksted. We stayed at Lon Southerland's Anchor Inn, situated right on the waterfront, overlooking historic Christiansted harbour. St Croix was discovered by Christopher Columbus on 14 November 1493 during his second voyage to the New World. In the eighteenth and early nineteenth century, enormous wealth was created for the Danish West Indian Company who had bought the island for the large sugar plantations. But as so often happens to a single-crop economy, a sharp drop in the price of sugar from 1820 onwards, the emancipation of the slaves, the development of sugar beet in Europe, planters' debts and land foreclosures and restrictive import laws of other countries all helped to bring St Croix's opulence crashing down and, by the end of the century, the 'fabulous sugar island' had become an economic liability.

During the 1914–18 War, the United States, fearing that Germany might seize the harbour of St Thomas and use it as a submarine base, offered $25 million for the three Virgin Islands and Denmark accepted it. Thus, in 1917, the Stars and Stripes replaced the Danish flag.

We obtained some idea of the past opulence when we visited Whim Great House, two miles east of Frederiksted. It was built about 1794 by a Danish sugar planter of Scottish ancestry. It is neo-classic in design and had been restored to an approximation of its original elegance. The interor contained furnishings appropriate to the period and, silhouetted against the sky, south-east of the Great House, we could see the chimney of the old sugar factory and the newly restored stone windmill.

Also in the grounds is the Plantation Museum and we were particularly interested in the cookhouse, the sugar boiling shed with its huge iron cauldrons or 'coppers', in which cane juice was reduced to sugar and molasses. Other exhibits on display included sugar and rum-making equipment such as a pot-still, various types of ironwork, implements and household articles.

A must for every visitor to St Croix is Buck Island. To come here and not visit it is like going to Niagara and staying away from the Falls. The Buck Island Reef National Monument is the only underwater National Park in the USA. Glass-bottomed boats, launches and sailing vessels await on the wharf at Christiansted and you can spend a half or full day swimming, snorkelling or picnicking on the sandy beach.

The reef is home to thousands of brilliantly coloured tropical fish and there is an underwater trail, marked out with signposts, so that with a snorkel and mask, you can explore the fantastic world of sculptured coral and its inhabitants. A great mass of Elkhorn coral extends like a horseshoe around the seaward side of the island, facing the trail from the open sea.

A holiday in the Virgin Islands is one you will never forget or regret.

In chapter 42, we described our tour of Jamaica but omitted to record our Swamp Safari to a crocodile compound. Ignoring the notice at the entrance 'Trespassers will be eaten', we came to a narrow causeway with pools of crocodiles on either side. Our guide told us: 'When I say go, run across and don't hesitate or stop to take photos.' The moment we started to cross, the reptiles made a bee-line for the causeway – and us! We just made it in time!

This was the location for James Bond (Roger Moore)'s encounter in the film *Live and Let Die* in which he uses the crocodiles as stepping stones to afford his escape.

CHAPTER FORTY-SIX

'California, Here I Come'

This land is your land, this land is my land
From California to the New York Island.
From the redwood forest to the Gulf Stream Waters,
This land was made for you and me.

Woody Guthrie, (Woodrow Wilson Guthrie) 1912–67,
American Songwriter

A LTHOUGH WE HAD MADE quite a number of trips to the West Indies, we did not set foot in the New World until 1978 with our visit to Miami. Now a year later, we were to venture further and go West to California, Arizona and Nevada.

But before this trip, we had our annual *Courier* New Year party, this time at the Hotel Vasco da Gama in Monte Gordo near the Spanish frontier in the Portuguese Algarve. It was raining on the last day of our week's break as we made our way to the airport. Having checked us in and passed us through customs, the Thomson representative disappeared and left our party in the departure lounge. Then came the announcement that our flight would be delayed eight hours and would not depart until the evening. With a party of sixty to look after, what was I to do? It was still raining and being a Sunday, the tour operator's rep could not be contacted and, furthermore, we were told that, having checked in at the airport, he was no longer responsible for us.

Being tour leader, I made several telephone calls and eventually contacted a coach firm that was willing to take our party on a tour of the countryside. I put the suggestion to our party and all agreed that this was a better idea than spending the afternoon sitting in the airport. Thus I was able to keep everyone reasonably happy and we visited Albufeira, Portimao and Praia da Rocha.

Our aircraft, a Britannia Airways Boeing 737 eventually arrived and we left the Algarve at 01.15 the next morning to arrive back at Gatwick at 3.30 a.m. Even then, my problems were not over. Later in the morning, I received a telephone call from two distraught ladies from East Molesey who had been in our party.

'Where is our luggage?' they asked.

'Did you put it on the coach at Gatwick?' I asked.

'No', they replied. 'We put it outside the main entrance and expected you to put it on the coach for us!'

I telephoned the airport and to my relief, their luggage was still awaiting collection. Fortunately for these ladies, if their cases had been left unattended in the 1990s, they would have been removed and blown up as suspected terrorist bombs!

In February, we met the directors of some of the Preferred Hotels of the World at a brunch in the Dorchester Hotel, London. One of them was Mr James Nassikas, president of the prestigious five-star Stanford Court Hotel in San Francisco. He invited us to stay as his guests if we should visit his city.

The following month, we caught the *Flying Scotsman* from King's Cross to Newcastle and boarded the Fred Olsen ferry *Dana Silvano* to Stavanger and Bergen in Norway. This was a press familiarisation mini-cruise, arranged by the Olsen press and public relations officer. A press conference on board was scheduled for the return voyage to Newcastle but this did not materialise as we ran into a Force nine gale in the North Sea and most of the journalists remained in their cabins including Margaret and I. As far as publicity value was concerned, this was a non-starter. Also on board were a young couple who were making the cruise as a prize in a competition. Afterwards, they said they would rather have not been the winners!

On 1 April, my birthday, we embarked on one of our most exciting *Courier* parties, a coach tour of California, Nevada and Arizona. Our party numbered thirty-three and we left Heathrow aboard a World Airlines DC8 to Los Angeles. As we started our descent at LA, we entered what we thought was fog but it was only when we landed that we discovered that the whole city lay beneath a dense layer of air pollution!

We booked into the Roosevelt Hotel in Hollywood and the next day were taken on a tour of the district which housed the stars of the silver screen. The following day was spent enjoying the attractions of Disneyland, followed by a visit to Universal Studios. Our next city was San Diego with its wonderful zoo park and Sea World, before crossing the Mexican border to the city of Tijuana. Here, we noticed the great contrast between affluent America and the poverty of Mexico. It was amusing to see street photographers inviting you to be photographed with their 'zebra'. It transpired that their 'zebra' was actually a mule on which white stripes had been painted on its body!

Back into California, our coach set off to Arizona and the desert. After lunch at Yuma, we were met by a representative of the tourist office who took us on to Tucson and the Ramada Inn. Old Tucson is a movie town where many famous western films had been made and here we wandered around the film sets and watched a mock gunfight. Later, during the afternoon, we visited the Sonoran Desert with its giant Saguaro cacti, coyotes, prairie dogs and a wide variety of fauna. Here, too, was the Desert Museum.

After lunch in Phoenix, we journeyed through the Coconino Forest and saw the colourful rock formations, before arriving in Flagstaff and the Yvavopi Lodge overlooking the Grand Canyon. We had two nights here and on the second day, we flew in a helicopter through the Canyon. We had wonderful views and, at times, it was quite hair-raising as we seemed to fly right up to the wall of the canyon and hovered a few feet away. After the helicopter, we repeated the journey but this time in a small Cessna aircraft and followed the Colorado River. During the flight, we observed a party slowly making their way down on mules along the Bright Angel Trail.

From the Canyon we travelled on through the desert to Las Vegas, via Kingman and the Hoover Dam. We were booked into the Mint Hotel for the night and as we walked through the main doors carrying our cases, an amazing sight met our eyes. We were in a huge room, hung with chandeliers and as far as the eye could see were row upon row of fruit machines and one-armed bandits. There was no sign of the hotel reception desk. Eventually, we found it at the very end of the long salon and booked in. Our room was at the very top of the huge skyscraper and we had a wonderful view of Las Vegas. Having deposited our bags, we made a tour of the gambling capital of the world. We watched some excellent aerial acts in Circus Circus and had dinner at Caesar's Palace. We finished the night watching the spectacular 1979 Revue at the Casino de Paris. We did try our luck on a fruit machine – I invested a dollar, doubled it and quit!

The next morning, we came down to the hotel's restaurant for breakfast and found there were even more slot machines and one of them was attached to our table! We had another surprise. There was a shortage of plates and saucers and when we enquired about this, we were told the plate washing machine had broken down.

'Why not wash the crockery by hand?' I enquired.

'Certainly not' was the reply. 'It is against hygiene regulations!'

We came across these regulations again a few days later when we were dining in a restaurant which was situated alongside a trout stream, full of fish. We remarked that the trout on the menu must be very fresh.

'Yes, we do catch our own fish,' we were told, 'but they have to be taken some twenty miles to the food and health inspectors to see if they meet the legal requirements, then they are frozen and returned to the restaurant!'

Leaving Las Vegas the next day, we crossed the Colorado River and had another look at the Hoover Dam before proceeding to The Oasis of Furnace Creek for lunch in Death Valley, the lowest and hottest point in the USA. Along the Sierras we gained spectacular views of Mount Whitney, the highest peak in North America.

Our overnight stay was at the Travelodge in the western style town of Bishop, from where we ascended 9,000 ft into the Sierra Nevada Mountains with their vistas of huge granite. The excellent mountain road was flanked by peaks capped by perpetual snow. Passing through Sacramento, we eventually arrived in the city of San Francisco for a three night stay. This was our chance to accept the invitation from Mr James Nassikas, given to us earlier in the year at the Dorchester Hotel, to stay as his guest at the magnificent five-star Stanford Court Hotel on Nob Hill.

A tour of the city the next day included lunch on Fisherman's Wharf and a ride on the famous cable car. Dinner at night was at the Blue Fox Restaurant. A visit to Chinatown the following day where we met one of the finest Chinese chefs and at night, we dined at another five-star hotel, the Intercontinental Four Seasons.

That concluded our western American tour and the next day, we flew back to Los Angeles where we boarded our overnight flight to Gatwick. This was a most enjoyable tour but halfway through, we encountered some harassment from some members of our party. We had arranged the tour with Jetsave Vacations who charged us £499 per person. All thirty-three members of our party were quite contented to begin with but unknown to us, another travel agent had booked another party on to our coach to make up a full complement. During the tour, it transpired that this other party had paid over £50 less than that which we were charged. We were blamed for this and accused of overcharging and pocketing the difference, which was quite untrue.

On our return to England we acted as press and public relations officers and assisted with the running of the Christchurch (Dorset) Ideal Home Exhibition. During that week, we received an urgent message that our apartment in Hinton Wood, Bournemouth, was flooded. On investigation, it transpired that friends we had allowed to stay in the flat the previous week for some unknown reason had blocked the overflow pipe in the bath with a tissue and the taps had not been fully turned off. In consequence, the bath had filled and overflowed, saturating the carpet and seeping through the floor to the apartment below. This was occupied by an obnoxious German couple who were most aggressive and insisted on us replacing the bedspread which had a slight water stain on it. At the same time, we received a tempting offer for the apartment and, as a result of the incident with the German couple, we decided to sell Hinton Wood.

It was then we did something which later we regretted. Being interested in fashion, we decided to purchase a ladies' boutique in Oxshott High

Street. It cost us £11,500 which included £2,500 for the lease, £1,500 for fixtures, fittings and equipment and £7,500 goodwill. In between a short trip to Seville and visits to the Nottingham Goose Fair, Liverpool and the Blackpool Illuminations, we visited a number of London wholesale fashion houses and made purchases for the shop.

On 12 November 1979, we opened *Rosaletta Fashions*, having staged a preview for some of our friends the previous day. Business was slow and our biggest sales were in tights. We were told the ladies of Oxshott did not like price tags displayed on garments in the window. They would come into the shop, examine and try on dresses and suits, then say they would wait until sales time! One lady bought an expensive dress but returned it the next day to say she had changed her mind about purchasing it. Margaret was convinced she had worn it for a function the previous evening, but we had to refund her money!

CHAPTER FORTY-SEVEN

A Biblical Safari

A good and spacious land, a land flowing with milk and honey.

Book of *Exodus*, chapter 3, verse 8

THE YEAR 1980 was a most significant year for us. It started with our annual New Year *Courier* party, the venue this time being the Hotel Santa Lucia in Palma Nova, Majorca.

By now, though, we were getting rather fed up with printers. Every few months, we were told the price of newsprint had gone up and so we decided to put the *Courier* up for sale. As soon as we advertised it, the Surrey Advertiser Group approached us. We met the Group chairman, Mr Ray Tindle, and the Chief Executive, Miss Murray, at the Hog's Head Hotel between Farnham and Guildford and discussed the sale. Not being ruthless business people, we agreed to a lower sum for the paper than what we wanted on condition that they retained our services as managing editors and that we continued to run the paper as before from our home. The Group would be responsible for the printing and publishing of the paper and would look after the accounts. Margaret, however, would prepare the advertisers' invoices for which she received the princely sum of £25 a month! John Douglas was retained as advertisement manager on a full-time basis and the sale was completed on 10 March 1980, fourteen years after we had started it.

At this time, Margaret was receiving heat treatment for an arthritic knee at the Epsom Hospital and things were not going well with *Rosaletta Fashions*. It was evident by the end of the first quarter of the year that our dabbling in the world of commercial retailing was not a success. In fact, from 17 November 1979 to April 1980, our gross profit was £4,389 and over the period, we had made a loss of £9,845. After some difficulty, we were able to sell the business though at a loss.

Following our sale of the *Courier*, we flew to Israel on a seven day familiarisation tour, visiting Tel Aviv, Nazareth, the Sea of Galilee, Tiberias, Capernaum, Acre, Haifa, Massada, Bethany, the Dead Sea, Jericho and Jerusalem. We scaled the Golan Heights overlooking Syria and visited the Lebanese border. Highlight of our visit to Jerusalem was the Garden

Tomb which many Christians believe was the actual burial site of Jesus Christ, rather than the Church of the Holy Sepulchre. It is situated outside the city walls in a garden, a short distance from the Damascus Gate. Inside the garden is a rock-hewn tomb which meets all the criteria as Christ's sepulchre. At the far corner of the garden is a rock outcrop, somewhat obscured today by surrounding buildings, which resembles in shape a human skull. The place was used for public executions and the New Testament calls the place of the Crucifixon *Golgotha*, meaning the place of the skull. If this is, therefore, the actual place where the Crucifixion took place, outside the city walls, and the tomb in the garden the place of burial, then surely the twelve stations of the Cross in the Via Dolorosa should be reversed, leading *out* of the city and outside the walls to Golgotha? Certainly food for thought!

Other highlights of our tour included the Garden of Gethsemane, the Mediaeval Hall of the Coenaculum where one can visualise the Upper Room where the last supper took place and the Mount of Olives.

We made two subsequent visits to the Holy Land – in 1993 and in 1996. The wish of devout Muslims is to make a pilgrimage to Mecca during their lifetime. For Christians, a chance to follow in the footsteps of Jesus and to visit places mentioned in the Old and New Testaments is an enriching experience. There are so many places mentioned in the Bible which one would like to see and we were determined to see as many as we could on our three visits.

Israel is the land of Divine revelations, the home of the people of the Old Testament, a country held sacred to Jews, Christians and Muslims alike. You can retrace the steps of Our Lord from His birthplace in Bethlehem, his boyhood home in Nazareth and through the years of His ministry in Galilee to His progress into Judaea and His final days in Jerusalem.

Starting at Nazareth, nestling in a circle of cypress-studded hills, we journeyed six miles north-east to Kafri Cana, a picturesque village, shaded by fig, olive and pomegranite, where Jesus performed the first miracle of turning water into wine (St John's Gospel, chapter two).

North-east on the northern shore of the Sea of Galilee lies Capernaum, where the first disciples, Simon and Andrew, were found casting their nets and were told by Jesus, 'Follow me and I will make you fishers of men'. (St Matthew, chapter four). It was also at Capernaum that Jesus healed the servant of the centurian.

Nearby is Chorazin, the wicked city overlooking the River Jordan, which Jesus upbraided 'Woe unto thee, Chorazin' (St Matthew, chapter eleven). There is a unique mosaic, south of Capernaum, depicting a basket of loaves and two fish and, not far away, a Franciscan chapel denoting the spot of the second miraculous draught of fish where Jesus bade Peter to 'feed my lambs' (St John, chapter twenty-one). Close inland is the Mount of the Beatitudes where Jesus delivered His sermon on the Mount (St Matthew, chapter five).

On the east coast is the port of Caesarea, built by Herod the Great and it is here that Peter baptised the first Gentiles and where Paul was held prisoner for two years until he appealed to Caesar and set sail for Rome on his last journey (Acts, chapter twenty-five).

Seventy miles south is the maritime town of Jaffa (Joppa in the Bible), today a suburb of Tel Aviv. Jonah embarked from here on his ill-fated voyage to Tarshish, during which he was swallowed by 'a great fish' (Jonah, chapter one). Here, too, is the house of Simon the tanner, with whom Peter stayed (Acts, chapter nine) and raised Tabitha (Dorcas) from the dead.

Between Jaffa and Jerusalem is Lydda, where Peter healed Aeneas (Acts, chapter nine).

This is also the legendary birthplace of England's patron saint, St George, and a church here contains his tomb.

Jerusalem, of course, is the ultimate destination for all pilgrimages to the Holy Land. On our 1996 tour, we were taken to Neot Kedumin, halfway between Tel Aviv and Jerusalem and ten minutes' drive from Ben Gurion Airport. It is a vast Biblical Landscape Reserve, covering 625 acres of gently rolling hills and villages. Hundreds of varieties of plants and trees mentioned in the Bible are grown here in their natural settings. These range from Cedars of Lebanon, hyssop, olive, fig and sycamore to grape vines, date palms and pomegranites and the 'atad' cruel thorn bushes from which Christ's crown of thorns most probably was made.

Reconstructed olive and wine presses, threshing floors, cisterns and ritual baths and archaeological excavations bring to life the world of the Bible. Stone by stone and tree by tree, Neot Kedumin has transformed once barren hills and valleys into a network of pastoral landscapes where sheep, goats, native cows and camels graze, representing regions of ancient Israel with the Judean Hills in the background.

Here, the visitor can grind wheat kernels between two stones, search for tares among the wheat and sit beneath a sycamore fig tree, the type which Zacchaeus climbed to see Jesus (St Luke, chapter nineteen). No visit to the Holy Land can be complete without experiencing Neot Kedumin.

CHAPTER FORTY-EIGHT

The Theme Parks of Florida

I like to be in America,
OK by me in America,
Ev'rything free in America
for a small fee in America.

Leonard Bernstein, 1914–1980,
West Side Story, 1957

NOT EVERYTHING IS FREE in America nor are the fees that small, especially if you are visiting the many theme parks in Florida with a family. Altogether, we have visited Florida six times, sometimes for a few days before embarking on a Caribbean cruise and other times for a longer stay to tour the state.

Our first trip was in 1980 and after a few days in Miami, we drove through the Everglades National Park and stayed at the Flamingo Inn. The night was far from pleasant, plagued by dozens of mosquitoes and midges. When we asked the manager for an insect repellent, we were told they were not permitted in the Everglades as insects were essential for the environment. So we suffered all night whilst the flying pests made a meal of us.

The Everglades extend right up to the outskirts of Greater Fort Lauderdale where we went on an airboat tour. We managed to steal close to a couple of alligators which looked as if they were asleep but we did not try to arouse them.

We then went on a board walk trail through the Fern Forest, a 254-acre wilderness. We saw curious woody projections like tree stumps which came from the roots of the bald cypress trees which bring oxygen to the trees and stabilise them against the wind. They are called 'Cypress Knees'. The bald cypress related to the giant redwoods is the dominant tree in the freshwater wetlands of south Florida, Texas and Delaware. It bears cones but unlike other conifers, it is deciduous, loosing its needles in the winter, hence its name 'bald'.

Another unusual tree is the Strangler Fig which supports its broad, spreading crown by sending roots down from its branches and when they

– 217 –

Margaret is kissed by a killer whale in Florida.

reach the ground, they grow in diameter and form new trunks. Its roots will eventually strangle and kill another plant. Among the animals we observed were the odd-looking nine-banded armadillo and furry racoons.

From the Everglades, we motored along the Florida Keys on Highway One to Key West, stopping at Humphrey Bogart's Key Largo where we explored the John Pennekamp Coral Reef on a glass-bottomed boat.

Arriving at Marathon, the heart of the Keys, the sky suddenly blackened and a tropical storm broke out. We were on the point of crossing the Seven-Mile Bridge, separating the Straits of Florida and the Gulf of Mexico but wisely, we waited until the storm had abated before making the nerve-racking crossing of this narrow single-lane bridge.

As dusk fell, we arrived at our final destination – Key West, the southernmost city in the USA. It was the home of the writers Ernest Hemingway and Tennessee Williams, an historic city of contrasts.

Retracing our journey along the Keys, we made our way to Orlando where most of Florida's theme parks are located. These include Sea World with its marine exhibits, live shows and the Penguin Encounter where hundreds of penguins of six species and alcids (birds native to the Polar regions) live among manufactured ice and snow. For most families, Florida means Walt Disney World – the Magic Kingdom and EPCOT (Experimental Protocol Community of Tomorrow). The latter comprises two main areas – Future World and World Showcase. To avoid the long queues as you enter Future World, by-pass it and start your tour around the World Showcase and then return to the first area.

Cypress Gardens is a 223-acre family park featuring a botanical garden, the world famous waterski revue and synchronised swimming. On the occasion of our visit, a pyramid of girl waterskiers displayed a banner on which was written the words, 'Welcome to Roy and Margaret Sharp from England.'

The biggest theme park in west Florida is Busch Gardens, called 'The Dark Continent'. Situated at Tampa, this is an African theme park plus white knuckle rides.

Fort Lauderdale is known as the Venice of America without the smells! Here, we boarded the river boat *Jungle Queen* for a three-hour cruise through Millionaires Row, magnificent waterside mansions. During the cruise, we visited an Indian village and watched an Indian wrestling with an alligator. I bought a traditional Indian beaded leather belt only to discover later it was stamped 'Made in Taiwan'!

Another stop was at a power station where warm water from the plant runs into a canal. In the water were hundreds of large tropical fish and fifteen feet long harmless manatees or sea cows, weighing up to a ton. They feed solely on vegetation.

We stayed a night at the famous Peabody Hotel in Orlando where each day the Duck Parade takes place. Twice a day, a drake and four hen mallards descend by lift from the fourth floor where they are housed to the hotel lobby and to the tune Sousa's 'King Cotton March', they waddle along a specially laid red carpet through the hall to a marble fountain in the foyer where they spend the day until five o'clock when they return to the lift and back to their quarters.

There is so much to see in Florida and you need time (and money) to see everything. One thing we discovered is that there is a lot more to Miami than *Miami Vice*.

The famed Overseas Highway linking the Florida Keys and Key West.

CHAPTER FORTY-NINE

Up, Up and Ha-waii

'Ua mau ke ea o ka aina i ka pono.'

'The life of the land is preserved in righteousness!'

NOT SO MANY YEARS AGO, a holiday on a beautiful island in the South Pacific, with blue skies, swaying palms, swinging hula girls in grass skirts, golden beaches and rolling surf was a mere fantasy, an exotic dream which would forever remain a vision of paradise.

On Sunday, 7 December 1941, American servicemen thought they had the posting of a lifetime to be stationed in Honolulu, that is, until 07.00 hours on that Sunday morning when the first wave of Japanese planes launched their unprovoked attack on Pearl Harbour. You can still see some of the results of that infamous attack as we did when we visited the USS *Arizona* Memorial, built over the hulk of the sunken battleship in Pearl Harbour. It is an awe-inspiring experience as you look down into the clear water and see the remains of the ship just below the surface with dozens of blue and yellow fish swimming around it. Here, 1,102 men lost their lives when the Japanese scored a direct hit.

On the first of April 1980, my birthday, we flew from Gatwick aboard a DC10 jet of Western Airlines, some three hours late because of a strike by air traffic controllers. Our flight took us over Iceland and Greenland, giving us an awe-inspiring sight as we looked down over the frozen Arctic Ocean and snow-covered mountains. Cracks were beginning to form in the sea ice as summer was just beginning and icebergs were forming. Crossing Alaska, too, was a beautiful sight with brilliant sunshine reflected in the snow and ice on the ground and on the mountains.

We touched down at Anchorage International Airport for refuelling. Leaving Alaska, our aircraft had to make a diversion to avoid Seattle and Washington State because on 18 May the previous year, a massive explosion blasted over 1,300 feet off the top of the 9,677 ft Mount St Helens. The subsequent fallout had spread hundreds of miles and made flying in the area too hazardous. This meant we were eight hours late in arriving in Honolulu and we missed the traditional welcome with floral leis being placed around our necks and the greeting *Aloha*.

After booking into the Ilukai Hotel and a short rest, we were taken to the Polynesian Cultural Centre and Park to watch the spectacular May Day Festival and procession of decorated long boats and canoes representing all the Polynesian and South Pacific islands, including Tonga, Fiji, Tahiti and Samoa and the Maori from New Zealand. Each craft carried dancers and musicians in their native costumes who performed as the boats slowly passed by.

Westerners are inclined to think of Hawaii as one island with Honolulu as its capital. But this is not the case. There are eight principal islands besides dozens of smaller ones. The largest is called Hawaii or the Big Island but this is not the one which contains Honolulu or the famous Waikiki Beach. These are found on the island of Oahu (pronounced Waa-hoo), meaning 'the gathering place'. It is the third largest in the group with an area of 608 square miles and a population exceeding 750,000, about 80 per cent of the entire inhabitants of the State.

Being America's fiftieth state, it has undoubted American influences but these do not overshadow traditional native culture. Honolulu, the bustling capital, has modern shops, fine hotels and exciting night life. From downtown centre to the tranquility of the Makaha Valley, there are miles of sugar cane and fields of pineapples and magnificent beaches. Because the tourist board had planned an exhausting programme for our two week stay on the islands, it was only on our final day that we were able to enjoy a couple of hours on Waikiki Beach. This is not the only attractive beach, though, on Oahu. Others include Ala Moana, a good family beach protected by a reef for safe swimming; Kailua beach which is ideal for surfing for beginners and Hana'uma Bay, ten miles east of Waikiki which has a spectacular lagoon-filled crater offering excellent snorkelling and swimming in a marine life conservation district.

Oahu's Sea Life Park, fifteen miles from Waikiki, features the Hawaiian Reef with a 300,000 gallon tank in the centre containing turtles, moray eels, eagle rays, hammerhead sharks and thousands of reef fish. A spiral ramp circles the aquarium enabling visitors to see marine life at various depths. Other attractions include the Whalers' Cove, the Ocean Science Theatre with dolphins, penguins and sea lions and the Pacific Whaling Museum.

Paradise Park in the Manoa Valley covers fifteen acres and features five ethnic gardens, over 500 colourful and exotic birds, a variety of shows and exhibits, many types of fruit trees, hau and bamboo jungles, waterfalls, native flora and a Polynesian restaurant.

Talking of restaurants, we made a special point of visiting The Willows at 901 Hausten Street, Honolulu in the residential district of Moiliili. Once a family estate of two acres, it is now a picturesque Hawaiian dining garden, an oasis in the middle of the city, with thatched roof pavilions built on stilts, overlooking tropical flora and a lagoon. Our main reason for visiting The Willows was to meet the chef de cuisine for the Kamaaina Suite, one of The Willows' intimate dining rooms, Mrs Kusuma Cooray, a Fellow of our Cookery and Food Association and Craft Guild of Chefs. She originally came from Sri Lanka and came to London to train at the Cordon Bleu School of Cookery. Subsequently, she worked in the Directors' Dining Room of Marks and Spencer in Baker Street, then at the Henri IV restaurant in Chartres, France and was personal chef for Doris Duke, the American billionairess, daughter of the founder of the American Tobacco Company. Having found her way to Hawaii, she acquired a flair for the distinctive flavours and styles of the island cooking and food presentation.

Maui – The Valley Island

Five days were certainly not enough to enjoy all the delights and attractions of Oahu but there were other islands in the archipelago to explore. We took the plane to the next island, Maui (pronounced Mou-ee), a distance of ninety-eight miles from Honolulu. It is the second largest of the Hawaiian islands, the ideal one for relaxation and gentle living. It has a coastline of 120 miles and our abode for the next few days was the beautiful Wailea Beach Hotel, situated on a picturesque crescent-shaped sandy beach and protected by coral reefs.

During our stay on Maui, we toured the zoological and botanical gardens, stood on the rim of the Haleakala Crater, the world's largest dormant volcano in the Haleakala National Park with its tropical rain forest and seven pools and visited the whalers' village. After spending their summers in Alaskan waters, humpback whales come to Hawaii for the winter and can be seen in the shallow waters between the islands.

The Big Island

The next island we visited is called Hawaii, the Big Island, a massive 4,038 square miles, bigger than all the other islands put together, and is the place where Polynesian voyagers first stepped ashore over 1,500 years ago. The island was formed by eruption out of the sea of five volcanos and two of them rise over 13,000 feet, making them the tallest in the Pacific.

There is so much to see on the Big Island, so we split our stay between the west side and the eastern. Our first venue was on the Kona coast and the Mauna Kea Beach Hotel, originally built by Laurance S.

Rockefeller in 1961. This is certainly one of the finest hotels in the world at which we have been guests. It contains more than 1,000 pieces of priceless art treasures and stands on a beautiful sandy beach. At night, large floodlights are turned on to the water's edge and within a few minutes, several giant manta rays appear and perform an underwater ballet. These huge bat-like creatures with their enormous wings and long tails are harmless, graceful and a great attraction for hotel guests.

If you really want to escape from the rest of the world, then you must seek out the hideaway Kona Village Resort. There are no direction or advertisement signs to show you where it is and it is so easy to miss. The entrance is on Highway 19 at Kaupulehu and is guarded by a thatched hut and a barrier across a rough lava track. After the gatekeeper has checked your identity and purpose of your visit, he eventually raises the barrier and lets you drive through the lava fields, a half-mile of no-man's land, a lunar landscape. Suddenly, you arrive at a group of native-style thatched buildings which make up Kona Village. This is where you leave the rest of the world and its problems behind you and become one of the natives!

The charm of Kona Village is what it does not have – no streets, no traffic, no shops, no disco, no radio, no television and no telephone! However, during our stay here, we discovered some guests had smuggled in portable radios and mobile phones. It is surprising what a difference it makes to one's life when you go without such every day 'essentials'!

At Kona, time stands still. You do not require a watch, you watch the sun. You need hardly any clothes – a swim suit, a hat, a wrap and sandals. Couples come to Kona Village to get married and to spend an idyllic honeymoon. Accommodation consists of beautifully-built thatched houses and cottages in Polynesian style, some of which are on stilts, some are on the sandy beach, some by the lagoon and some in the tropical gardens, hidden among the palm trees. At the time of our visit, there were ninety-five such dwellings, built in ten different styles, ranging from Tongan and Fijiian to Tahitian, Somoan and Hawaiian.

Both Hawaiian and international cuisine are provided in the resort's Hale Moana dining room. The highlight of our stay was the traditional Hawaiian Luan, an outdoor feast with a roast pig as the principal attraction. Prepared as it has been for centuries, the animal is cooked in an underground 'oven', called an 'imu'. A pit is dug in the ground and the Kalua pig is stuffed with large stones which have been heated in a fire. Then the pig is covered in rock salt and wrapped in ti leaves (large, aspidistra-type leaves, similar to the ones used by Hawaiian girls to make their traditional huala skirts). Next, the whole animal is covered with more very hot stones and the pit is filled in with pulverised volcanic lava. It is then left for twelve hours and the heat from the stones, both inside and outside the animal, slowly cooks the meat.

When the time arrives for the Luau, the pit is ceremoniously opened, the stones and outer covering removed and the roasted pig is lifted up and carried in a torchlight procession to the open-air dining area to be served to the guests. This was the most delicious tasting roast pork we have ever had and makes our barbecued offerings at home a tasteless sacrifice of a pig!

Reluctantly, we had to leave paradise and return to 'civilisation' to motor from the Kona coast to the eastern side of the Big Island. We drove through the privately-owned Parker Cattle Ranch to the town of Honokaa, where the macadamia nut factory is located. Then we took pictures of the Alaka Falls, where the water plunges 420 feet over a cliff, and the Wailuku River with its Rainbow Falls.

Our destination was Hilo (pronounced Hee-low), the largest city on the Big Island. This part is a complete contrast to the Kona coast. The town sprawls along the edge of a crescent-shaped bay with the mountain Mauna Kea rising behind it.

Here, everywhere is lush and rich with tropical vegetation, thanks to frequent short tropical showers. Here is the centre for orchids, anthuriums of many colours and many other tropical flowers and fruits. This is also volcano country and a drive to the Volcanos National Park is essential. Smoke and steam emerge from the ground and the numerous craters.

After our stay in the Maniloa Surf Hotel, it was off to another island, Kauai (pronounced Koo-ai).

Kauai

Known as the 'Garden Isle', Kauai is indeed beautiful, the place where Mitzi Gaynor 'washed that man right out of [her] hair' in the film version of *South Pacific*. Other exotic films have been shot here, including *King Kong*.

A Grayline coach tour took us to *Bali Hai* (*South Pacific*) beach, to the Botanical Gardens at Wailua, known as 'Paradise Pacifica', to pineapple plantations, the Fern Grotto, the Opaekaa Falls, the Spouting Horn where the sea gushes forth from a hole in the rock in a spectacular fountain, and the Waimea Canyon, the Grand Canyon of the Pacific and almost as impressive as the one in Arizona.

One of our most delightful dining experiences was at the fabulous Coco Palms Hotel in its Coconut Palace Dining Room, a vision of fantasy and gastronomic delight. One of the first courses was onion soup but not as we usually have it. A very large onion had its inside scooped out and the soup was poured into the hollow outer skin. The top of the onion was placed over it to form a lid – a wonderful way to present this entrée.

The hotel is situated at Wailua Beach amidst 2,000 coconut palms, many of which were over a hundred years old. Built on a former homestead of Queen Deborah Kapule, it is a unique complex of individual low-rise buildings and thatched cottages, surrounded by lily-covered lagoons and gardens. Numerous films and television scenes have been located here. Each night, before dinner, an historic torchlight ceremony takes place to the accompaniment of conch shell trumpets and drums, as malo-clad youths sprint along the banks of the lagoon and in and out of the coconut palms, swinging flaming torches to light a further hundred ground torches situated throughout the grounds to create a tropical fairyland.

Alas, paradise on earth does not last forever and reluctantly, we had to return to Honolulu for our return flight home. Our chef friend, Mrs Kusuma Cooray and her husband were at the airport to see us off and to present us with the floral lei that we missed on our arrival in Hawaii.

Back in the UK, it was business as usual with press luncheons, theatre visits, familiarisation tours and, of course, the production of our *Courier* newspaper and the *Food & Cookery Review*.

On 29 July 1981, Prince Charles married Lady Diana Spencer in St Paul's Cathedral and on the previous day, we watched the Royal Firework display in Hyde Park. Other activities this year included *Courier* parties to Boulogne and Amsterdam, a gourmet visit to Oxford and Oxfordshire and our fifteenth cruise aboard the P & O liner *Canberra*, visiting Malaga, Granada, Malta, Sicily, Naples, Sorrento and Gibraltar.

We had been in our Oxshott house now for twenty-five years and we felt it was time for a move. We liked the Oxshott house, it had style, character and individuality but it would soon need rewiring and various repairs and the heavy clay soil in the garden made it very hard work to cultivate. We had seen an advertisement for a modern four-bedroomed two garage detached house in Great Bookham, two miles from Leatherhead, with an attractive medium-sized rear garden and terrace and open-plan front garden. After prolonged negotiations, during which the vendors had changed their mind re selling and then put it back on the market, we eventually completed the purchase and managed to sell our Oxshott house.

When removal day arrived, it transpired that the vendors had not completed their removal arrangements, so we had to put our furniture into store and moved into the Bookham Grange Hotel for a week. Eventually, we took up residence at No. 45 West Down, Great Bookham, on 15 October 1981.

CHAPTER FIFTY

A Ruby Celebration

A wife of noble character, who can find? She is worth far more than rubies.

Book of *Proverbs*, chapter 31, verse 10

She is more precious than rubies and nothing you desire can compare with her.

Proverbs chapter 3, verse 15

THE YEAR 1983 was a very special year for us; it marked our 40th wedding anniversary, our Ruby Wedding. But before I describe our celebrations, I must go back to the previous year. This we started with a Caribbean stay on the island of St. Lucia. For nine days, our base was the Cunard Hotel La Toc, a beautiful five-star establishment a few miles south of the capital, Castries, overlooking the extensive golden sand beach.

St Lucia has never quite made up its mind whether she is British or French. Both countries struggled to own the island for the best part of 200 years. In 1841, the final victory was won by Britain and St. Lucia became part of the Commonwealth. In towns like Soufriére, the second largest on the island, and Vieux Fort, an old form of French is still spoken and lots of buildings look distinctly Provençale, ornate and delicately pastel-painted. The original inhabitants were Amerindians, who tried to defeat the invaders by eating them! They liked the taste of Frenchmen but found the Spaniards unpalatable. Perhaps frogs and garlic had something to do with it!

During our stay, we toured Pigeon Island National Park, visited the drive-in volcano near Soufriére and drove through a freak fissure in the rock, parking inside the crater amidst smoke and steam and the nearby sulphur springs. Two volcanic spikes of sheer rock, the Pitons, rise 2,700 feet straight out of the sea and are the island's landmark. Marigot Bay is a secluded spot and was the location for the tropical island scenes in the film *Doctor Dolittle*, starring Rex Harrison.

When we arrived back in England on 10 January, we found Luton Airport under several inches of snow. We were very apprehensive about driving back to Surrey, but once we got on to the M1 conditions were much better.

In June, I received a personal invitation from Sir Geoffrey Howe, Chancellor of the Exchequer, to a cocktail party in No. 11 Downing Street. This enabled me to see inside this historic building.

The year ended sensationally. Our grandson, Michael, aged nine, was playing with a cigarette lighter in his bedroom and set the curtains alight. The fire brigade was called but fortunately, the fire was extinguished before very much damage was sustained.

Now I return to our anniversary year, 1983. We enjoyed two cruises – the first on the Fred Olsen ship *Black Watch* to Madeira and the Canary Islands, and later on a small Dutch vessel *Vacationer*.

To celebrate our Ruby Wedding, we booked a weekend at the Holiday Inn, Bristol and invited Margaret's sisters Winnie, Iris and Florence, my sister Eileen and her husband Eric and friends Cliff and Betty Bore. During the weekend, we organised a car treasure hunt starting in Bristol and proceeding to Wookey Hole Caves and a cheese factory.

The following weekend, we arranged another celebration party at our Bookham house. Not knowing what the weather would be like in July, we had a canopy erected over the terrace in the event of rain. As it turned out, it was a very hot day, so the canopy provided welcome shade. We placed tables and sun umbrellas on the lawn and our neighbours lent us their tables and umbrellas as well. We decked the garden with flags and bunting and an outdoor caterer came along to assist us with the food. We provided forty-seven different buffet items including paté de foie gras, smoked salmon, roast turkey, York ham, ox tongue, an assortment of salads and cheeses and desserts, plus a special anniversary cake.

After everyone had eaten their fill, entertainment was provided by Rex Cooper, a member of the Inner Circle of Magicians (Gold star) and the International Brotherhood of Magicians. He put on a wonderful display of magic and illusions, as well as balloon creations and close-up magic. We then had Country and Western dancing, accompanied by Doris Thomas and the Bookham Country Dance Band to round up our anniversary celebration.

Having made several applications to join the Guild of Travel Writers and been turned down each time because we also wrote on other subjects besides travel, I decided to form our own travel group within the Freelance Division of the Institute of Journalists. I was elected first chairman of the group and organised familiarisation visits to France and various UK locations. Margaret went to Inverness and Skye to see the Scottish salmon farms. In the autumn, we attended the annual conference of the Institute of Journalists in Blackpool and visited Lancaster, Morecambe and the

National Savings Premium Bond headquaters and saw their random selector, ERNIE in action.

In April, I met the film star Diana Dors who came to Leatherhead to open a dry cleaners in Church Street. Much to everybody's surprise, Miss Dors arrived before time! Most notable was the fact that she was no longer slim and curvaceous as we had seen her on screen but had put on considerable middle-aged spread!

Our house in Great Bookham.

CHAPTER FIFTY-ONE

Gastronomy at High Speed

'The Age of Steam is just a memory but rail travel is still a joy.'

American folk song

DOCTOR BEECHING axed over 2,000 stations and many lines throughout the country in the 1960s but thanks to the enthusiasm of many devotees, the new millenium has seen many of these branch lines reopening by railway preservation societies and old steam locomotives have been lovingly restored and put back into service to provide the public the opportunity to once more experience the Age of Steam.

We have been on many journeys by train, both steam-hauled and electric-driven but the most memorable ones have been aboard the famous Venice-Simplon-Orient Express. Our first trip was in 1984. The year had begun with an invitation from the Gibraltar Tourist Office to update ourselves on the latest developments in the Crown colony. We stayed at the Holiday Inn and were VIP guests at the Three Kings' Cavalcade through Main Street. We met the Minister for Tourism and then transferred to the Rock Hotel where we were interviewed for Gibraltar Television and the Gibraltar Forces Radio. We also gave our impressions on tourism to the daily newspaper, the *Gibraltar Chronicle*.

On 4 May we arrived at Victoria Station, London and made our way to platform eight. A bewiskered, beaming conductor, dressed in uniform such as was worn in Edwardian times, greeted us and directed us to the magnificent First Class Pullman Parlour Car bearing the name *Cygnus* where we were welcomed aboard and shown to our compartment. The construction of *Cygnus* commenced in 1938 but completion was deferred due to the war until 1951. It was used in the special Festival of Britain train, reserved for use by royalty and visiting heads of state. It also formed part of Sir Winston Churchill's funeral train in 1965 and made its last journey for British Rail as part of the 'Golden Arrow' in 1972. There are twenty-four seats in this coach and other Pullman coaches making up the British section of the Orient Express, dating from 1925. They total twelve in number, having been restored at Carnforth, Lancashire. No detail had been overlooked. Pink lampshades, still in their original places on the tables, provide an authentic link with the past. No evidence of plastics or synthetic materials can be seen – it is rosewood and oak panelling all the way with exquisite marquetry in its original gleaming state, with four free-standing seats in the discreet coupes and extending tables.

As soon as we were comfortably seated, we were served with a glass of champagne, together with a tray of canapés. Then exactly at 11.44, the British section of this famous train pulled out of Victoria *en route* for Folkestone. Lunch was served as soon as we were underway, starting with leek and watercress cream soup, followed by chicken and lobster mayonnaise, nutty rice salads, a delicious blackberry and apple fool with Scottish shortbread and coffee.

Since the British Rail night ferry service ceased, trains no longer make the Channel crossing aboard ship. Passengers, therefore, leave the train at Folkestone and board a Sealink ferry for the two and a half hour crossing to Boulogne. A special first class lounge was reserved for the exclusive use of Orient Express passengers, who were served with tea, coffee and biscuits during the crossing.

Among our fellow passengers were a young honeymoon couple. For the newly-wed bride, this journey was a complete surprise as her fiancé had refused to tell her where they were going or how they were going on their honeymoon. All he said was, 'Take your passport, we are going abroad.' There were a large number of American passengers who had flown to England in order to travel on the Orient Express.

After a mere glance at our passports by the French authorities, we were directed to the continental sector of the journey, standing alongside the quay. The Wagon-lits comprised no fewer than seventeen coaches plus two diesel locomotives. Ten of the coaches were sleeping cars which, during the day are converted into seats and tables. There are two kitchen-restaurant carriages and a dining salon, plus a lounge with a bar and a grand piano, where a pianist entertains during the evening. The rest of the train is made up of baggage cars and a staff carriage. All the coaches are decorated in their original blue and gold livery and are just as magnificent as those used on the British sector.

The sleeping compartments accommodate two persons on bunk beds arranged one above the other. During the day, the top one folds up and the bottom one converts into a comfortable settee. Each compartment has its own washbasin, with hot and cold water, concealed behind a folding door. There is also a toilet. Certain compartments open up with the adjoining one to form a double cabin for a family of four.

The coaches are heated by charcoal boilers, situated at the ends of each carriage, just as they were before the war. An attendant sits by to keep it stoked up!

At precisely 17.44 European time, five hours after leaving London, the

Venice Simplon Orient Express was on its way *en route* for Paris and Venice. Visions of intrigue, espionage and murder came to our mind as we settled back in our seat and we recalled films such as *The Lady Vanishes*, *From Russia with Love* and Agatha Christie's *Murder on the Orient Express*. Would we, we wondered, be the victims of a new 1984 thriller?

Our reflections were interrupted by the steward who informed us that the first sitting dinner was about to be served. We changed into evening dress and black tie, as did the majority of fellow passengers, and made our way to one of the dining carriages. A few of the guests were sporting fashions of pre-war days. Vases of fresh flowers, the finest Limoges china, beautiful Cristallin glassware, silver plated cutlery engraved with the art nouveau VSOE motif, linen damask table cloths and napkins adorned the tables – only the very best for the 'king of trains and the train of kings'.

A delicious *table d'hôte* dinner was served comprising fillets of fish in pastry, fillet steak, French cheeses and desserts, rounded off with coffee and les Mignardises.

A stop in Paris to pick up some more passengers and then we were on our way through the night, travelling through Dijon and the heart of France. After a night's sleep in our cabin, we were awakened at our request by our steward at six o'clock as it was getting light. We did not want to miss any of the scenery as we passed through Switzerland. A short stop was made at Lausanne in the early hours to take on provisions and freshly-baked croissants. These were served to us with our breakfast by the steward in our cabin. Another stop at Brig, in Switzerland, was made so that our diesel engines were exchanged for electric locomotives and then we were off again and heading for the twelve-mile Simplon Tunnel taking us from Switzerland into Italy.

After running along the shores of Lake Geneva, we caught a glimpse of the Matterhorn before entering the tunnel. There was another short technical stop at Domodossola where a second locomotive took over and then we pulled into Milan station at 9.15 a.m. Here, we had a twenty-five-minute wait so were able to get off the train and stretch our legs.

Once beyond the industrial sprawl of Milan, we were once again in the countryside, passing through Brescia and then Desenzano at the southern end of the huge expanse of Lake Garda, home of the famous Gorgonzola cheese. In this rich agricultural area, the densely cultivated acres of wheat and maize, bisected by little streams, gave way to the orderly rows of vineyards as we approached the lovely city of Verona and the area which produces the red Valpolicella and white Soave wines. This is the city that Shakespeare used for the setting of his plays *Two Gentlemen of Verona* and *Romeo and Juliet*.

Resuming our journey, the steward brought us a copy of the day's *New York Herald-Tribune* and told us it was now time to once more proceed to the dining car for brunch. This included fruit juices, scrambled eggs with bacon and a very appetising dish called 'L'Assiette Mata Hari' after the famous War World One spy who travelled frequently on the Orient Express. This consisted of smoked salmon, a chicken liver mousse, tomatoes stuffed with crabmeat, vegetable terrine and salad. The main course was Boeuf Stroganoff with paprika sauce and the meal finished with a dessert called La Gourmandise, described as a 'sweet tooth'.

Now we were nearing the end of our journey and, as far as we were aware, there had been no murders committed during the trip, no suicides and we did not see James Bond or any SMERSH agents among the passengers. But who knows what fascinating tales could be told by our fellow passengers? Some had flown the Atlantic just to make the journey, others must have saved a lifetime to experience a twenty-four-hour never-to-be forgotten train journey across Europe.

A long causeway connects Mestre, on the mainland, with the island setting of Venice and the glories of the city are revealed as the Orient Express finally pulls into Santa Lucia station.

Robert Benchley (1889–1945), a newspaper correspondent, on arriving for the first time in Venice, sent a telegram back to his editor in New York saying, 'Streets full of water – please advise'. After a short stay here, we flew back to England.

We paid a second visit to Venice in March 1996, this time to board the Orient Express for the reverse journey to London. During our two day stay in the 'Bruges of the south', we were invited to dine in the famous five-star Hotel Cipriani, situated on Giudecca Island in the lagoon. We were picked up from St Mark's Square by the hotel's own launch and we discovered that this is the only hotel in Venice with its own garden and outdoor swimming pool. The cuisine here is all one would expect as the hotel is owned by the Orient Express company.

Our second invitation was dinner at another superb hotel, the Danieli, once a fifteenth century Doge's palace and now part of the luxury collection of ITT Sheraton Hotels. The palace was converted into an hotel in the early nineteenth century and still offers the luxury and style of a bygone age. Situated overlooking the lagoon, the Danieli is a few hundred yards from St Mark's Square and its beautifully restored public rooms include an impressive galleried entrance hall, elegant lounge, bar and rooftop restaurant with spectacular views.

It was now time for us to begin our journey home. We boarded the water taxi which took us to the railway station. The train follows the same route through Milan and Switzerland but this time, we had a chance to see the scenery we missed when we travelled through the night on the outward journey. This time, our night journey went through the Jura mountains in Switzerland and in the following morning through the

Burgundy wine district centred around Dijon, the region of Nuits St Georges, Pommard, Morgan and Volnay. Breakfast was served *en route* to Paris where we arrived at Austerlitz station soon afterwards. Here, the train stopped for forty-five minutes. As soon as we arrived, porters and railway staff formed a chain and loaded supplies into the kitchen car.

From Paris, we crossed the countryside of northern France to Boulogne and the cross-Channel ferry to Folkestone. Here, we transferred to the British Pullman train for the journey to Victoria Station, London. A very English afternoon tea was served during the journey and at 5.30 p.m., we reluctantly left one of the world's most exciting and romantic trains.

This was not our last encounter, however, with the VSO Express. In August 1994, we joined a press party aboard the British unit of the train for a tour of the Kent orchards and countryside as guests of Britain's Apple and Pear Board.

Our fourth trip on the Orient Express took place on 26 June 1998. We set off from Victoria but this time, we only journeyed as far as Zurich, where we disembarked for a couple of nights before taking a train to St Moritz. Our Swiss adventure is described in chapter 53.

These gentlemen are among the staff of the V.S. Orient Express.

CHAPTER FIFTY-TWO

California Revisited

California here I come, right back where I started from ...

The year 1985 was an exciting year. We enjoyed another cruise; visited Normandy D-Day beaches, toured Florida and its theme parks; participated in a Murder Weekend and Margaret and I were presented to Her Royal Highness Princess Anne, the Princess Royal.

The following year was just as exciting with a week in Mojocar in Spain and visiting Granada and the Alhambra, the gipsy caves and fishing village of La Garrucha and Almeria. This was the year of Hotelympia, the International Hotel and Catering Exhibition in London and I was privileged to accompany and photograph Queen Elizabeth the Queen Mother as she toured the Salon Culinaire.

Shrove Tuesday was marked in Leatherhead with a pancake race down the High Street. The *Courier* was represented in the race by our advertisement manager, Mr John Douglas, dressed as a waiter. He made a supreme effort but just as he reached the finishing line in first place, he fell and broke his arm.

In March, Bookham was shaken at breakfast time by a loud explosion. I immediately went to investigate and found a house in the High Street had collapsed, following a gas leak. Fortunately, no one was injured and I was able to send photographs and a report to the *Surrey Advertiser*. At the end of the month, we watched a magnificent firework display on the River Thames to mark the end of the Greater London Council. An even bigger spectacle was provided by the fire at Hampton Court Palace.

I organised a tour for the IOJ travel specialists to Cumbria and the Lake District, visiting Ambleside, Penrith and Ullswater, and the former homes of William Wordsworth and John Ruskin. We had travelled to Cumbria by train and for our return journey, our guide took us to Oxenholme station to catch the London train. Unfortunately, the tourist office gave us the wrong train times and we found there was no train stopping at this station for six hours. I am not a person who lets a little matter such as this deter me so I went along to the station master's office and explained our predicament that we were a party of important journalists and travel writers and it was imperative we got to London as soon as possible. The station master was very helpful and telephoned British Rail offices in Carlisle. The outcome was that the non-stop *Royal Scot* from Scotland made an unscheduled halt at Oxenholme to enable our party to board.

On 2 June, we flew to the USA on a Pan-Am Boeing 747 to Los Angeles for our second visit to California. As we circled the city, the whole area was obscured by what we thought was cloud. On landing, we discovered that the 'cloud' was in fact smog, created by the fumes of thousands of motor vehicles.

For three nights, we stayed in one of the state rooms in the former Cunard liner, SS *Queen Mary*, now permanently berthed at Long Beach, southern California. The former holder of the Blue Riband, this grand old lady of the seas had been converted into a tourist attraction and a floating hotel, with 390 state rooms, restaurants, banqueting and conference facilities. The most elegant restaurant was now called Sir Winston which is decorated with photographs and memorabilia of Britain's wartime prime minister.

Much of the Queen's splendour has gone but the Grand Salon is still there and now features 1,250 sq. ft of food displays for the extensive Sunday champagne brunch.

Also at Long Beach is the *Spruce Goose*, Howard Hughes' all-wooden 200-ton flying boat. It only made one flight of less than a mile at a very low height. Whilst in the area, we took a boat to Santa Catalina island, twenty-two miles off the coast. One of the features to be seen there is its herd of wild buffalo.

Although we have been to Venice in Italy a number of times, we had never been on its canals in a gondola. Long Beach has four twenty-five ft Venetian gondolas, propelled by traditionally costumed gondoliers, and a thirty-two ft vessel with two gondoliers. We took an hour long cruise through the canals of Naples Island, whilst our gondoliers serenaded us with Italian songs and music.

After our three days in Long Beach, we took the AMTRAK train to San Diego where we booked into the US Grant Hotel. Originally built in 1910 by Ulysses S. Grant Junior in honour of his father, it is the grande dame of the city's hotels, hosting in the past such luminaries as Albert Einstein, Charles Lindberg and Presidents Woodrow Wilson, Franklin D. Roosevelt, Harry S. Truman, Dwight D. Eisenhower and John F. Kennedy.

This was our second visit to San Diego and we loved its beautiful natural harbour and its many other attractions. One of these is Balboa Park, 1,400 acres of cultural and recreational activities with galleries, museums, theatres, sports facilities and garden walks with their sub-tropical plants and ponds.

We again visited the world famous zoo with its 1,500 species, the world's largest collection, and thirty miles to the north in the San Pacqual Valley, the 1,800 acre Wild Animal Park and Game Reserve.

From San Diego, we took the AMTRAK train to Anaheim in Orange County and booked into the Disneyland Hotel to experience once again the thrills and excitement of this fantasy world. Back in Los Angeles, we spent our remaining four days in California in the luxurious five-star Biltmore Hotel. Whilst in LA, we toured the *Los Angeles Times* newspaper offices. In the building is a museum and on display there are out-of-date printing presses. They may have been out-of-date in the States but the *Surrey Advertiser* in Guildford were still using similar machines!

On 16 October, we attended a family luncheon at The Green Man, Great Offley, Hertfordshire to mark my father's forthcoming 90th birthday on 24 December. Present were my sister Eileen and her husband Eric, their daughter Hazel and her children Andrew and Christine.

To mark the twentieth anniversary of our newspaper, the *Courier*, we organised a celebration dinner for our readers and advertisers at the Leatherhead Leisure Centre.

The year 1987 started with two deaths in the family. John Bamford, husband of Margaret's eldest sister, Winnie, died on 4 December. John had served in the army during the Second World War and was one of those who managed to escape at Dunkirk in 1940. He had arrived back in Nottingham dirty and exhausted but after two days, he had to rejoin his unit and was then shipped out to the Western Desert where he joined the Eighth Army as a tank driver.

The second death was that of my father at the age of ninety years. He had been admitted to the Lister Hospital, Stevenage, on his birthday, Christmas Eve, after a heart attack but was allowed home after some days, only to be readmitted in February 1988. On 24th of that month, I telephoned the hospital to enquire how he was and was told by the sister that he had collapsed on the way to the bathroom and died that morning.

Another casualty was our appointment as editors of the Cookery and Food Association's journal, *Food & Cookery Review* which we had edited from December 1971. The reason given was the cost of production and the Association thought they could run it more cheaply in-house with the Association's general secretary editing it. He produced one issue and that was the last. The magazine has not since been published.

Travel writers always seem to be travelling and we were no exception. We did a lot of tours in 1987, starting with Majorca in January where it rained most of the week and on 14 January, snow fell on Palma, a very rare occurrence.

We were involved in two royal occasions this year, the first in May when we met the Duke and Duchess of York in Leatherhead and in

July with Prince Edward when he opened the Chessington World of Adventures.

During the night of 15–16 October, southern England experienced a hurricane. We had 100 mile an hour winds in Surrey, trees were uprooted, roofs blown off, houses damaged, roads blocked and telephone, gas and electricity supplies were cut off.

In Bookham, several giant cedars of Lebanon were blown down and at the National Trust property Polesden Lacey, half a mile from our house, hundreds of trees were uprooted. In our garden, our front fence was blown down, one fruit tree was destroyed and our Bramley apple bent over at an angle of forty degrees. I was, however, able to upright it and it survived. In Oaks Park on the borders of Sutton, Reigate and Banstead, 15,000 trees were down and similar devastation was experienced in Kent and the home counties.

Beside the wind, eight inches of rain fell during the first weeks of October, making it the wettest October that century. A red flood alert was issued for the River Mole.

We had a repeat performance in 1990 although not as strong as the 1987 hurricane. But the winds did manage to uproot the remaining giant cedars of Lebanon in Bookham. The bad weather was not confined to Britain as parts of Europe also experienced hurricane conditions.

On 3 March 1990, we left Gatwick for an inspection tour of Barratt's Homes villas and apartments which they had for sale for time-sharing on the Costa del Sol. We flew on a GB Airways Boeing 737 and were supposed to land on Gibraltar. Hurricane winds were blowing when we approached the Rock and the pilot had difficulty in approaching the runway from the east. He was undecided whether to make for Tangier or Malaga and finally decided on the latter.

Barratt's representatives met us and took us to the Villacana apartments where we were to stay for the next three days. The wind was so strong that it almost bowled us over. We also went to see other Barratt's properties at Dona Lola, Duquesa and the Leila Golf Club. On 6 March, we were taken to Gibraltar and after a tour of the Rock to see the storm damage, we flew back to the UK.

CHAPTER FIFTY-THREE

Cheese, Chocolate and Cowbells

*They say that if the Swiss had designed these mountains, they'd
be rather flatter.*

Paul Theroux, 1941–,
The Great Railway Bazaar

THE BRITISH have been coming to Switzerland on vacation for well
over one hundred years. We have visited Switzerland on several
occasions, both in winter and summer, and have always enjoyed the Swiss
hospitality, their food and the exquisite natural beauty of the country. We
decided to go there again for our forty-fifth wedding anniversary which
occurred on 3 July 1988. As already related in chapter fifty-one,
we travelled there in style aboard the Orient Express, disembarking in
Zurich.

After two nights here, we took the train to St Moritz, using the Swiss
Holiday Card which is only available to non-residents and has to be
purchased before departure from England. It entitles the holder to un-
limited travel on practically all the major railway routes, boats and postal
coaches, as well as buses and trams in twenty-four towns and cities.

This was the first time we had been in St Moritz in summer. Our hotel
was the four-star Schweizerhof in the centre of the town overlooking the
lake. On our previous visit, the lake was frozen and covered with snow.
According to official statistics, the sun shines in St Moritz on 322 days
a year and overcast skies are rare in the canton of Engadine. The tourist
board describes it as a 'Champagne climate'.

On the second evening of our stay, we made our way down for dinner
in the hotel when a horse and carriage pulled up at the entrance. The
local tourist board had laid on a carriage ride just for us to Bei Pontresina
and a special dinner at the Hotel Roseggletscher, much to our surprise
and delight.

Having travelled across France to Switzerland in the luxury of the Venice
Simplon Orient Express, we took the opportunity to make another trip of
a lifetime, a train journey across the country from St Moritz to Zermatt
aboard the famous Glacier Express, truly one of the most spectacular

railway routes in the world. Using our Swiss Travel Card, plus a small supplement and reservation fee, we boarded the train at 8.30 a.m. and set off on the eight hour journey, covering some 185 miles. Hardly an express speed but no one wants to dash up and down mountains without admiring the views.

The Express is run by three railway companies, forming a network of one-metre gauge mountain track and as each company takes over the train, the locomotives are changed. At one point, we descended to 1,980 ft at Reichenau and then ascended to 6,670 ft through the Oberalp Pass. Luncheon is served on the journey as well as drinks and snacks.

Our journey ended in Zermatt, one of our favourite Swiss resorts, a delightful holiday centre in both summer and winter. On leaving the station, we were confronted by an array of what looked like electric-driven milk floats. They were, in fact, the local hotel courtesy cars and taxis. Only electrically-propelled vehicles are allowed in the town, thus helping to ensure a pollution-free atmosphere.

We stayed in the four-star Mirabeau Hotel, one of the most pleasant hotels in which we have stayed. We were greeted by the owner and his wife and shown to a very comfortable room with spectacular views of the Matterhorn and the Rothern Mountains. The meals could not be faulted and both the proprietors were on duty throughout the meal, supervising the service and ensuring everything was piping hot and to everyone's satisfaction. Here, we celebrated our wedding anniversary.

There is so much to do in Zermatt, both in summer and winter, with all-year-round skiing on the Kleine Matterhorn, the highest in Europe at over 12,500 ft, and a cable car will take you to the Breithorn Plâteau. The cog railway took us to Riffelberg and Gornergrat (10,170 ft) where we had lunch on the terrace of the restaurant, surrounded by snow-capped peaks. Then we took the cable car to the summit of Stockhorn (11,155 ft).

Another enjoyable mountain trip was by 'Metro'; a railway which runs through a tunnel in the mountainside from Zermatt to Sunnegga. Emerging from the tunnel, we transferred to the cable car to Blauherd, then another cable car to the summit of the Unterrothorn (10,180 ft).

Zermatt itself is a very pleasant small town with attractive shops, restaurants, an alpine museum, gardens and sporting facilities, a place we intend to revisit.

Reluctantly, we left Zermatt by train and, three hours later we were in Montreux, famous for its various festivals. Described as the 'Pearl of the Swiss Rivieras', it is situtated on the shores of Lake Geneva and is surrounded by the majestic Swiss Alps and the French Savoy Alps. Small hidden beaches, picturesque harbours and quaint old stone villages can be found along the fifteen kilometre shoreline.

Our four-star Hotel Suisse et Majestic on the Avenue des Alpes over-looked the lake.

Adjoining Montreux is Vevey, the headquarters of the Nestlé Company. The promenade from Vevey to Montreux consists of gardens and flower displays, a very interesting and pleasant walk. The whole of the surrounding area is covered with vineyards, the source of Swiss wines.

After a too short a stay, we left Montreux by another special train, the Panoramic Express. This was, perhaps, the slowest express in the world, taking ninety minutes to cover a distance of forty-five miles but it takes in more spectacular scenery on its journey to Zweisimmen, where we changed trains for Spiez. Another change here for the train to Interlaken and on to our final destination, Lucerne, a town which is twinned with our south coast resort, Bournemouth. We stayed at the Hotel Montana which is part of the Swiss Hotel Management School.

Lake Lucerne is one of the most famous of the Swiss lakes, surrounded by wooded hills above which tower mighty mountains. Lucerne itself is a charming town, with its watch towers, churches, solid town houses, ancient wooden bridges with paintings under their eaves, and sturdy city walls dating back to mediaeval times. The petrified Glacier Garden gives you a glimpse of twenty million years of the earth's history.

In two weeks, we had travelled across half the country by numerous forms of transport, climbed mountains, cruised on lakes, stayed in superb hotels, enjoyed some really delicious meals, sampled lots of chocolates and cheeses and, above all, experienced the great welcome and hospitality of the Swiss people. Switzerland is certainly a country for all seasons and, like a magnet, will draw you back time and time again.

Swizerland was not our only overseas venture in 1988. Earlier, we had cruised on the Fred Olsen *Black Prince* to the Canary Islands. Among the ports of call was the island of Gomera, a unique island and rich in ecology. It is an amazing landscape where mountains, valleys and flora reflect God's creative beauty. It was the last Spanish island where Christopher Columbus anchored before sailing for America.

The population numbers about 18,000, distributed in its six towns and the main occupations are fishing, agriculture and tourism. The capital is San Sebastian, which is also its port. The coastline is abrupt with high cliffs and the mountainous interior is bisected with luxuriant valleys. Unique to the islanders is their language of whistles, whereby they communicate with each other from one mountain to another.

The 1988 National Garden Festival was held in Glasgow which also gave us an opportunity of seeing the Burrell Collection, Mackintosh House and the Art Gallery. On our return, Margaret had an operation in the Ashtead Hospital for the successful removal of a cataract.

What could be more romantic and exciting than to stay in a house and sleep in a room which had, in the past, been used by such famous personalities as Frederick Prince of Wales (father of George III), the Duke of Sutherland, Queen Victoria, the Duke of Westminster, William Waldorf Astor, Lady Nancy Astor, Sir Winston Churchill, Lord Curzon, prime minister Arthur Balfour, Rudyard Kipling, Henry James, George Bernard Shaw, Lawrence of Arabia, Charlie Chaplin and many more?

The place is Cliveden, Britain's only stately home which is now a hotel. Overlooking the River Thames at Taplow, Buckinghamshire, it is set in 376 acres of National Trust gardens and parkland. One of the great pleasures of Cliveden is eating. In the main dining room the chef combines classical English dishes with some of the best contemporary cuisine. The French Dining Room, with its original Madame de Pompadour Rococo decoration is the finest eighteenth century boiserie outside France. Breakfast is served here in the morning at a traditional long table.

The bedrooms are enormous in size and each bears the name of a famous former occupant. The first time we stayed here, we had the Prince of Wales' suite with a huge four-poster bed. In 1988 we stayed in the Mountbatten Room.

On arrival at Cliveden, having driven down the long tree-lined drive and past the Fountain of Love, we were greeted at the entrance by a footman, whilst another took our car to the car park. A chambermaid asked us if we needed any assistance to unpack our case and the butler brought us a pot of tea and cream cakes. Before retiring for the night, we found that our night attire had been ironed and carefully laid out. This is what we call living!

Alongside the main house is the Pavilion with an indoor swimming pool. In front of the Pavilion is a large heated outdoor swimming pool and whirlpool. It was here that Christine Keeler frolicked with the Minister of War, John Profumo, in 1963.

During the year, we were invited to afternoon tea with the ex-king Constantine of Greece and Queen Anne-Marie at Dorincourt, the workshops of the Queen Elizabeth's Foundation for the Disabled at Leatherhead.

By way of relaxation, I built a small greenhouse at the bottom of the garden, measuring eight feet by six feet. In spite of its size and being unheated, I still managed to raise seventy boxes of bedding plants the following spring. In the summer of 1991, the Leatherhead Horticultural Society presented us with the second prize in the Joseph Birtwistle Awards for the small garden that had given particular pleasure to the passer-by.

CHAPTER FIFTY-FOUR

Battlefields

When the hurlyburly's done,
When the battle's lost and won ...

William Shakespeare,
Macbeth, Act 1, Scene 1

ALTHOUGH I SERVED THREE YEARS in the Forces during World War Two, I was fortunate not to have been involved in any bloody battle. Margaret, too, escaped conflict, being in a reserved occupation but her city, Nottingham, had its air raids and she was required to do fire-watching duties.

In 1985, we took a *Courier* party to France with Epsom Coaches and we toured the Normandy area – Dieppe, Rouen, Arromanches and Honfleur and the British and Canadian landing beaches, Sword, Juno and Gold. We paid a visit to the Observation Point, the Musée du Débarquement and the remains of the Mulberry Harbour.

In the same year, we went to visit another field of battle, Bosworth, near Leicester, which took place in the year 1485. On the death of King Edward V, a Welshman named Henry Tudor, Earl of Richmond, fought against King Richard III. With Henry was a small army of zealous supporters, plus a few French and English adventurers with the aim of gaining the English crown. This was the last battle in the War of the Roses and took place on a bare Leicestershire upland. Richard was killed and Henry Tudor was crowned Henry VII soon afterwards.

Four years later (1989), after a tour of Kent attractions including the Battle of Britain Museum at Hawking, we took the Sally Lines Ferry from Ramsgate to Dunkirk for a coach tour of World War One battlefields in Flanders and Ypres; also visiting the Menai Gate, war graves and the trenches. Our granddaughter, Maria, had previously made this tour with her school and had told us how interesting it was.

Cambrai in the French Nord is famous for a tank battle in World War One, which took place on 20 November 1917, during which the British army employed 300 tanks. We visited the town and the site of the battle, and the British War Graves Cemetery in 1999. We stayed in the Hotel

Beatus, the owner of which, M. Philippe Gorczynski, is an expert on the Battle of Cambrai and he personally conducted us on a tour of the various villages involved in the conflict. He had the previous year, discovered a damaged British tank buried in a field, which he had raised and was having it restored and exhibited.

Cambrai is a town of art and history; an old fortified place with its Middle Age relics and fort, the Château du Selles, with an exceptional defence system. The town is also the seat of an archbishop with fine examples of religious architecture dating from the end of the seventeenth century to the first half of the eighteenth. In St George's Church is displayed Ruben's masterpiece 'Christ laid in the tomb'.

Around the lively town square, le Grand Place, the streets are dotted with houses in various styles from the sixteenth century to the 1930s. The local tourist office is housed in a mediaeval building called the Spanish House. The museum has been transformed from an unheated, unlit nineteenth century establishment into a fully equipped modern building of historical artefacts, sculpture and fine art from pre-history to the present day. Among the exhibits is a statue of John the Baptist by Rodin. The painter Henri Matisse was born at Cateau-Cambrésis, twenty-four kilometres from Cambrai.

Back to 1987, one of the places we found most interesting was the former prisoner-of-war camp at Malton, midway between York and Scarborough in North Yorkshire. This was built in 1942 to house the steady stream of enemy prisoners of war captured in North Africa. The site was named Eden Camp and the first inmates were 250 Italians They were put to work to construct a larger, permanent camp consisting of forty-five huts. Later, both Germans and Italians were housed here.

In 1985, a coal merchant named Stan Johnson, discovered that POW Camp 83 was still intact and that thirty-five of the original huts were roughly in the same condition as when the last of the 1,200 inmates left for the Fatherland in 1948. Subsequently, Mr Johnson bought the site, together with all the existing huts and invested £750,000 to re-establish Eden Camp as a theme park and a Museum of Modern History.

The huts were re-equipped to tell the story of the British people at war and Mr Johnson and his project director, Ron Beamish, constructed realistic tableaux with moving figures, authentic sounds and appropriate smells.

In 1989, my sister Eileen and her husband, Eric, sold their house in Bexhill-on-Sea and moved to a bungalow in Verwood in Dorset, to be near to their daughter, Hazel, who had divorced her husband and was now living in Salisbury.

An interesting invitation reached us from the Fuji Company. They were operating an airship around Surrey and asked us if we would like a flight

We flew over Surrey in this airship in 1989

in her. We eagerly agreed and made our way to Woking where the ship was waiting. We walked across the field where a team of men were holding it down with ropes and climbed on board. Our advertisement manager, John Douglas and a photographer from the *Surrey Advertiser* also joined us for an hour's flight over the county. It was a pleasant sensation, slowly gliding along at varying heights and hovering above our house and the offices of the *Surrey Advertiser* in Guildford. This was a unique experience which not very many people will have experienced.

Also this year, we spent a night in the bedroom of the late Sir William S. Gilbert, librettist of the Savoy Operas, in his former home, Grim's Dyke Manor in Harrow Weald, Middlesex.

CHAPTER FIFTY-FIVE

Murder Most Foul!

Truth will come to light, murder cannot be hid long.

William Shakespeare,
The Merchant of Venice, Act 2, scene 3

MARGARET'S SISTER, Renée, the youngest of the five daughters, and her husband decided in 1967 to leave Nottingham and emigrate to Australia on the government's £10 scheme. They had three children, the eldest, Sheila and Jill, were both adopted by them as babies and the youngest Alison was their natural child.

Before leaving England, husband Ernest had been a bank manager in Nottinghamshire but he thought there were greater opportunities down under. They settled for a time in Melbourne then moved west to Perth. Jill, however, decided to remain in Melbourne where she had made a number of friends. In 1989, her boyfriend, Michael Rice, moved into her flat. He was aged forty-one and Jill was thirty-five and he was an American.

In October 1989, Jill's niece, Sheila's daughter, was getting married and Auntie Jill arranged to fly to Perth to join the family for the celebrations. She bought new clothes for the wedding, a gift for the bride and booked her airline ticket and, according to her boyfriend, he drove her to the airport and saw her on the flight.

But Jill never arrived in Perth. Her parents waited in vain and made enquiries to find out where she was or what had happened to her. Had she missed the flight or changed her mind at the last moment?

Jill was a civil servant and worked as a clerk in the Melbourne Health Clinic and in her spare time ran a rock 'n' roll dance studio. She had finished work on Friday 13 October, promising to be in on Monday morning to finish work on a report before going to Perth. On the following day, she used her credit card to draw some money and to purchase some lingerie and then spent the weekend with Michael at the Ringwood Lake Motel outside the city. It is believed she wanted to end the friendship and that this was their parting date. She had told him she wanted him to vacate the flat. They booked into Room 21 at the Motel and that was the last time Jill was seen by anyone. What happened in Room 21 remains a mystery. She did not turn up for work on Monday morning to finish her report.

Her parents began to suspect foul play and asked the Melbourne police to investigate but they came up with nothing. Ernest was not satisfied and went to Melbourne where he spent two months making enquiries, questioning friends and acquaintances, probing and searching for answers. He went to see Michael Rice who maintained his story. The wedding outfit and the wedding present were still in Jill's flat.

Ernest kept meticulous notes of his enquiries, visiting acquaintances of Jill and kept in constant touch with the police investigations. He appealed for information on television, hired a private detective and even consulted a clairvoyant, all to no avail. Eventually, he persuaded the police to re-open the case.

'It was just commonsense and determination to find out what had happened,' he told the press.

In 1993, four years after her disappearance, a policewoman from the Missing Persons Bureau re-opened the case and decided to search for Rice's car. It was traced to a garage on a Mount Eliza farm, outside Melbourne. Inside the garage was a forty-four-gallon drum and on opening it, Jill's body was found inside, immersed in lime. Her feet were bound and she was wearing a black negligée and her partly decomposed, mummified body was wrapped in plastic. The pathologist was unable to give a conclusive cause of death but had found a tiny bone in her neck broken, which could have been caused by strangulation.

In June 1993, Mr and Mrs Cave came to England and stayed with us for our golden wedding anniversary celebrations. During their stay with us, they received a call from the Melbourne police to report the finding of Jill's body. They had to return home to identify it.

The police set about tracing Michael Rice. Credit card records showed that on 25 October, he had bought a considerable amount of the lime product 'Limil' from a Fitzroy garden supplier. On the same day, still using his credit card, he hired a van and rented a self-storage space in a Melbourne suburb. He made as many as fifty-four trips to the store in the following eighteen months until 17 March 1991, when he checked out of the self-storage unit and hired a utility. He drove to the small farm outside Melbourne, whose owner agreed to store some of Rice's things, including the forty-four-gallon drum, whilst he made a trip to America. He also left his car at the farm, where it was eventually traced by the police.

Being bigger and stronger than Rice, the farmer obliged by rolling the padlocked yellow reconditioned drum into a shed. Rice told the farmer it contained computer equipment. When he noticed some white powder lying in a thin film on the back of the utility, Rice told him it was to protect the equipment in the barrel. Two days later, Rice flew to the United States.

Six months later, the farmer became concerned because the drum had started to leak and Rice had not returned. He contacted the police who, in turn, contacted the policewoman who was making a search for Rice's car.

In the meantime, Rice had moved to Baltimore and married. But the Melbourne police were able to trace him through his credit cards. Detectives from Victoria's homicide squad flew to the States to interview him. On 13 September 1994, he was arrested and charged with Jill's murder. After a few weeks in Baltimore's notoriously tough prison, Rice waived his right to fight extradition and agreed to return to Australia to fight the charge.

At his subsequent trial, he remained silent throughout and refused to answer questions. His defence lawyer argued that there was no evidence as to how Jill Cave had died, in spite of the pathologist's evidence regarding the broken bone in her neck. To the dismay of her parents, Mr Justice George Hampel upheld the defence's submission that there was insufficient evidence for a murder charge but the jury subsequently convicted Rice

Jill's parents Ernest and Reneé Cave with Margaret at the National Trust Fête in Claremont Gardens, Cobham, Surrey

Margaret's niece, Jill Cave who was murdered in Melbourne in 1989

on the lesser charge of manslaughter. He was sentenced to seven years' imprisonment and was required to serve a minimum of four.

The Court of Appeal ruled that the trial judge should not have ordered the jury to acquit Rice of murder. The three appeal judges said the jury could have found from the evidence that he used such violence as to kill Jill Cave and that the deceased had died as a result of unlawful and dangerous violence on the part of the applicant.

Rice's appeal counsel argued that Miss Cave could have died from natural causes and that his client had panicked.

'What did he have to fear if her death came to light?' asked Justice Brooking. 'Any reasonable person must have realised that, by concealing her body and her death and telling lies, ran a great risk, if the body was discovered, of being charged with murder'. His appeal was dismissed.

CHAPTER FIFTY-SIX

End of an Era

For solitude sometimes is best society
and short retirement urges sweet return.

John Milton 1608–74,
Paradise Lost, Book 9

Aʟʟ ɢᴏᴏᴅ ᴛʜɪɴɢs ᴍᴜsᴛ ᴄᴏᴍᴇ ᴛᴏ ᴀɴ ᴇɴᴅ, so they say. I was now in my sixty-eighth year and already in receipt of my State Old Age Pension. But I was still very active and gave no thought of retiring. Together with Margaret, we had been running and editing the *Courier* since we founded it in 1966 and had continued to do so after the *Surrey Advertiser* took it over. Our contract with the company was due for renewal at the end of 1990 but it came as a shock to be told that our services were no longer required and that Mr Ian Tait, the editor of *Esher News & Advertiser*, part of the group, was taking over.

But all was not lost. I was still a freelance journalist and travel writer and was not yet prepared to lay down my pen. Ian Tait was most sympathetic and agreed to continue to print our travel articles in the *Courier*, though he was unable to offer us any remuneration for our work.

At the beginning of the year, we had spent a week in San Augustin in Gran Canaria and on our return, southern England experienced another minor hurricane, resulting in forty-five deaths. The remaining cedars of Lebanon in Great Bookham succumbed to the storm and the side fence of our house was blown down.

On 31 January, I had a cataract operation on my left eye at the Ashtead Hospital. This was the first time I had been in a hospital and although I told the surgeon he could start without me, nevertheless he insisted I should be present. When the attendants came to take me to the theatre, they placed me on a trolley and almost ran with it, singing 'Here we go, here we go, off to the theatre we must go!' It was soon over. I felt no pain or after effects and went home the next day, my eyesight much improved.

At the end of March, Britain suffered Poll Tax riots in Trafalgar Square and other parts of the country, and in Manchester there was a prison riot.

The coach and tour company, Epsom Coaches, was organising a coach tour of parts of Yorkshire and Lincolnshire and a visit to the annual Spalding Flower Parade. Their director, Mr Roy Richmond, invited us to join the party and we made our way north in May. Spalding lies in the heart of the Fen District, an area which was once marshland, but drainage and reclamation have provided the district with rich fertile soil, ideal for growing bulbs. The fields in springtime are carpets of colour with daffodils, hyacinths and tulips. The climax of tulip time is the Flower Parade, a mile-long procession of flower-decorated floats and brass bands through the streets of the town. Each float is covered with tens of thousands of tulip heads. When the tulips reach full bloom, the heads are cut off at the top of the stems to ensure the strength in the bulbs is conserved and it is these heads which are used to decorate the floats in the parade. Flower heads are also used to form a series of beautiful mosaics.

That is the theory. However, 1990 was an unusual year with regards to the weather and the tulips came into bloom weeks earlier than they should have done. The result was that there were no flower heads available to decorate the floats. But the parade still went ahead, using artificial flowers and coloured paper tissues instead. It was still a colourful and spectacular procession but not as good as the real thing.

The 3 July was our forty-seventh wedding anniversary and coincided with a visit to Nottingham, so we took the opportunity of going to the Bridgeway Hall Methodist Church where we were married. It was not the same building as the original church in which we were joined as man and wife. This had since been demolished and a new one built in its place.

After a tour of Gloucestershire, we had dinner and spent the night in a four-poster bed in the Mountbatten Suite in Lady Astor's stately home, Cliveden, at Taplow. Another gourmet treat was dinner and night at Le Manoir aux Quat' Saisons at Great Milton, Oxfordshire. Owned by the famous chef Raymond Blanc, we were persuaded by him to sample his special ten-course dinner. Fortunately, portions of each course were very small but on reflection, we would rather have made our own selection from the à la carte menu.

On the international stage, Iraq invaded Kuwait on 2 August which led to Britain being involved in the Gulf War. We do not know whether the setting alight of the Kuwait oil wells had anything to do with it but we in Britain experienced thirty-seven days without a drop of rain! Mrs Margaret Thatcher resigned as prime minister on 22 November and John Major took over.

If 1990 was a momentous year for us, 1991 was even more so. Not only were we no longer editors of the *Courier* but we decided to move our abode from Surrey to England's Garden resort by the sea – Bournemouth. But more about that later.

Although our journalistic activities were now considerably reduced, we still continued to write as freelance journalists and travel writers. A glossy monthly magazine entitled *Surrey Occasions*, agreed to use our articles and pay us a small remuneration. I also took over the editorship of the local newsletter, the *Bookham Bulletin*, but for no fee.

On 16 January, the Gulf War with Iraq commenced and this continued until 28 February, following the liberation of Kuwait City and airport. A ceasefire was agreed on 3 March.

In Febuary, we flew to San Juan in Puerto Rico to embark on what was to turn out to be one of our best cruises ever. It was aboard the Chandris Line Celebrity Cruise liner MV *Horizon*. This took us to Martinique, Barbados, St Lucia, Antigua, St Thomas (one of the US Virgin Islands), and back to Puerto Rico. The food on board was exceptionally good, but it could not have been otherwise because the famous French chef, Michel Roux, created the menus for the ship.

A month later, we again crossed the Atlantic, flying first to St Lucia and then to Port of Spain, Trinidad, where we booked into the Trinidad Hilton. One of the many attractions we visited was the Asa Wright Nature Reserve, the Scarlet Ibis Sanctuary, the Caroni Swamp, the Wild Fowl Trust at Point-à-Pierre, the Emperor Valley Zoological Gardens and the annual flower show of the Trinidad and Tobago Horticultural Society.

Five days later, we flew to neighbouring Tobago. This was our third visit to Robinson Crusoe's island and we booked into the Blue Waters Inn, Speyside. We have visited many exotic locations around the world to see the flora and fauna but we have never seen so many varieties of birds in their natural habitat. The island boasts no fewer than nineteen different species of humming birds and there are hundreds of varieties of colourful butterflies and fascinating reefs swarming with tropical fish.

We experienced a number of tropical showers both in Trinidad and Tobago. During one of them, we were sitting in the lounge of our Tobago hotel when a very wet and bedraggled parrot walked through the door and very plainly said 'Good morning'. It turned out that he was a regular visitor to the hotel and was very friendly. Guests had taught him to say 'Good morning'.

One of the most beautiful spots on the island is Pigeon Point with a smooth warm sea and soft white sand. Other fine beaches include Store Bay where brown pelicans can be seen diving to catch fish; Man o' War Bay at the opposite end of the island and Mount Irvine and Bacolet Bays. Off the north-west corner of Tobago are a series of reefs, the most famous being Buccoo Reef. A continuous stream of glass-bottomed boats take passengers to the reef where multitudes of coral creatures can be seen among the colourful coral gardens. Away from the reef and almost out of sight of land is an area called the Nylon Pool, a small sandbank which is exposed at low tide. It is a queer sensation to stand in about three feet of water in what appears to be in the middle of the ocean.

At the other side of the island is Speyside where our hotel was located. Here is the Tobago Dive Experience, the centre for scuba diving and snorkelling and visits to the reef. It is also the departure point to Little Tobago Island, a nature reserve where Sir David Attenborough and his BBC Wildlife film crew filmed the magnificent frigatebirds, the yellow-billed tropic birds and the brown boobies.

The capital of Tobago is Scarborough, a town with many quaint houses which spill down from the hilltop to the waterside. Overshadowing the town is King George Fort, built in 1779 during the many struggles between the French and the English. Nearby is the small town of Plymouth with its tombstone inscriptions dating from 1700.

The population of the two islands is made up of British, Americans, Venezuelans, American Indians, East Indians, Chinese, Africans, Syrians and Lebanese, a truly mixed race! This has led to a varied cultural life; the diversity of which is reflected in costume, religion, architecture, music, dance and place names. The most popular pastime is 'liming' or talking for talking's sake, the subject uttermost above all others is cricket!

The main event of the year is the Trinidad and Tobago Carnival which takes place on the two days immediately preceding Ash Wednesday in Lent. The run-up starts immediately after Christmas when the Calypso Tents open and the Calypsonians perform their latest compositions and arrangements. During Carnival itself, normal life grinds to a halt and the whole of Trinidad and Tobago is absorbed in the festivities. A week before the Carnival proper is staged Panorama, a grand drum tournament when all the big steel bands parade and demonstrate their skill around the Savannah, the large park in the north of Port of Spain.

Tobago ranks among the top destinations among all our world-wide travels but we regret we are unlikely to go there again.

CHAPTER FIFTY-SEVEN

Beside the Sea

I do like to be beside the seaside,
I do like to be beside the sea...

Music Hall Song

O N THE 13 JUNE 1991, our first great-grandchild was born, a boy, to Rosalind's daughter Maria. He was named Shaun. This really made us feel we were no longer in our prime years! Now that we were no longer tied to producing the *Courier*, we turned our thoughts to semi-retiring on the coast. At first, we had thought of returning to Nottingham but Margaret's sister, Iris, said we would not like the city after living in Surrey. Nottingham had changed greatly since we left there in 1955 and not for the better.

As we had been invited to the Imperial Hotel, Torquay for their famous Summer Gastronomic Weekend, we decided to look around for a suitable property but found Torquay a bit too hilly. On our way back to Surrey, we stopped in Bournemouth and asked an estate agent to show us some apartments.

The first one we viewed was in Westbourne on the West Cliff Road, next to the Middle Chine. It was on the third floor of a three storey apartment block which consisted of twelve flats and a penthouse. It had a large lounge with a balcony overlooking a large communal garden, a

large dining room, a kitchen, three bedrooms and two bathrooms. This seemed to be the ideal residence, just the sort of place for which we were looking and although we visited several other flats, this was the best. We decided there and then to go ahead and purchase it and put our Bookham house up for sale.

After several would-be purchasers had viewed our house, it was eventually sold to a Mr and Mrs Walker. We had to reduce our asking price as we did not want to lose the Bournemouth property. Incidentally, ten years later, we hear that the Bookham house is on the market for double the price we sold it for!

Now began the task of moving. We had to dispose of some of my filing cabinets and photocopying machine and Rosalind had our garden tools and lawn mower. We also took a load of goods to a local car boot sale. Being novices at this game, no sooner had we driven our car on to the ground where the sale was taking place than we were surrounded by a horde of people anxious to relieve us of our goods. Only later did we discover that they were dealers who immediately put our goods up for sale on their own stalls at a higher price! We had over one hundred long-playing records and one man bought the lot. He said his brother was a disc jockey in Majorca and could use them.

We had several offers for our greenhouse but we turned them down because we said this went with the property. We later learned that Mr Walker sold it immediately he moved into the property! He turned out to be a very awkward customer.

On the day of removal, there were a few items which we could not get into the removal van or our car, so we asked him if we could leave them in the garage and my daughter would collect them. (We had two garages, so he could still use one for his car.) When Rosalind called for them, Mr Walker refused to release them, saying we had left a lot of rubbish and wanted £100 before he did so. The so-called rubbish turned out to be some shelving and cupboards we had left as fixtures in the garage. Our solicitor recommended we offer him £50 to close the matter.

Before we moved, we had one more press trip to undertake – a grand tour of Austria with Inghams. This we describe in our next chapter.

Meanwhile, Rosalind's divorce from Tony Simpkins was made absolute and on 14 September 1991, she married chef Andrew Ruddock at the Epsom Registry Office, with a reception afterwards at the Bookham Grange Hotel.

At last, our removal day arrived, Wednesday 25 September, and we finally made our way to the seaside, having been up all night doing the last-minute packing. We arrived in Bournemouth at 2.30 p.m. and our removal men completed unloading by 8.30. We were very tired and very hungry. We motored round the town centre but could not find a restaurant which was still open. Eventually, we were recommended to try Chez Fred's at 10 Seamoor Road, Westbourne. This is a prize-winning fish and chip establishment, run by father and son Peter and Fred Capel. It proved to be an excellent choice and we have used them many times since then.

We had only been in 'sunny Bournemouth' three days when the town had three inches of rain. This caused a landslide in the Middle Chine.

When we moved to Bournemouth, we anticipated a quiet, restful life but we soon discovered that retirement is for a younger person – there is so many things we wanted to do! We made frequent visits to London by train and by National Express coach and saw several West End shows.

Travel writing and familiarisation tours kept us busy and the *Courier* continued to publish our articles. Towards the end of the year, I was made part-time features editor of the *Independent Weekly Post*, a Bournemouth publication. I provided travel articles, hotel and restaurant write-ups, theatre reviews, senior citizen news and gardening notes (I was by-lined as 'Our Gardening Expert'!)

A General Election took place in April 1992, which was won by the Conservatives with 334 seats to Labour's 270, Liberal Democrats 22 and others 24. John Major became Prime Minister.

At the end of the month, we flew by Delta Airlines Tri-star to Miami and stayed a week in the Cavalier Hotel on Ocean Drive, Miami Beach. This was an area in which Art Deco had been revived on the front of hotels and other buildings. One of the best ways of seeing Miami and district is to take a round trip on the Old Trolley, a converted tram-car which passes all the principal attractions and enables you to get on and off at will.

A week later, we flew from Miami by British West Indies Airlines to St Kitts via Antigua. With its sister Caribbean island, Nevis, it became an independent state within the Commonwealth. A few weeks earlier, Diana, Princess of Wales had relaxed on the islands following her separation from Prince Charles. It was rather ironic that the capital of St Kitts should be called Charlestown. No doubt she had a smile on her face when she came upon the magnificent ruins of Fort Charles on Pelican Point, built in 1690 to defend the island from the French.

Christopher Columbus, on his second voyage of exploration to the New World in 1493, sighted the islands known to the Carib inhabitants as Liamuiga, meaning 'Fertile land' and Oualie meaning 'land of many waters'. He named the first island St Christopher and the second Nevis because the perpetually cloud-capped peak of Mount Nevis reminded him of the snow-capped Sierra de las Nieves in Spain. In the course of time, St Christopher gave way to the phonetically simpler St Kitts.

Nevis is only thirty-six square miles in area and has long stretches of golden sandy beaches, fringed with coconut palms. Princess Diana was photographed by the world's press on the southern tip of the island on Indian Castle Beach, a secluded spot hardly mentioned in the guide books. It is on the Atlantic coast where the royal party, which included Princes William and Harry, tried surfing the breakers.

The Princess's holiday residence was the lovely Montpelier Plantation Inn, one of the pleasantest places in the Caribbean. It is situated in sixty acres of lush grounds and at 650 ft elevation, has some spectacular views of the island. There are only sixteen guest rooms and these are housed in cottages spread throughout the grounds. We were priviledged to stay in one of these. In the main house is the Great Room lounge and bar, library and card room, drawing room, breakfast room and dining terrace. In the grounds is a large swimming pool, the surrounding walls of which are covered with colourful murals of the island, painted by Belinda Beaumont from Northumberland. The hotel is personally run by an English couple, James and Celia Milnes Gaskell, whose family have owned Montpelier since 1964. Their cuisine is excellent!

The inn has been built on the site of the Montpelier Great House where, on 11 March 1787, Captain Horatio Nelson, then commanding HMS *Boreas*, married a local lady, Frances Herbert Nisbet.

The waters around the two islands offer the snorkeller and scuba diver a wealth of experiences, viewing the colourful reefs and reef life and the numerous shipwrecks. One of the attractions on St Kitts is the rain forest.

Our stay in the islands was much too short. They must rank among the top holiday destinations for discerning pleasure-seekers who want an exotic location, a pleasant climate, warm hospitality and escape from everyday troubles.

Viscount Lord Admiral
Horatio Nelson.

CHAPTER FIFTY-EIGHT

Grand Tour of Austria

To the tent-royal of their emperor
Who, busied in his majesty, surveys
The singing masons building roofs of gold.

William Shakespeare,
King Henry V, Act 1, scene 2

A USTRIA IS A LAND OF CONTRASTS, of mountains and lakes, historic towns and cities and enchanting settings for both summer and winter holidays. Although it has been a republic since the Kaiser Karl was forced to give up the throne of the Austro-Hungarian Empire in 1918 at the end of the First World War, there are reminders and monuments throughout the country of the 645 year reign of the Hapsburgs. It was to follow the trail of the Hapsburg Dynasty that we set out on our grand tour of Austria in 1991.

One of the most popular Hapsburg monarchs was Maria Theresa (1740–80), daughter of Karl VI, who built magnificent palaces and carried out financial and administrative reforms. Her son, Josef II, continued this reorganisation. In 1806, Franz II renounced the title of Head of the Holy Roman Empire and adopted that of Emperor of Austria under the name Franz I.

Everywhere, you can still see portraits of Emperor Franz Josef (1848-1916), Europe's longest reigning monarch. We visited his tomb and that of Maria Theresa and other members of the Hapsburg dynasty in the Capuchin's Crypt in Vienna, where twelve emperors, sixteen empresses and more than 100 archdukes are buried.

Most tourists see only a small part of the country – Salzburg, Vienna, the Tyrol or the Carinthian Lakes. But our tour operator, Inghams, provided us with this grand tour lasting fifteen days. It started with a flight from Gatwick to Salzburg, the city of Mozart and *The Sound of Music*. The Salzack River divides the town into two. The Old City has an Italian flavour and many impressive baroque-style buildings, the work of Italian architects.

Dominating the city is the Hohensalzburg Fortress, dating back to the Middle Ages and the largest totally preserved fortress in central Europe.

Salzburg had for centuries been the residence of the Prince-Archbishops who were responsible for building the magnificent baroque cathedral (the Dom) and the Glockenspiel Tower from which the carillon of bells ring out on the hour during the day, as well as the palace and gardens of Mirabell. A must for devotees of Mozart is a visit to the Mozart Museum and No. 9 Getreidegasse where the composer was born.

Salzburg was the setting for the famous play and subsequent film *The Sound of Music* starring Julie Andrews. It was based on the story of Captain Georg von Trapp, his seven children and their governess. Various parts of the city were locations for the film including the summer house where I attempted to sing 'I am sixteen, going on seventeen', the Mirabell Castle, and outside Salzburg is the Salzkammergut holiday region where Julie Andrews comes prancing through the meadow singing 'The hills are alive with the sound of music'. In the village of Mondsee is the attractive church where the wedding scenes were filmed.

Salzburg's most famous shopping street is the Getreidegasse, a pedestrian only thoroughfare where most of the buildings and shops have retained their original seventeenth and eighteenth century façades and elaborately decorated wrought-iron business signs.

Prince Archbishop Markus Sittikus engaged an Italian architect to design his Hellbrunn Palace and Gardens. He was a practical joker and his Palace Water Gardens incorporate hidden water spouts and fountains which spasmodically spray visitors as they walk around the gardens.

After three days based in Salzburg, we left by luxury coach for the capital, Vienna, known throughout the world as the city of the waltz. The dance was introduced to Vienna by Josef Lanner and Johann Strauss senior about 1820 and reached its greatest popularity under his son Johann Strauss junior. *The Blue Danube* was composed for one of the carnival balls, to be followed by *The Artist's Life, Tales from the Vienna Woods* and the *Emperor Waltz*.

Other great musicians associated with Vienna include Haydn, Mozart, Beethoven, Schubert, Brahms, Bruckner, Mahler, Stolz and Kalman.

Vienna is a city of palaces and stately buildings, many of which were commissioned by the royal house of the Hapsburgs during the baroque period. Some of the most majestic are to be found in the Hofburg, a town within a town. It was the Imperial Palace and favourite residence of the Hapsburgs and was progressively enlarged over the centuries. Empress Maria Theresa's apartments are now used by the President of the Austrian Republic. Here, too, are tombs of the Hapsburgs.

Within the Hofburg is the Spanish Riding School where the white Lipizzaner stallions perform their haute école in the colonnaded white baroque-style hall. We found three days in Vienna was not long enough as there are so many places to visit.

Our tour then went into Styria, a province of forests, mountain chains and meandering valleys. Graz, its capital, is one of Europe's finest surviving mediaeval towns. The Landhaus, former seat of the Diet of Styria, is a remarkable Renaissance building built between 1557 and 1565.

Not far from Graz is the village of Piber, where the Lipizzaner horses are bred. When born, the foals are black or grey and they do not change to white until they are at least four years old and, sometimes, only when they reach the age of ten.

Carinthia was our next destination, Austria's southernmost province with its countless lakes, small attractive resorts and picturesque villages. The largest lake is the Worthersee. Legend has it that a dwarf drowned the land and its people because they ignored his warnings to forsake their wild revelries and immoral ways, thus forming the lake. There are about 1,270 lakes in the province, the heritage of the ice age. Some 200 of them are so pure that you can drink the water and in summer, you can bathe in them, the water temperature reaching 28 degrees centigrade.

The Worthersee is a popular holiday region with Portschach and Velden the top resorts. We enjoyed three days in Portschach with its colourful promenade of flowers, its lakeside walks and sporting facilities of all kinds. There are some 100 kms of marked paths through the hills and woods. Regular steamers ply across the lake to Maria Worth and to Klagenfurt, the business, administrative and cultural capital of Carinthia. Klagenfurt has an abundance of historic buildings and attractive courtyards dating from the Middle Ages.

Leaving the Carinthian Lakes, our journey took us eastwards through Villach to Lienz, a town just inside the Tyrol in the shadow of the Dolomites and the chief town in the Eastern Tyrol district. Then we turned north and re-entered Carinthia, following the River Moll to Hei-ligenblut, a fairly undiscovered part of Austria as far as British tourists are concerned. Our two-night stay here was at the delightful four-star Hotel Post.

Heiligenblut is situated at the foot of the snow-capped Grossglockner Mountain which rises to 3,798 metres. It is an area where nature holds sway with fast flowing mountain streams, meadows, fields of maize and rural countryside. Most outstanding are the beautiful displays of pink, red and mauve trailing ivy-leaf geraniums which cascade over every balcony and windowsill of houses, farms and restaurants.

The area is ideal for mountain walks but we were taken by coach along the Isel and Vergin valleys to Pragraten, where the road ends. We then had to revert to shanks's pony for the forty-five minute walk to the Umbal waterfalls.

After two days at Heiligenblut, we took the Hochalpenstrasse road up the mountains of the National Park. The road wound its way through

Alpine landscapes, climbing above the treeline. A stop was made at 8,000 ft at the Franz Josef Hohe, the highest point reached by the former Emperor, and here we climbed the 131 steps to view the Pasterzen Glacier extending six miles, above which towers the Grossglockner. We then followed the road down with its twenty-six hairpin bends until we emerged from a tunnel in the mountains into the Tyrol.

Our first stop in the Tyrol was at the winter sports resort of Kitzbuhel, then on to the resort of Seefeld, twice the venue for the Winter Olympic Games. Seefeld is an attractive small town with excellent skiing facilities, cable cars, chair lifts and sporting activities. Here, we took the funicular tram (Bergbahnen Roashutte) to the middle station from where we looked down on the town. Here, we had a choice of two cable cars – one to the top of Harmelekopf; the other to Jochbahn from where you can climb up to the Seefeld Joch with its spectacular views of glaciers and snowcapped peaks. Seefeld also has a small lake which freezes over in winter for skating.

The capitol of the Tyrol is the town of Innsbruck, host of the Winter Olympics in 1964 and 1978. The climb to the Olympic ski jump reveals how nightmarish this sport really is and can be of little comfort to the competitors to see the cemetery at the bottom of the run! The town has many connections with the Hapsburgs. Emperor Franz Stefan died here two days after the wedding of his son, Leopold. The triumphal arch commemorating the event depicts both joy and sorrow.

Empress Maria Theresa frequently stayed here at the Hofburg, her summer palace, which was built between 1553 and 1563 to house the tomb of Emperor Maximillian who died in 1519 but was, in fact, never placed in it. He was buried elsewhere as the townsfolk of Innsbruck decided they did not want the body of the emperor. The large marble sarcophagus is surrounded by twenty-eight more-than-life-size bronze statues of emperors, twenty busts of Roman emperors and twenty-three small bronzes of the Hapsburg family saints. Other attractions not to be missed are the Tyrolean Museum of Folk Art, the botanical gardens, the Alpine zoo and the Hungerburg cableway.

Our Austrian tour was drawing to a close and after a Tyrolean evening and a buggy ride, we left the Tyrol to complete our circuit back to Salzburg and the airport. On the way, we took a short cut through Bavaria, Germany, close to Hitler's mountain retreat at Bertchtesgaten.

CHAPTER FIFTY-NINE

A Golden Celebration

The world's great age begins anew.
The golden years return ...
Heaven smiles and faiths and empires gleam.

Percy Bysshe Shelley, 1792–1822, *Hellas, 1060*

O UR JOURNEYING continued throughout 1992 and included a cruise
aboard the new Royal Caribbean Cruise ship *Majesty of the Seas*,
calling at Playa del Carmen, Mexico, where we explored the Mayan Ruins
at Tulum on the Yucatan Peninsula; Cozumel, the Grand Cayman Islands,

Celebrating our Golden Wedding with daughter Rosalind, her husband
Andrew and grandson Matthew – 1993

Ocho Rios (Jamaica) and Coco Cay on Little Stirrup Cay in the Bahamas. The star artiste in the cabaret aboard the ship was Petula Clark.

We enjoyed another cruise later in the year aboard the *Victoria Cruiziana* along the River Rhine from Cologne to Strasbourg and then a coach tour of Switzerland from Basle to Berne, Interlaken, Lucerne and Brienz before returning to the boat and sailing back to Cologne with stops at Rudesheim, Heidelberg and the Mozelle Valley.

In contrast was a sail down the River Thames aboard the Dutch three-masted *Minerva* and then back to Bournemouth to cruise around the Isle of Wight and on to Lulworth Cove aboard the paddle steamer *Waverley*.

Every ten years, Holland stages the greatest flower show on earth, the 'Floriade' at Zoetermeer. Here are acre upon acre of floral displays and gardens, sights which must never be missed. We had a fantastic day there and intended to go again in 2002 but, regrettably, did not make it.

In September, I was invited to give a lecture in the Dorking Halls, Surrey on freelance journalism during the Mole Valley Arts Festival. A stay in a Welsh farmhouse in Upper Trewalkin, Talgarth in Pengenffordd, the home of Mrs Meudwin Stephens, whose delicious meals included the finest Welsh lamb; another night at Cliveden; a tour of Devon and Cornwall and a visit to Blenheim Palace, Woodstock, completed a very busy year of 'retirement'!

The year 1993 was a golden year for us, our Golden Wedding anniversary, which we celebrated on Saturday 19 June in the Oxshott Village Centre in Surrey. Among the guests were all members of our two families including Margaret's sister, Renée and her husband Ernest, who had come over from Australia for the occasion. In addition, my best man, Jim Lodge, and his wife Josie came down from Nottingham. Son-in-law Andrew, assisted by Rosalind and another chef, undertook the catering comprising a six-course buffet. For entertainment, we screened a sixty-minute video which we had put together from films and photographs which I had taken depicting our Golden Years.

Our actual anniversary day, 3 July, was celebrated aboard the *Cunard Princess* cruise ship, during which voyage we called at Katakolon, Alexandria, Israel, Cyprus, Bodrum (Turkey), Kos and Athens. From Alexandria, I went by coach to Cairo and visited the Pyramids and Sphinx at Giza and the Cairo Museum with exhibits from the tomb of Tutankhamun. Margaret did not accompany me on the Cairo tour – some passengers put her off and said it was too hot and too dangerous, which proved to be greatly exaggerated. However, she did make it on another cruise in 1996.

Besides our Golden Wedding, two other family events took place. On 25 April, Rosalind's son, Matthew, was christened at St John's Church, Merrow, Surrey and on 13 November, her daughter Maria and her partner

Margaret with her sisters in 1993
Left to right: Winnie, Iris, Florence, Margaret, Renée

Glenn made their union legal at the Epsom Registry Office. To end an eventful year, Margaret had a successful laser operation on her left eye.

1994 was another year of full activity and travel. My appointment as features editor for the *Independent Weekly Post* terminated with the company going bankrupt and owing me several months' fees, which I never recovered. However, a small parochial monthly, the *Canford Cliffs Independent* asked me to contribute entertainment and travel articles for them and shortly afterwards, I became features editor (freelance) for it and we renamed it the *Dorset Independent*.

Following the demise of the *Weekly Post*, the advertisement manager and several of the editorial staff, including myself, set up a new weekly paper called *Dorset on Sunday*. After the initial launch, the financial backer decided to pull out, thus the first issue of the paper became the last!

The year had begun with a flight to Gibraltar in the company of the former Conservative prime minister, the Right Honourable Sir Edward Heath for the start of the Europa Round the World Yacht Rally from Europa Point. Later, we were entertained at the Royal Gibraltar Yacht Club and occupied the VIP seats next to Sir Edward to watch the Three Kings Procession through the Main Street on Twelfth Night.

I made two visits to Belgium in March and May as guest of the Belgian

National Tourist Office. The first was to tour the Ardennes and the area of the Battle of the Bulge in the Second World War (December 1944). The May visit was to Parc Paradiso in Belgian's Hainaut province, a few miles from the historic city of Mons. It is a 130-acre development featuring ornithological, botanical and historic exhibits, the home to more than 2,500 birds from all over the world and contains 300-year-old trees, a ruined Cistercian abbey and a neo-classical château.

In between my Belgian trips, I made a two-day visit to the wonderful fairyland park Efteling in Holland. Margaret was not with me on this occasion but we both went there the following year, a description of which is given in the next chapter. I also made a solo visit to Amsterdam in August.

June took us to Euro-Disney at Marne La Vallée near Paris, staying at the Sequoia Lodge Hotel. One of the highlights was dinner at the Buffalo Bill's Wild West Show.

We embarked on our thirty-second cruise in July aboard the Fred Olsen *Black Prince*. This was a Midnight Sun cruise up the coast of Norway, visiting various ports including Bergen, Narvik, Stavanger and Kristiansand. On 13 July, we crossed the Arctic Circle with due ceremony and a visit from King Neptune and continued beyond up to Honningswag and the North Cape. Anticipating cold weather up north, we took warm clothing, only to find the temperature at the North Cape in the seventies and some ladies were sunbathing in bikinis. It did not get dark at night and I was able to read a newspaper on deck at two o'clock in the morning.

In February, Margaret's sister, Florence, was burgled during the night. The intruder cut out a pane of glass and entered the house in Radstock Road, Nottingham. She was asleep in bed but woke up and confronted him. She went for him but he punched her in the face and threatened her with a knife. He tied her hands and then escaped through the back door, taking very little with him. Florence managed to get free and went across the road to a neighbour. As a result of her ordeal, her church, the Bridgeway Hall Methodist, helped her financially and enabled her to move to a residential flat in the Meadows.

The fiftieth anniversary of D-Day, the Allies' invasion of Normandy, was celebrated throughout the country. We were on holiday in Newquay, Cornwall, and attended a D-Day service in the Wesleyan Methodist Church.

Margaret entered the Royal Bournemouth Hospital in October for an operation to replace her right knee as she was having great difficulty in walking and suffered pain from it. It was successful but for the next three months, she underwent physiotherapy and hydrotherapy at Christchurch Hospital.

Another great-grandchild arrived on 7 November to Maria, a boy she named Daniel.

A Golden Celebration

Christmas Eve fell on a Sunday this year and we had seen a notice outside Christ Church in Alumhurst Road, Westbourne, announcing a carol service. We decided to go and were most warmly welcomed by the church members and, after the service, coffee and mince pies were served. We had drifted away from the church since leaving Surrey and we felt that this was God calling us back into His service. Christ Church is an independent evangelical Church of England with very active membership and attracts people from other denominations. Taking active part in the services are former Plymouth Brethren, Salvationists, Methodists and the retired Baptist Minister from the Westbourne Baptist Church, the Reverend Michael Ridgeon. There are very few empty seats at Sunday morning services.

In the following years, we have become more and more involved in the church activities. Margaret is on the flower arranging rota, I am responsible for the outside noticeboard and posters and we are both members of the Welcome Team.

Roy and Margaret cut their Golden Wedding Cake

CHAPTER SIXTY

The World of Efteling

*When the first baby laughed for the first time, the laugh broke
into a thousand pieces and they all went skipping about and that
was the beginning of fairies.*

Sir James Matthew Barrie,
1860–1937, *Peter Pan*, Act 1

EVERYBODY AT SOME TIME in their life believes in fairies. As children,
we all enjoyed fairy tales. We went to the pantomime and cheered
the fairy queen and booed the demon king. English gardens have gnomes,
at Christmas we have fairy lights and even in the kitchen, many housewives
use Fairy Liquid!

Situated in south Holland and an hour-and-a-half drive from the ferry
port of Vlissingen in the town of Kaatsheuvel is Efteling, a theme park
for all ages. It is indeed a wonderland, a fairyland, and has been awarded
a Golden Apple, Europe's premier award for tourism and recreation and
an international jury unanimously crowned Efteling with the Applause
Award which is given to the best amusement parks in the world.

Margaret was still undergoing hydrotherapy treatment for the first few
months of 1995 but by the end of May, she was able to walk with her
new knee without pain or discomfort. This enabled us to undertake a
river cruise aboard the *Rhine Princess* from Holland, through Germany to
Switzerland.

Last year, I paid a brief visit to Efteling and was so impressed that I
was determined to go again, this time with Margaret. I contacted the
Automobile Association's Overseas Route Service to prepare an itinerary
for me and we drove our car to the Channel Tunnel terminus near
Folkestone and, with no fuss or trouble, drove on to Le Shuttle. The
train journey through the tunnel under the English Channel takes only
thrity-five minutes and is so smooth and quiet that you hardly realise you
are moving at all. We just had time to get out of the car and go to the
toilet before we emerged into daylight in Calais. We were waived through
customs and Passport Control and we were on our way.

Our journey to Efteling was practically motorway all the way via Dunkirk,

Bruges, Ghent, Antwerp, Breda and Tilburg, a total of 190 miles. Hard to believe is the fact that we did not come upon any roadworks whatsoever on the entire journey, something we could not have done if travelling in Britain.

There is so much to see and do in Efteling and the park is so large you need at least a full day to enjoy it. A night at the Efteling Kaatsheuvel Hotel next to the north entrance to the park is recommended. A three-star hotel, it could have come straight from fairyland with its four towers and a moat. It has 121 rooms, all with en suite facilities and every room has a fairy-tale mural in it. Ten of the rooms are really different from the rest. They are themed rooms, designed and decorated in various styles. For example, the 1950s Room is decorated with memorabilia from the period and the bed takes the form of a 1952 Chevrolet Bel Air. The room even has a jukebox and there are pictures of teddy boys and girls in petticoat dresses. There is a Sleeping Beauty and a Hansel and Gretel suite; you can imagine yourself as a sheik in the Fata Morgana suite or a big-top performer in the Circus Room, designed as a caravan. In the Golfer's Room is a miniature putting green and the John Pemberton Room, named after the man who first brewed Coca-cola, there are drink dispensers and the two double beds are separated by an illuminated partition made from hundreds of empty Coca-cola bottles.

Dining in the hotel is a treat not to be missed. It is more like a picture gallery with paintings by famous artists adorning the walls and the room is lit by glittering chandeliers. A herald announces that dinner is served. Children have a surprise awaiting them at dinner time. When it comes to the dessert course, the waitress invites them to come into the kitchen where they are provided with a chef's hat, given a dish and allowed to create their own sweet from tubs of ice cream, sweet decorations, cherries, etc. Proudly, they return to their table wearing their chef's hat and display their own special dessert.

Efteling is first and foremost a world of fantasy and enchantment with attractions such as the Fairyland Forest where Hansel and Gretel, the Sleeping Beauty and Little Red Riding Hood are to be found among the forty or more life-size animated fairytale characters. The Village of the Laafs is sheer delight where these comical characters can be seen in the bakery kneeding the dough, the patriarchal mother with her house full of babies, the distillery and the schoolroom.

The Haunted Castle is one of the largest in Europe and Fata Morgana boat ride through the mystical East is similar to Disney's 'Pirates of the Caribbean'. Joki's Carnival Festival is a round-the-world tour of colourful national characters dancing and singing as you ride past, and not to be missed is the Dream Flight through Fairyland.

Efteling is open from spring to autumn. The attractions we have

The christening of our third great grandchild, Charlotte Narey,
with brothers Daniel and Shaun and cousins Isabella and Matthew and
parents Glenn and Maria and Rosalind and Andrew Ruddock in 1997

described were those in operation when we were there in 1995 and I
expect they have been updated and new ones added.

We visited another theme park in August, Port Aventura in Spain on
the Costa Dorada, near Salou. We were on our thirty-fourth cruise aboard
the *Black Prince*. On our return voyage through the Bay of Biscay, we
encountered a Force 9–10 gale with very rough sea. When we were ready
to sail from Gibraltar, one passenger, a lady, was missing. The captain
delayed our departure while they tried to locate her but eventually, her
baggage and belongings were put ashore and we sailed without her. Perhaps
she had an inkling of the rough passage ahead. Eventually, she was traced
and flew home.

Family affairs were a mixture of good and not so good news. In March,
1995 Jill Cave's murderer was found guilty and sentenced to imprisonment
in Australia. In August, Sean and Daniel Narey, our great-grandchildren
were christened in St Mary's Church, Leatherhead and on 12 October,
our fifth grandchild, Isabella, was born to our daughter, Rosalind and her
husband Andrew. The news concerning our niece, Hazel, daughter of my

sister Eileen and husband Eric was not so encouraging. She had been diagnosed as having breast cancer and underwent two operations at the end of the year.

A very eventful year ended with a Turkey and Tinsel week at Warner's Norton Grange Village in Yarmouth, Isle of Wight.

Efteling Hotel.

CHAPTER SIXTY-ONE

An Escape to Prague

Prague ... the most precious stone in the stone crown of the world.

Johann Wolfgang von Goëthe, 1749–1832

IN 1944, FELLOW TRAVEL WRITER Christopher Portway escaped from a German prisoner-of-war camp in Poland and was befriended by a Czech family on a farm in Czechoslovakia. He fell in love with the farmer's daughter, Anna, and for many years after the war, he made repeated and hazardous crossings of the Iron Curtain in search of her and to bring her back to England and to marry her. His persistent illegal entries into the country without a visa or papers and fleeting meetings with Anna often ended in arrest and imprisonment. Eventually, he succeeded in his quest and Christopher and Anna were married in England in 1952 and now live in Brighton. He tells his fascinating love story in a book entitled *Czechmate*, published by John Murray.

In a subsequent book entitled *Pedal for your Life*, published by Lutterworth Press, Christopher gives further details of his encounters in Czechoslovakia and a bicycle journey from the Baltic to the Black Sea. I strongly recommend you get a copy.

Czechoslovakia is now split into the Czech Republic and Slovakia and they are no longer ruled by the communists. Christopher makes frequent trips to the Czech Republic and he told us how exciting a country it is, so in the spring of 1996, we decided to take a City Escapades weekend in Prague, the Czech capital and see for ourselves.

This was our fifth year in Bournemouth and we were still very active. Margaret continued with her physiotherapy for her replaced knee and was taking water tablets to keep down her blood pressure. On 3 March Rosalind's fifth child, Isabella, was christened in Brockham Parish Church in Surrey.

The year had begun with a wonderful concert by the Bournemouth Symphony Orchestra entitled 'The Magic of Vienna'. Later in the year, we enjoyed 'Friday Night is Music Night' in the Winter Gardens with the BBC Concert Orchestra and, just before Christmas, Ron Goodwin conducted the Bournemouth Symphony Orchestra in his annual Christmas Concert

A visit to Leeds in February enabled us to preview the new Royal Armouries Museum and to see the city's spectacular Tropical World.

We flew with British Airways on a scheduled flight for our weekend in Prague. The journey took ninety minutes in a Boeing 757. As we arrived, Prague was enjoying a heatwave with temperatures in the eighties.

The city escaped destruction in the Second World War and the architecture of almost every building is a work of art. You literally walk along the streets with your head in the air to admire the buildings but at the same time, you must keep looking down as many of the pavements are uneven and in need of repair. It is a city of spires, steeples, dramatic façades and winding cobbled streets. Six hundred years of classical architecture is on display, ranging from Gothic and Baroque to Renaissance and Art Nouveau.

Dominating the city since the ninth century is the castle and is a 'must' for every visitor. You need at least half a day to see everything within the castle precincts, from its giants guarding the western gateway, the Holy Cross Chapel in the second courtyard, the Old Royal Palace and the Castle Picture Gallery to the biggest enclave of all, the third courtyard in which stands the majestic Cathedral of St Vitus. Finally, there is the Golden Lane, a narrow cul-de-sac of tiny, pastel-coloured houses built into the ramparts and originally occupied by archers defending the castle.

Other sights not to be missed include the Sternberg Palace, St George's Basilica and Convent, St Nicholas' Church, the Wallenstein Palace, the National Theatre, the Charles IV Bridge, guarded at both ends by towers, the former Jewish ghetto district, the Old Town Square with its astronomical clock and Good King Wenceslas Square with his statue still looking out. The 'Square' is not a square but a 700-metre long boulevard, with the king mounted on his spritely steed.

Wining and dining offers the visitor a wide choice of venues with Czech and Slovak cuisine, International fare and exotic eating, plus pubs, bars and cafés. We chose to combine sight-seeing and entertainment with our meals and on the first evening, we took a dinner cruise along the River Vitava. For our second night, we went along to the Hotel Ariston for a Bohemian party. This turned out to be a ninety-minute spectacular revue, featuring ballet, folklore, music, dancing and the famous Prague Black Theatre. A three-course dinner was served before the performance and dancing followed the show. Altogether, an excellent combination.

On our return, we watched the first flight into Bournemouth International Airport by Concorde to mark the extension of the airport's runway. Since then, a number of flights have been made from Bournemouth by

Concorde to various destinations. We have not flown in Concorde but we have had a meal aboard whilst it was on the ground at Heathrow.

After tours of East Anglia and of Somerset and Avon with Epsom Coaches, we were invited to a press visit to the trial grounds of Dobie's and Sutton Seeds near Paignton. Prior to setting off to Devon, Margaret had a 9.00 a.m. appointment at the Royal Bournemouth Hospital for a routine check-up. I waited in reception for her and an hour later, a nurse called me and told me to go and see the doctor. He told me that Margaret had blood clots on her lungs and must be admitted at once as an in-patient. Devon was out as far as we were concerned and Margaret remained in hospital for seven days. Fortunately, they were able to relieve the situation and she was declared fit for our next press trip which was a 'Steaming Break' in Yorkshire, taking in the National Railway Museum in York, the Moors Railway, the Embsay Steam Railway and the Keighley and Worth Valley Railway.

For senior citizens, steam locomotives are among their cherished memories of years gone by. We have forgotten the smoke and grime associated with steam trains, only remembering the mighty monsters which took us to work or on our holidays.

We remember famous engines of the Merchant Navy and Battle of Britain classes, the famous LNER *Mallard* (No.4468) which holds the world speed record for steam traction at 126 miles per hour, made on 3 July 1938, and other locomotives like *Sir Nigel Gresley, City of Truro, Silver Link* and *Coronation Scot.* Gone are those prestige trains such as the *Flying Scotsman, Golden Arrow, Cornish Riviera, Cheltenham Flyer*, the *Bournemouth, Brighton* and *Devon Belles*, and the *Yorkshire Pullman* to name just a few.

The infamous Doctor Richard Beeching axed over 2,000 stations and many lines throughout the country in the 1960s. Today, many of those branch lines have been reopened by railway preservation societies and operated by enthusiastic volunteers. Old steam locomotives have been lovingly restored and put back into service to provide the public the opportunity to once more experience steam travel. In the South, we have the Watercress Line in Hampshire, the Swanage Railway in Dorset (the line has now been extended and linked up with the main railway at Wareham), the South Devon Railway, the Paignton & Dartmouth Steam Railway and the East and West Somerset Railway. Steam trains are also running on the Isle of Wight.

Yorkshire has a number of these privately-run railways and it were these we travelled on during our 'Steaming Weekend'.

With so many worldly pursuits, we had let our Christian devotions slide, but God in His mercy had not abandoned us. As mentioned already, He drew our attention to the Carol Service on Christmas Eve 1995, after which we were led to become regular attenders of Christ Church in Westbourne. We went to the morning service and communion on 25 February and the vicar, the Rev. Brian Ruff, invited us to attend a 'Way-In' introduction course at the Vicarage. It had dawned on us that, if either of us had died before then, we would have had no church in which to hold a service or a minister to conduct it.

There were four other couples attending the course and it proved to be most uplifting and from then onwards, we became fully involved in the activities of the church. (Incidentally, the home-made cakes of the vicar's wife, Judith, were mouth-watering!)

The year 1997 was full of activities, surprises and problems. The Grand National steeplechase at Aintree was cancelled because of an IRA bomb alert; the Labour Party won a large majority in the General Election and Tony Blair became Prime Minister and in March, we had a good sighting of the Comet Hale-Bopp.

On 31 August, Diana, Princess of Wales, was killed in a car crash in Paris. We were on a short cruise from Southampton to Le Havre aboard the Norwegian Cruise Line's SS *Norway* when the news came over the public address system. On arrival in Le Havre, we were besieged by French journalists who wanted to know our reactions to the news.

Margaret was still experiencing breathing problems and attended the hospital for check-ups. She also had a tear duct problem and received drops for her eyes. In September, having seen her doctor for thrombosis, she was admitted to the Royal Bournemouth Hospital for treatment and remained a patient for seven days. After the blood clots had gone down, she was allowed home, although her breathing was not that good and she was back on steroids and warfarin.

In November, she found a lump on her ear lobe which was operated on in Poole Hospital. The problem recurred the following year and she had another operation which removed it. When asked what was the growth, the surgeon said it was Chrondrodermatitis Nodularis Helicis or 'taxi driver's ear'. The surgeon was even able to spell it!

Our niece, Hazel, had a recurrence of her cancer and she died in Salisbury Hospital on 27 July at the age of forty-nine. Eileen and Eric were devasted at their loss. The previous year, they had celebrated their Golden Wedding. Regrettably, we were unable to attend as we were abroad, neither were we present when they got married in 1946 as Margaret was giving birth at the time.

Maria's daughter Charlotte was born on 19 June and we attended her blessing in Brockham Parish Church, Surrey. In November, Rosalind, Andrew and family left Dorking and moved into a house in Littlehampton, West Sussex.

Church activities now took up quite a bit of our time. In March, the

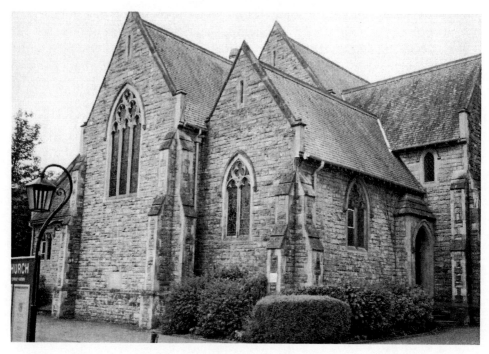

Christ Church, Westbourne, Bournemouth where we worship each
Sunday *(Photograph by Roy Sharp)*

West Cliff Council of Churches staged the Roger Jones musical *From
Pharaoh to Freedom*, the dramatic story of the Jewish Passover and the
escape from Egypt by the Children of Israel. It was staged in our church
and the large cast of singers, musicians, actors and dancers came from all
the Westbourne churches. I was responsible for the posters and handbills
and general publicity.

Every two years, Christ Church holds a church family weekend. In 1997,
and again in 1999 and 2001, it was held in Sidmouth, south Devon and we
all stayed at the Methodist hotel 'Sidholme'. The weekend programme
included Bible studies, talks, entertainments and games, as well as visits to
local beauty spots and attractions. It is due to be repeated in May, 2003.

'Sidholme', in the Elysian Fields, is a gracious Victorian mansion beside
the River Sid. It was originally built for the sixth Earl of Buckinghamshire
in 1826.

A wealthy banker, Benjamin Davidson, bought the Lodge in 1876 and
eight years later, it was renamed 'Sidholme'. It opened as a Christian
guest house for young Methodists in 1931. It is a Grade II listed building
of special historic and architectural interest.

After our weekend in Sidmouth, we continued south to Torquay and
went on the trail of one of Devon's most famous citizens, the mystery

crime writer Dame Agatha Christie. No fewer than fifteen of her novels have specific connections with the area and there are some fifty sites which can be explored by visitors to the district that played an important part in her life and work.

The English Riviera Tourist Board and South Hams Tourism have devised four trails which one can follow, ranging from the Agatha Christie Mile in Torquay to a romantic steam train and river boat tour.

These four trails are described in a book entitled *Exploring Agatha Christie Country* and is available, together with information on where to stay, from the English Riviera Tourist Board, The Tourist Centre, Vaughan Parade, Torquay, South Devon, TQ2 5JG, Telephone: 01803 296296.

Among the celebrities interviewed by Roy were Stan Laurel and Oliver Hardy and film star Diana Dors.

CHAPTER SIXTY-TWO

Exploring Burns' Country

*O ye'll tak' the high road and I'll tak' the low road
and I'll be in Scotland afore ye.*

The Bonnie Banks of Loch Lomond,
Famous Scottish song

IT MAKES A VERY PLEASANT CHANGE to have someone else in the driving seat when on holiday. In 1997, we decided we would like to tour the West Highlands and Burns' Country but did not fancy motoring all the way to Scotland from Bournemouth.

We looked at various coach firm's brochures and decided the one from Shearings Holidays looked the most promising, especially as they have won the travel industry's major awards for the last three years.

Shearings is the largest coach holiday operators in Europe, carrying over 450,000 holidaymakers throughout the United Kingdom, as well as abroad. It is also one of the UK's top ten hotel groups with thirty-eight establishments from the south coast to the Scottish Highlands, trading as Coast & Country Hotels. We understand that this subsidiary has now changed its name to Shearings Hotels.

Shearings was created from the merger of three companies and its history dates back to 1903 when it began as Smith's Happiways. Eight years later, William Shearing founded Shearings in Oldham. Smith's Happiways and Shearings amalgamated in 1987 and merged with National Holidays in 1989, creating Shearings Holidays.

What pleased us was the convenient picking-up point, Bournemouth's Interchange coach station, from where the feeder coach took us to the Scratchwood services on the M1 where we transferred to our Scottish touring coach. We have never seen so many coaches belonging to one company assembled in one place – the whole of the coach park seemed to be occupied by Shearings, ready to depart for tours throughout the country.

Our journey to Scotland had two rest stops, the first at Exhall, near Coventry, and at Gretna Green. The latter is famous as the place where runaway couples from England used to come to get married. The ceremony would be carried out by the blacksmith at his anvil in accordance with eighteenth century Scots' law by means of a declaration before witnesses.

In 1856 an Act was passed requiring the couple to reside north of the border for three weeks before the marriage could take place. Today, Gretna Green is a tourist attraction with shops, restaurants, a pub, museum and, of course, the smithy.

Our base for our holiday was the Glenmorag Hotel in Dunoon, which is one of the Shearing hotels. The company has invested heavily in the development and refurbishments of all their hotels, spending over £8 million in 1996.

All the bedrooms in our hotel had private facilities and we enjoyed excellent Scottish breakfasts and three-course dinners with a choice of menu each night. A gala dinner was provided at the hotel on one evening which, of course, included Scotch salmon and haggis.

Three full day excursions were included in the cost of the holiday. The first took us across the Kyles of Bute and the ferry to the Isles of Bute and Rothesay.

Our second excursion headed across the Clyde to follow the Ayrshire coast to Ayr and Alloway, in the heart of Burns' Country.

Our third inclusive tour took us over the 'Rest and be thankful' Pass and past Arrochar at the northern end of the long and narrow Loch Long to the famous Loch Lomond, the 'Queen of the Scottish Lakes', and the exceptionally pretty village of Luss, at the mouth of Glen Luss on the Loch's western shore.

In 1998, we took another Shearings' tour, this time to the Highlands of Scotland. On the way, we broke our journey north at the Shap Wells Hotel, near Penrith, Cumbria. The next day, we continued our journey to Gairloch, on the Wester Ross coast, opposite the Isle of Skye. Our base for the next three days was the Gairloch Hotel, another Shearings' Coast & Country establishment. During our stay here, we visited the Beinn Eighe Nature Reserve, the picturesque village of Shieldaig, the superb Inverewe Gardens and the Glens of Carron and Docherty.

From Gairloch, our journey took us farther north into the Highlands, with stops at Corrieshalloch Gorge, the fishing port of Ullapool and the Shin Falls, finally arriving at Dornoch on the Dornoch Firth on the east coast. This was another Shearings' hotel with similar standards and cuisine as at Gairloch. Trips from Dornoch included a day in Inverness and a tour of the Black Isle, a visit to the Caithness Glass factory, Thurso and the ultimate destination, John O'Groats. Our return journey south took us through Pitlochy and Perth with an overnight stop in Middlesbrough.

CHAPTER SIXTY-THREE

A Taste of Scandinavia

Come: and strong within us
Stir the Viking's blood.

Charles Kingsley, 1819–75,
Westward Ho (1855)

BRITAIN HAS BEEN INVADED many times in the course of history but among the earliest raiders were the Vikings, the Saxons and the Danes and they have left their mark in York and other parts of the country. Now it is our turn to 'invade' their territories and short breaks to their capitals – Oslo, Stockholm and Copenhagen – can be an enjoyable and rewarding experience.

The Norwegian capital Oslo claims to be the Viking capital with more than fifty unique museums, plus numerous art galleries. Among these are two very contrasting attractions – the Viking Ship Museum and the Kon-Tiki/Ra Museum.

The former houses three recovered Viking ships, together with small boats, richly-carved sledges and wagons, textiles, harnesses, tools and kitchen utensils which have been discovered in Viking burial grounds.

The vessels from the Thor Heyerdahl expeditions are on display at the Kon-Tiki Museum, including the original Kon-Tiki balsa wood raft on which Thor and five companions crossed the Pacific Ocean from Peru to the Tuamotu Islands near Tahiti in 1947. Also on display are some of the mysterious stone statues from Easter Island.

Other museums include the Norwegian Folk Museum, the National Gallery and the Ski Museum, adjoining the terrifying Olympic Ski Jump.

The Vigeland Sculpture Park is one of the biggest outdoor displays of statues, the creations of Gustav Vigeland and comprising of hundreds of nude figures.

The best way to see the attractions of Oslo is to take one of the sightseeing tours by coach and boat. Very useful is the Viking Card. Costing approximately £12, it gives you a day's free transport on the underground, trams, buses, suburban trains and ferries within the city boundaries, free admission to most museums and attractions, a free mini sightseeing cruise and discounts in restaurants.

Stockholm

Stockholm, capital of Sweden, is called 'Beauty on Water' with magnificent buildings, clean safe streets and large areas of undisturbed woodlands, meadowland and the sea. It is a city comprising of fourteen islands and, in 1998, it was Europe's cultural capital.

Portsmouth has the remains of the *Mary Rose* but this is nothing compared to the splendid battleship *Vasa*, salvaged after it had sunk 333 years previously and over ninety per cent intact. Now completely restored, its splendour is indeed breathtaking.

You can take a guided tour of Stockholm by boat, bus, on foot or a combination of all three which we did. The sightseeing walking tour through the Old Town's narrow, winding streets and vaults was like stepping back into the Middle Ages.

Copenhagen

What can we say about 'Wonderful, wonderful Copenhagen' except wonderful? There is so much to see and a grand coach tour from the City Hall Square is an ideal introduction to the capital. On this tour, we visited the Royal Palace, the Nyhavn, Christiansborg Palace where Parliament meets, the Carlsberg Glyptotek, the Tivoli Gardens and the Little Mermaid statue, sitting on her rock at the water's edge, inspired by Hans Christian Andersen. Nearby is the Gefion Fountain, depicting the legend of the Nordic goddess who turned her four sons into oxen to plough the island of Zealand out of Sweden.

Opposite the City Hall are the famous Tivoli Gardens, a vast amusement park with dozens of restaurants, live shows and beautiful gardens, which are lavishly illuminated at night. Part of our walking tour took us along Stroget, Europe's longest pedestrianised street, 1.2 kilometres in length, a shoppers' paradise.

Tallinn, Estonia

This was our first visit to Estonia, known as the Baltic city with a difference. Our tour commenced with a drive round the old town of Tallinn, the mediaeval capital with its ancient walls. Then our coach took us into the Upper Town, Toompea or Cathedral Hill, where we commenced our walking tour. We visited the Russian Orthodox Church, inaugurated in 1900, the thirteenth century gothic-style Dome Cathedral and viewed the castle, now the seat of the Estonian Parliament.

Helsinki, Finland

Known as the Daughter of the Baltic and the White City of the North, our tour of the Finnish capital took in the Uspenki Cathedral; the ice breakers moored up for the summer; Senate Square with its Lutheran Cathedral and along the Esplanade shopping street until we came to Mannerheim Street, in which is located Parliament House, the National Museum and the concert and convention centre, Finlandia Hall.

Our next sight was the Olympic Stadium where the 1952 Olympic Games were held. This was followed by the new Opera House, completed in 1993 and then the unique Temppeliaukio Rock Church which was blasted out of solid rock. In Sibelius Park, we saw the famous monuments comprising 527 steel pipes dedicated to the great composer Jean Sibelius.

Leaving the city, we followed the coastal road to Porvoo, the second oldest town in Finland, dating back to 1346, where we had lunch before wandering round the town and looking at the mediaeval Cathedral before returning to our ship.

Berlin

We had wanted to visit Germany's capital for a long time but now we had the opportunity. *Black Watch* anchored in Warnemunde, a thirty-minute drive to Rostock. We boarded a coach which took us on the three-hour drive to Berlin. The countryside contains hundreds of lakes surrounded by flat land, formed by the last ice age. Reaching the capital, we were then taken on a sightseeing tour of Berlin's main highlights, including the Olympic Stadium, Charlottenburg Castle, Tiergaarten Park, the Victory Column, Bellevue Palace, the Reichstag and the Brandenburg Gate.

After lunch, we entered the former Eastern Zone along the Unter den Linden boulevard and Checkpoint Charlie. We saw the remains of the Berlin Wall and obtained a piece as a souvenir. The remaining section of the wall has become an art gallery with paintings depicting the trauma of the years 1961 to 1989.

The final leg of our cruise was through the Kiel Canal.

CHAPTER SIXTY-FOUR

Emerald Celebrations

Brightly dawns our wedding day,
Joyous hour, we give thee greeting.

Sir William S. Gilbert, 1836–1911,
The Mikado, Act Two

THE YEAR 1998 was a special one for us. It marked fifty-five years of married bliss. We have had our problems and troubles over the years but our love has never waivered, no quarrel or disagreement has lasted more than a few minutes and the secret of our happy married life lies in the fact that we are both Christians, that our faith and trust in God and His Son, Jesus Christ, who through His death on the Cross and Resurrection, we have been saved and promised Eternal Life; and that we have shared everything together – what is mine is Margaret's and what is Margaret's is mine.

The year started with two spectacular shows. The first was the Canadian Le Cirque du Soleil, a completely new conception of circus, in the Royal Albert Hall, and a wonderful new stage production of Walt Disney's *Beauty and the Beast* at the Dominion Theatre.

We also tried a Saga holiday in Majorca, staying in Cala d'Or, an enjoyable break and not too hot.

To celebrate our Emerald Wedding, we had a family thanksgiving service in our church in Westbourne, followed by an excellent luncheon in the church hall with Eileen and Eric, Rosalind and family and the vicar and his wife, Brian and Judith Ruff.

The next day, as part of our celebrations, we motored to East Anglia, stopping on the way at the National Rose Society Gardens in St Albans and an overnight stay at the famous Smoke House Inn, Mildenhall. We took the opportunity of calling on my cousin, Charles Sharp at Burwell, Cambridgeshire, whom I had not see since we were teenagers. Our destination was Warner's Holiday Village at Gunton Hall, Lowestoft, a most enjoyable stay; good value, good activities and entertainments and excellent meals. This is an adults-only holiday and to our surprise, the management presented Margaret with a huge bunch of flowers for our anniversary.

Whilst at Warner's, we had a two-hour cruise on the River Waverney and Oulton Broads; toured the Suffolk Wildlife Park at Kessingland; took a brief look at Great Yarmouth (not a patch on Bournemouth!); spent half a day at the Pleasurewood Hills Theme Park and made a tour of Somerleyton House and Gardens.

The date of our anniversary was, actually, on 3 July and this we spent at the University Arms Hotel, Cambridge, where we had a celebration dinner and another bouquet. The next day, we transferred to the Moat House Garden House Hotel overlooking the River Granta and the Backs of the colleges. The last time we stayed here, in 1972, the hotel burnt down just after we left! It did not happen again this time!

Whilst in Cambridge, we called upon another cousin, Dorreen Felts, in Cherry Hinton Road, whom we had not seen since schooldays; and an old school chum, Ron Elborn, who had also served with me in the Royal Air Force during the war in Gibraltar. We were sorry to see he was confined to a wheelchair through arthritis. Both passed away in 2002.

We attended morning service at my old church, St Paul's, which had been completely altered inside and refurnished. The balcony had been converted into a recreation room, and in the nave the congregation now faces west instead of east. Here, we met my second cousin, Lucy Cornwall (we knew her as Lizzie). Her mother was the sister of my grandmother. She celebrated her 100th birthday in April 2002. She still seemed very active and alert in her advancing years.

As a boy, one of my special treats was sticky Chelsea Buns from Hawkins, the Cambridge confectioners and caterers. These were *real* Chelsea Buns, oozing with syrup, not the sugary rounds of dough you find in most places these days. But there is one firm that does still make real, sticky buns, Fitzbillies in 52 Trumpington Street, Cambridge. Established in the early 1920s by the Mason brothers, it soon became famous for its Chelsea Buns and dons, undergraduates and townsfolk daily joined the long queues for them. The bun consists of six tightly rolled, overlapping ribbons of dough, permeated with butter, brown sugar, treacle and currants. Subsequent owners (there have been only three) have guarded the secret recipes and the present owner, Mrs Penny Thomson, has kept the tradition going. Only Hawkins, which no longer exists, have rivalled this delicious product.

I do not know whether we carry a jinx around with us but a short time after our visit, Fitzbillies was burnt down. But that was not the end of the story. The firm moved to temporary premises and now a new restaurant and bakery has been erected on the old site. Our home group leader, the Rev. Michael Ridgeon, who is still a director of the builders' merchants in Cambridge, attends board meetings in the city and often brings back some Chelsea buns for us.

For years, I have been searching for the unique Cambridge Cream Cheese which we used to enjoy pre-war. We were told by many authorities that it was no longer in production. But at last, we found someone who is still making this delicacy, though regrettably, not on a commercial basis. She is Eleanor Gale of Beck Farm, Histon, in Cambridgeshire. Mrs Gale sent us some of this cheese to try but it was delayed in the post and was not in a perfect condition when we received it. However, it was very similar to the pre-war version which was made from cow's milk, whereas Eleanor uses goat's milk. The distinctive feature of this white cheese is the yellow, creamy streaks running in layers through the product. The original was sold on its own small straw mat but hygiene regulations do not allow today's product to be so presented.

Cambridge Cheese is made from a very old recipe and was mostly produced at Sutton, near Ely by Baden Powell and his brother after the First World War and was continued by the family until the outbreak of World War II. The product is neither leathery as some cheeses nor in 'pinheads' like today's cottage cheese. Another cheese no longer available but still made by Mrs Gale is Cottenham Cheese, last made on a commercial scale about a hundred years ago. Made from the same recipe as the Cambridge Cheese, it was then pressed and wrapped to give a finer cheese with good keeping qualities.

Mrs Gale has a flock of sixteen British Saanen goats which provide both milk and meat, as well as chickens and ducks, and she and her husband, Bob, also breed and show Appaloosa horses which have a spotted coat and originated in North America. Besides her Cambridge and Cottenham cheeses, Eleanor also makes her own curd and cottage cheese and, occasionally, mozzarella.

1999 did not give us much time to put up our feet and rest, in spite of Margaret's asthma and glaucoma. At the end of April 1999, we embarked on yet another cruise on the *Black Watch*. But this time, we were not only passengers as I was also engaged as a lecturer. I gave four lectures on board as we cruised around the Mediterranean. Illustrated with slides, they were on Gibraltar at peace and war; the Mediterranean and its place in history; 'In search of Robin Hood' and Royal Occasions. The last named included historic footage from British Movietone newsreels which I had selected and made up into a video.

My search for Robin Hood began in the city of Nottingham and the award-winning attraction 'The Tales of Robin Hood', which is situated on Maid Marion Way. It consists of a vehicular ride through mediaeval England and into Sherwood Forest, narrowly escaping the Sheriff's men as you watch the tales unfold. The scenes have been recreated in three dimensions with sight, sound and smell. The next stop is Nottingham Castle, the former home of the Sheriff. The original castle was destroyed after the Civil War in the seventeenth century and rebuilt as a fine ducal mansion. Below the castle are the dungeons and Mortimer's Hole, a unique system of caves which run under the castle to various parts of the city and to Sherwood.

We continued our search by taking the A146 road out of the city and headed north through Sherwood to the village of Edwinstowe, the very heart of the Robin Hood legend. In the twelfth century church of St Mary, Robin and Maid Marion are said to have been married. Nearby is the Sherwood Forest Visitors' Centre with its walk-through exhibition depicting more tales of the outlaws. From here, we took a fifteen minute walk through the forest to the Major Oak, a tree thirty feet in circumference and now supported by props and ropes, in whose hollow the Merrie Men may well have hidden from the Sheriff.

Beside the churchyard path of St Mary of the Purification at Blidworth is the grave of Will Scarlet, one of Robin's most trusted followers, and at Hathersage in the Derbyshire Peak District is the grave of John Little, better known as Little John. Alan-a-Dale, the minstrel, was married in Papplewick parish church of St James's to a young maiden rescued by Robin from the clutches of a tyrant knight.

Not far from the Visitors' Centre is 'The World of Robin Hood' at Haughton, which takes the visitor back to the time of the Crusades to witness life as lived in the forest, using sets from the Kevin Cosner film *Robin Hood, Prince of Thieves.* On our latest familiarisation visit to Nottingham we dined with the current Sheriff in the Council House who turned out to be a lady! I wonder what Robin Hood would have done about that!

The Robin Hood statue in Nottingham below the Castle walls.

CHAPTER SIXTY-FIVE

French Dressing

Some refer to it as a cultural Chernobyl: I think of it as a cultural Stalingrad.

J.G. Ballard, 1930–, *Daily Telegraph*, 1994

WE HAD ALREADY BEEN to the Disney theme parks in California and Florida and now, in September 1999, we paid our second visit to EuroDisney (the first was in 1994), We took the Eurostar Express through the Channel Tunnel from Waterloo and after a swift, pleasant journey, we arrived at Marne-la-Vallée station, right next to the entrance to EuroDisney. A shuttle coach took us to the Newport Bay Hotel, one of the seven Disney themed hotels.

After our visit, we rejoined the Eurostar Express at Marne-la-Vallée station and alighted at Lille, the birthplace of General Charles de Gaulle and its Museum of Fine Arts, second only to the Louvre in Paris.

During our short break, we were able to enjoy Lille's many other assets, such as fine shops selling everything from designer clothes to hand-made chocolates; restaurants, cafés, crêperies and pâtisseries.

Having sampled the delights of Lille, we were taken to the town of Cambrai, famous for its tank battle in World War One. We have described Cambrai in chapter fifty-four.

Earlier in the summer, we were able to try out the new Condor Ferry service from Poole to St Malo.

St Malo is a very romantic city with some genuine historic characters, including the navigator Jacques Cartier who sailed out of the port in the sixteenth century and discovered Canada. It is hard to believe that during World War II, eighty per cent of the city was destroyed by Allied bombardment. Later, it was rebuilt almost exactly as it was before the war, using original plans and materials.

There is a great deal to admire about this beautiful city. It has a magnificent cathedral, a city history museum, a wax museum, the Old Market Hall, a Maritime College and a Grand Aquarium. For a guided tour of the Old Town without wearing out your feet, we commend the Little Train of St Malo which departs every hour from St Vincent Gate with a commentary in English.

The River Moselle is undoubtedly the most beautiful tributary of the Rhine, meandering leisurely through Cochen, Beilstein, Zell, Traben-Trarbach, Knov, Bernkastel-Kues, Trier and Koblenz, where at the 'Deutsches Eck', it finally meets Germany's greatest river.

The Moselle Valley provides many vistas of tranquil beauty at every bend – the silvery gleam of the water, the attractive little wine towns and villages, the steep vineyard slopes, the tree-clad hills and the romantic castles perched high on cliff-tops, all inviting you to sample the sparkling Moselle wines, mostly Riesling, in their vaulted cellars.

We decided to take advantage of Ryanair's daily flight from Bournemouth International Airport to Frankfurt-Haln to discover some of the delights of this region. There is a coach service from the airport to Frankfurt's main railway station from where you can take a train to anywhere in Germany.

No other city in Germany possesses such a rich heritage from Roman times as Trier, one of the major trade centres of the Roman Empire, and many monuments erected in those days still survive including the Porta Nigra city gate, the living quarters of the Imperial Palace, the Imperial baths and the amphitheatre. An excellent hotel in Trier is the Deutscher Hof on Sudallee 25.

Nearer the airport is the romantic mediaeval town of Bernkastel-Kues, a photographer's paradise. On every side, round every corner are stunningly beautiful half-timbered buildings and the picturesque market square with its late Renaissance-style town hall, built in 1608.

Among the fine hotels and cosy wine taverns in the town is the Hotel Doctor Weinstuben, built in 1668 which provides guests with transport from the airport. Towering above the town are the ruins of Landshut Castle, testimony to a turbulent past.

Our latest trip across the Channel was a grand tour of France with Shearings Holidays. In two weeks, we travelled from Calais to Normandy and the landing beaches of D-Day; then on to Rouen to the châteaux of the Loire, Cognac and Bordeaux before heading up the Dordogne valley to Carcassone and to Nice and the French Riviera.

Returning north, we took in Lyons and Avignon to Paris before heading back to Calais and the Channel. Altogether, a very interesting if somewhat exhausting tour.

Thus we come to the year 2000, Millenium Year. There is always a great danger of overkill when the media get hold of something of interest. The world, which normally shows little interest in the birthday of Jesus except as an excuse to have a party, was suddenly fascinated as the year of His birth clicked round from 1999 to 2000.

There is only the slenderest chance of Christ being born on 25 December but the actual date does not really matter. What we do know is that God sent His Son to Earth to be born as a baby to the Virgin Mary.

I wonder how many people these days make their own Christmas pudding, stirring the mixture around the time of the last Sunday before Advent. This was known as 'Stir up Sunday' because the old Collect (prayer) for that day began 'Stir up, we beseech thee O Lord'. Advent, of course, is the four Sundays before Christmas when we prepare to celebrate the birth of Jesus and look forward to his second coming.

Regrettably, Christ is left out of so many traditional Christmas festivities. On the face of it, Satan seems to be winning. Christianity is being eliminated from our country. It is no longer Christmas in Birmingham; the City Fathers have decreed that it would be the Winterval Festival. In Glasgow, it is the Winter Festival and in Luton, where there are more than 20,000 Muslims, the council has rebranded its Christmas lights and calls them 'luminos', a word from the Harry Potter books. According to one newspaper report, Muslims in Britain now outnumber professing Christians!

In 1647, the Long Parliament passed a law abolishing Christmas but we still celebrate Christ's birthday. The year 2000 is Millenium Year, 2,000 years after the birth of Jesus. Or is it? A dating system was created in 525 AD, which divided time into BC (Before Christ) and AD (Anno Domini, the years after His birth). In the ninth century, it was agreed to be inaccurate but we are stuck with it. Given that the first Christmas may have been in 5 or 6 BC, the twenty-first century had already begun! But does it really matter? The fact remains that Christ was born in Bethlehem about 2,000 years ago, that He was crucified, rose again on the third day and seen alive by more than 500 people (as recorded in the New Testament) and ascended into Heaven and is coming again but we know not when.

In spite of all the criticisms and brickbats, we thoroughly enjoyed our visit to the Millenium Dome at Greenwich. The day was not long enough to see everything. One of the most successful projects to mark the Millenium is the Eden Project, already being dubbed the Eighth Wonder of the World. We visited it on a Shearings' coach tour of the gardens of Cornwall, staying in St Ives. Having toured the lost Gardens of Heligan and the Abbey Gardens of Tresco on the Isles of Scilly, our visit to the Eden Project was the icing on the cake. Nestling in a giant 50 metre crater, a former china clay pit, it consists of two huge plastic domes, called biomes, and the entire area would cover thrity-six football pitches. In one biome is a tropical rain forest with growing balsa, teak and mahogany trees, a giant waterfall, cocoa, coffee and rubber plantations and every conceivable tropical plant, fruits and flowers. It is the world's largest greenhouse, 47 metres high.

The second dome is the warm temperature biome, filled with plants, trees, fruits and flowers of the Mediterranean, South Africa and California. The Eden Project is certainly the triumph of Millenium Year.

CHAPTER SIXTY-SIX

A Coach and No Horses

Nine coaches waiting – hurry, hurry, hurry.

Thomas Middleton, 1580–1627
The Revenger's Tragedy

NOT NINE COACHES but three hundred make up Shearing Holidays fleet, the largest coach operator in Europe, carrying around half a million passengers a year.

We have used all means of transport in our travels – planes, ships, trains, trams, buses, ferries and our own car. One advantage to using your own vehicle is that you can pack everything you need from bikinis to overcoats and be prepared for all weathers. But whilst you are concentrating on the road ahead, you are likely to miss things of interest or be unable to stop to admire them or the view because there is a tail of traffic behind you. That is why we often choose a coach tour. The driver knows where to go, where to stop and to point out items of interest on the way.

A good example was of our tour of the gardens of Cornwall with Shearings. Our itinerary included a visit to the marvellous Eden Project. As we approached the venue, we passed a mile-long queue of cars waiting to reach the attraction, whereas our coach (and other coaches) have priority and can drive right up to the entrance. If you are planning a visit to the Eden Project, then take our advice, take a coach!

Other tours we have made with Shearings have included the Scottish Highlands, the Isle of Man and southern Ireland and all have been satisfactory. We have also been with them on a grand tour of France. Shearings was created from the merger of three companies and its history dates back to 1903.

A company with whom we have had very good relations is Epsom Coaches. When we ran our Surrey newspaper, we used to organise tours with them for our readers. Founded in 1920 by Herbert Richmond, the son of a Norfolk farmer, the company's first 'charabanc' was garaged in Epsom High Street. By the outbreak of war in 1939, the company operated six coaches and had six horse boxes.

After the war, Mr Richmond's son, Roy took over the firm and received the MBE in 1998 in recognition of his services to the industry. Today, Epsom Coaches run touring holidays throughout the UK and on the continent, as well as day trips to places of interest. Their fleet now exceeds fifty vehicles.

Mention must be made of National Express coaches. We find them very economical and the fare much lower than by train. It is Britain's only express coach network to around 1,200 destinations in the UK. They are the natural successors to the stage coach.

It is certainly a pleasure to sit back in a coach and let somebody else do the driving.

Two of the early coaches or "Charabancs" operated by Herbert Richmond in the early 1920s

CHAPTER SIXTY-SEVEN

The Best is Still to Come

*For God so loved the world, that He gave his one
and only Son that whoever believes in Him
shall not perish but have eternal life.*

St John's Gospel, chapter 3, verse 16

As YOU HAVE READ through the pages of my life, I think you will agree that there has never been a dull moment. God has been very gracious to me and to my wife Margaret. He has met our every need as He promised to do. I have let him down many times but He has not forsaken me.

We are living in perilous times. Evil is everywhere, disasters abound. As the Bible foretold: 'Nation will rise against nation and kingdom against kingdom. There will be famines and earthquakes in various places' (St Matthew's Gospel, chapter 24, verses 7 and 8).

But all is not gloom and doom. According to the Bible, everyone who is a Christian and accepts Jesus Christ as their own personal Saviour, knows that a time is coming when He will return and there will be no more suffering, no more pain, no more tears, no more death. Every day is one more day nearer to that day. We are looking forward to that day – are you?

If we are spared to the year 2003, this will be a great year for us. Margaret and I will be celebrating our Diamond Wedding; our daughter Rosalind will reach her fiftieth birthday; grandson Michael will be thirty and I will be eighty!

If you, the reader, would like to know more about how to become a Christian and have Jesus Christ as your own personal Saviour and friend, you can write to me care of the publishers: Serendipity, Suite 530, 37 Store Street, Bloomsbury, London, WC1E 7QF.

NOT THE END!

If you are in the vicinity of Bournemouth in July, 2003, you will be very welcome to attend our wedding anniversary thanksgiving service on Sunday 6 July in Christ Church, Westbourne at 10.30 a.m.